NO COWARD
=SOUL=

VOLUME 1

My Story So Far

BY
ANNE PORTER

Published for Anne Porter by
Verité CM Limited,
Unit 2, Martlets Way, Goring Business Park,
Goring-by-Sea, West Sussex BN12 4HF

+44 (0) 1903 241975
email: enquiries@veritecm.com
Web: www.veritecm.com

British Library Cataloguing Data

A catalogue record of this book is available from
The British Library

Cover photo: 'After the Storm' – taken by the author when in Bermuda, after surviving two hurricanes in two weeks

Design and Typesetting by Verité CM Ltd

Printed in England by Page Bros, Norwich

Contents

No Coward Soul is Mine

No coward soul is mine
No trembler in the world's storm-troubled sphere.
I see Heaven's glories shine,
And faith shines equal, arming me from fear.

O Christ, within my breast,
Almighty, ever-present Deity!
Life - that in me has rest,
As I - Undying Life - have power in Thee!

Vain are the thousand creeds
That move men's hearts, unutterably vain;
Worthless as withered weeds
Or idlest froth amidst the boundless main,

To waken doubt in one
Holding so fast by Thy infinity
So surely anchored on
The steadfast rock of immortality.

With wide embracing love
Thy Spirit animates eternal years
Pervades and broods above,
Changes, sustains, dissolves, creates and rears.

Though earth and moon were gone,
And suns and universes ceased to be
And Thou wert left alone
Every existence would exist in Thee.

There is not room for death
Nor atom that his might could render void
Thou – Thou art Being and Breath
And what Thou art may never be destroyed.

Emily Bronte

Prologue

Why am I writing this story? Well, here goes. I'm beginning writing in my "65th year to heaven", 2011, and I am so grateful for the years God has given me, the things He has taught me and taken me through, the amazing things I have seen and experienced, and the beautiful people He has brought into my life. I have learned some priceless lessons, most of which probably can't be passed on without the experiences that go with them, but perhaps some could be, and the people most likely to read this book are the ones I would like to impart them to. Why do we spend our "three-score years and ten" accumulating wisdom, apparently only to take most of it to the grave with us? I personally don't believe that anything is wasted eternally, but I have observed, sadly, that here on earth, as we get older, we are less and less likely to be heard and heeded, especially by the ones that we would like to benefit from our years of life! Something else happens as we get older, too. It becomes more and more important to be known as we really are. So here, with these two things in mind, is the story of my life, warts and all.

1 – Sutton Road

I was born on the 2nd November 1946 at Hedon Road Maternity Hospital in Hull, East Yorkshire. The time was 12 noon, and I was told I had arrived in time for lunch and never stopped eating from then on. Sixty-four years later this could still be true! I was named Anne – just plain Anne – no second name. My Mum was an avid reader all her life, and "Anne of Green Gables", by Lucy Maude Montgomery, was one of her favourite stories. My hair was bright red when I was born, and so Mum decided to name me after the red haired Anne Shirley of the book. It later "faded" to strawberry blonde, much admired by others, but hated by me as a teenager (I wanted to be ash blonde like Brigitte Bardot and Twiggy). My Mum was Joan Osborne, nee Dawson, and my Dad was a Devon man called John Richard Osborne – known as Jack. They had married the day before D-Day, and had less than 24hrs together before Dad had to rejoin his regiment in Sussex before going off to France to fight. I was their first child, and the first grandchild on my Mum's side of the family.

Mum was a staff nurse at what was then the Infectious Diseases Hospital in Cottingham, Dad became a Plasterer working for Hull City Council, after being demobbed from the army at the end of World War 2, a year before I was born. They had met in the bus station in Hull after a night out with their friends, and caught the same bus home – Dad back to his Barracks in Willerby, Mum back to the Nurses Home at Castle Hill Hospital. They dated, fell in love and were engaged 3 weeks later! Mum's family lived in Hull –

at 98 Sutton Road. Her father was William Dawson, whose maternal family originally came from the West Riding. His Dad was George Dawson, the Bridgemaster at Hull's North Bridge, and his second wife was Harriet Gill. She had come to Hull to look after George's first wife and children, who had smallpox. Only the children survived, and Harriet stayed on to help take care of them, eventually marrying George. He was a barge owner at that time, and was away a lot, so Harriet's parents would only give permission for them to marry if he got a job locally, which is why he became a Bridgemaster. There were seven children. Two, Sam and Edith, were the smallpox survivors from the first marriage, then there were five with Harriet. They were George, William (my Grandad), Maudie, Albert, and Amy. Three more children died in infancy. I can vaguely remember an Auntie Maude, but Sam married a Maude Wetherhog from Huddersfield, so it could have been her. Amy is the only one I can really remember. She had bright red hair and was always laughing. William married Ruth Bell, my Grandma, who came from Stockton-on-Tees. She was the daughter of Frederick Bell, an engineer from Thirsk, who married Mary Elizabeth Todd, from Melbourne near York. They moved to Stockton-on-Tees where work was available and settled down in a little house in Walter Street. Ruth was the sixth of their eight children, Walter, Gertie, Millie, Hugh (known as Julo) Harold, then came Ruth, George and Evelyn. Evelyn was a bit of a black sheep. She had a mad passionate affair with Harry Bright, the brother of Geraldo, who was a famous dance band leader, and she had a daughter by him, called Fay. He never married her, but she later married Baden Millward and had two more daughters, Katherine and Anne, whom I remember well. I loved their Stockton accents! Ruth was a clever girl and went to High School, then worked as a Nanny for a farmer at Castle Eden. After that she was Nanny to a family called Tate in Sheffield, then moved to York to live with her mother's sister and worked in the Army Pay Corps Office, where she met William, who was in the army at that time. I remember Grandma telling me about the great Spanish Flu epidemic of 1918. She caught it, as did most of the young women she worked with, and when she eventually recovered and got back to work, she found that almost half of her workmates had died from it. After the Armistice in 1918, William came back to York, and eventually he and Ruth married at Yarm Lane Methodist Chapel on September 13th 1922.

Joan was the oldest of their 5 children, born 10th December 1923. Next in line was Eileen – 14 months younger, then Frank, followed by Mary and then Keith. My Dad, Jack, came from Plymouth. He was born 24th November 1918, the middle child of 3, Evelyn being the oldest, and Ethel the youngest. His Mum, Annie (nee Oaten), was a Cornish woman, from the Delabole area. She died from the consequences of childhood Rheumatic Fever when Dad was quite young. Grandad (John Robert Osborne) remarried, to a harpy of a woman named Minnie, who moved in with him, along with her son, Albert. She was very unkind to my Dad and his sisters, and they all left home as soon as they could, but remained very close and affectionate towards one another. Albert, on the other hand, was spoilt rotten, and I remember my Dad telling me that his Mum still wiped his bum when he was 8 (the butt of a joke to the others, I guess). It all made for interesting family dynamics, which would surface in all kinds of ways later. My Grandad Osborne died when I was a toddler, so I don't remember him, although there was a photo of me in his arms at the age of 2 or so. Dad became an apprentice plasterer and completed his training in Plymouth, then in 1939 he signed up for the Territorial Army, thinking that by doing this he would avoid having to fight in the 2nd World War. It didn't work, and he was in the thick of the war from day one, a Sergeant in the RASC. His life experiences, both as a child losing his Mum and coping with Minnie's ill will, then fighting in the war, scarred him for life, and he always struggled with depression and anger. Not only did he fight in North Africa, Italy, France and Germany when he was only 21 years old, but he was posted missing after Dunkirk. He only escaped from the beach at the third attempt, his previous 2 rescue boats were blown up and he had to get back each time and try again. Added to this, he was among the first of the Allies to enter the Bergen-Belsen Concentration Camp at the end of the war. I recently found out that one of the jobs they had was to bulldoze the bodies into mass graves. Enough said, and in those days they hadn't even put a name to "post traumatic stress", let alone offer anything like counselling for it. In fact it wasn't so long since those suffering from it and going AWOL, or being unable to carry on fighting, were labelled cowards and traitors, and some were executed by firing squad.

Dad was a real "artisan". Some of his decorative plasterwork can still be seen in the stairwell of the Wilberforce Museum in Hull, and also on the ceiling of the Guildhall. Mum was a stoic, she "held the fort" when Dad was ill with a serious nervous breakdown (when I was about 10), and worked really hard all her life – as did Dad. Mum was the epitome of self-sacrifice, she always put us first. She was a brilliant nurse, a real instinctive carer, and eventually became a Deputy Matron at the local Nuffield Trust Hospital – later to become B.U.P.A. – and she received many presents from grateful patients throughout her career.

When I was born Mum and Dad were living at Grandma and Grandad's house, 98 Sutton Road. They had bought it for £400, plus another £100 for a vacant plot which they shared with their next door neighbours, the Newloves. The Newloves were a really nice family, but we all thought they were a bit strange, because they went abroad on holiday

– even to France! Mrs. Newlove was German, her family had been held on the Isle of Man with all the "suspicious foreigners" during the war. She used to sunbathe in the garden in very small swimsuits, and Grandad used to say she was the only woman in Hull with a sunburnt fanny. They had a daughter called Paulette, which was a very exotic name for someone from Hull! Just before I was born Grandad was very ill with pneumonia and had almost died. Everyone reckoned that I had saved his life by giving him a reason to pull through (or maybe it was looking at Mrs. Newlove!). I was his first grandchild, and he would sit next to my crib, which was in the corner of the living room by the coal fire (no central heating then) and gaze at me. I think that my birth, so soon after the austerity and anguish of the second World War, was symbolic of new life and hope, not only to him, but the whole family. He was a wonderful man, I loved him so much. He had served in Egypt and France during the First World War, joining the Army at 16 initially, but he was brought back by his Mum, only to join up again when he was old enough! He was gassed in the trenches on the Somme, so his lungs were always delicate. Of course, smoking cigarettes didn't help, but no-one then realised how dangerous they were. He had the most amazing set of false teeth. The "gums" were a vivid brick red, and the teeth looked like white tombstones. He hated wearing them, and wouldn't eat with them in, so he took them out as soon as he stepped in through the door after going out, or to work. He kept them in a glass of water on the kitchen windowsill, and I can still see them sitting there grinning at me. He always had time for me. I can remember as a little girl sitting with him on the back doorstep at 98, podding peas for lunch, or picking cooking apples and big fat blackberries from their garden, so that Grandma could make jam and pies, filling their little kitchen with the most heavenly perfume. Their kitchen always smelled so good. He had a lovely garden and grew the best peas in the world. To this day, whenever I smell a garden fire I am back in the garden at 98, helping Grandad to throw old leaves and garden refuse on the fire, precious memories unclouded by health and safety rules! As I'm writing, I'm realising afresh the strong association of memories with our sense of smell. I can still remember the oily smell of the garage where he had his workshop, and the smell of his work clothes – a combination of garden fires, workshop, sweat, and cigarettes. He left school at 14, which was the norm back then, but had worked hard at "bettering himself", going to night classes for years, and eventually became head of Welfare Services in Hull. Grandma was a great cook, and her gravy was world-class. The whole family would talk about it! She was a stoic, too. I never saw her cry or show any excessive emotion. She nagged Grandad a lot, and I can still see him in my mind's eye putting his teeth in, donning his trilby and raincoat, and escaping to his local pub, "The Cross Keys" on Beverley Road, to play dominoes with his mates.

I loved being at their house. They had no indoor toilet. The "cludgy" was downstairs next to the kitchen. The door was next to the back door of the house. Keith kept all his "Eagle" comics out there – along with a few "Beano" and "Dandy". I loved the adventures of Dan Dare, Harris Tweed, The Bash Street Kids and Minnie the Minx, and spent hours sitting on the loo so I could read them. For some reason the comics never came into the house! A lot of the time there was only squares of newspaper threaded on string instead of toilet paper, but then "prosperity" came, and there was horrible shiny stiff "Izal" toilet paper – everyone preferred the newspaper, but it wasn't as posh as the Izal, so we suffered in silence! We had some great family parties at 98, we always spent Boxing Day there, and played silly games such as "Family Coach", and listened to Keith's Fats Waller records on the gramophone. Dad used to play the piano – usually "The Barcarolle" from the "Tales of Hoffmann", or "I can See the Lights of Home" – it was lovely. He would sing too, "If I were a Blackbird" or "Oh my Beloved Father" (O mio Babbino Caro). He had a beautiful tenor voice, which had earned him and Grandma lots of free drinks from appreciative listeners in pubs over the years. Uncle Frank always used to say his own favourite game was "Sleeping Dolls" – really an excuse to have a snooze after lunch! As well as all the Dawsons and their spouses and kids, every family gathering included Auntie Enid, Grandma's cousin from York. She never married, and worked as a resident "house mother" in a local orphanage, so, on her days off, number 98 became her home. She was a crabby old thing, but always gave us nice presents at Christmas so we put up with her! Her nickname was "Neddy", a corruption of "Nedi" – an anagram of her name. She was frequently the butt of jokes, her nickname being an example. I found out in later years that Eileen had come home one day and found Grandad and Neddy in bed together! That would explain Eileen's attitude to her Dad – she was always very snippy with him, and also why Neddy hung around there so much! She was the only person I ever heard call him Billy, Grandma just called him Dad, and he called her "Mother", which could explain a lot.

My very earliest memory was of Frank coming to visit us, walking across our garden in deep snow, wearing his navy uniform, bell-bottoms and all. I can remember the clear blue sky and the sun shining on the snow, his bright blue eyes, black hair and tanned skin – I think he had just come back from the Far East. (I was always a bit in love with him, he was so gorgeous and so much fun!) I must have been about a year old then, as it was the snowy winter of 1947. By this time Mum, Dad and I had moved out of 98 and into a little prefabricated council bungalow about 30 minutes walk away, number 682 Sutton Road. We were very happy there. In 1948 my little sister Elizabeth arrived. I was always a bit jealous of her. She was rather sickly, and would get bronchitis every winter. She also had a squint, which had to be corrected by surgery, so she was in hospital a few times. This meant she was fussed over more than me, as I was a strapping healthy type! Added to this she had the unspeakable nerve to be the first one connected to the Dawson family to be given a middle name – Helen – which I thought was desperately romantic in later years. She wore little round pink rimmed glasses and looked so cute, Dad's family called her "little 'Buth". I always felt embarrassed about my appearance, as I had no front teeth until my second ones came through. I had knocked my front milk teeth out not long after I got them, when I had crashed to the ground with the handle of my doll's pram in my mouth. Liz and I were never really close as we grew up. I think that had a lot to do with the fact that because of being the first born after the war, I was expected to achieve great things. The hope for the future was through education and hard work, and the whole family urged me to "do well at school". However, I never felt as if I had ever done quite enough, and Liz seemed to be protected and coddled, and able to enjoy just being a little girl. I also resented having a little sister hanging around when I was playing with my friends, and as we grew up we went to different schools and had completely different outlooks on life. I had delusions of grandeur, and thought I was too intelligent to mix with the people she used to hang around with! This was shown when we hit 18 and started going out "to the pub" – she went to "The Gardeners' Arms" which was full of darts-playing beer swillers, I went across the road to "The Haworth" – which was full of beer swilling University students!

We didn't see much of Dad, he worked really long hours, riding his push bike to and from work, sometimes 12 miles a day. He also did a bit of "moonlighting" to earn more money. Mum went back to work when we started school. She rode her bike too, from Sutton Road to Cottingham, 3 or 4 nights a week. She worked nights back at Castle Hill hospital where she had trained, sleeping during the day whilst we were at school. They must both have been exhausted much of the time, but would have been super fit with all the cycling if it wasn't for the fact that they both smoked like chimneys! I can still remember waking up in the mornings, hearing Dad cleaning out the grate and lighting the fire before bringing us a cup of tea. I had a really happy childhood, we would play out in the fields around our house all day, and it seemed that all the summers were long and sunny and warm, whilst there was always snow in winter. Dad made us lovely things - dolls-houses and cribs and rabbit hutches and swings in the garden. We had bikes, and went for long rides – nobody worried about us – the world was a relatively safe place for children then. I think my eclectic taste in food started back at Sutton Road. We never ate "Foreign Muck", as Dad called anything non-British, but because of lack of money and post-war austerity we must have eaten every kind of offal that was going. A favourite weekend roast was half a pig's head, and I clearly remember eating the brains, which makes me cringe now. I don't think we ever had tripe, because Mum had bad memories of eating it (stewed and smelly) at home when she was a child. I didn't like tongue, because of the texture and also because of the thought of what it actually was. Chewing on something that had come out of something else's mouth seemed almost cannibalistic.

Hardly anyone had a car, so I remember specially our neighbour Dennis Chadburn's car. He would take us all to the seaside at least once a year, it was such a treat. Their dog, Jess, would come with us. The Chadburns lived across the road from us. There was Mum and Dad and sister, Jill, plus Uncle Walt, who kept racing pigeons. Mrs. Chadburn used to make wonderful rice pudding in the little oven at the side of their coal fire. I have never tasted anything so delicious as that – especially the golden crust on top! I can still remember the sad day when Jess died, we were all so upset. Another car I remember was a huge Mercedes, which rolled up at our little house one day. It contained Mum's old school friend Sheila and her husband Angus, who was a diplomat in what was then Malaya. We went for a ride in it, Dad drove it – I'll never forget the look of delight and envy on his face. He had a motor bike (a "Matchless") by then, but didn't ride it to work, as petrol was too expensive. Another car I remember was Uncle Keith's first. It was a black Citroen with big running boards, like something out of a gangster movie. He used to go off every Saturday night to Bridlington and Scarborough, where they had jazz bands playing at dances. We thought he was really cool! He met his wife, Muriel, at one of these dances. They married in about 1959 I think, but in the Registry Office because Muriel was divorced. They went on to have 3 boys; Philip (who was born on my birthday), Ian, and Nicholas. I loved Auntie Mary. When I stayed at Grandma's house I slept with Mary, and used to love snuggling up in her feather bed, listening to her loud alarm clock ticking away in the darkness. She was chubby and pretty, and had lovely boyfriends. She married one of them, Jim Thrustle, and Liz and I were bridesmaids. Jim was a scout leader when Mary was a cub mistress at St. John's Church, Newland (where I would eventually get married). They had a car too – a funny little Morris Minor.

My early school days were really happy. I went to Sutton Road School, a little prefab building about 15 minutes walk from home. My teachers were lovely, and I clearly remember my very first day at school. I cried so much the teacher sat me on her knee and cuddled me most of the day

– not allowed now, sadly. The headmistress was called Miss Daulton, and she liked me. I was pretty smart, and she got on well with Mum, so she "chose" me to be a friend of her neice, Judith, whom she brought to school every morning. I always went to her Birthday parties, very exciting for me as we never had enough money for such frivolities! Miss Daulton also took some of us to the Hull Guildhall to listen to Organ Recitals from time to time. Mostly it was desperately boring, and I really don't like organ music even now – about the only kind of music I don't like. It was good getting out from school though, and of course we got to ride in a car! I had lots of friends, Janet Botham and Lindsay Johnson were my best friends. We had such fun together. Another family we were friendly with was the Roberts. Their daughter Rosemary had Polio and was partially paralysed, but still managed to get up to mischief with us. They had a big rain barrel in their garden and used to rinse their hair with the rain-water to make it soft and silky – I had never heard of such vanity! There were lots of kids in the area, and we had street parties and school PTA events. I remember a big party for Queen Elizabeth's coronation. Mum made a cake in the shape of the crown, everyone said it was amazing! Janet and I together won loads of Fancy Dress prizes, the best one was as Queen Elizabeth 1st and Sir Francis Drake, but another good one was when we dressed as a Bride and Groom. I got to be the "girl" both times, as Janet was slightly taller than me. We used to love Bonfire Night – I looked forward to this time of year, as my birthday (2nd November), Grandad's birthday (4th November), and Dad's birthday (24th November) all came in that month, and we also knew that Christmas was just around the corner. Bonfire Night was really exciting because there was fierce competition for the biggest fire. There were no regulations then, anyone could have one, and some of them were massive! Night-time raiding parties would go out for a couple of weeks before the 5th, stealing prime stuff from rivals to build up their own fires. In the last few days before the big event the Dads would even post a guard to prevent such disasters. I nearly got caught by someone's Dad when we were out on a raiding party in their back garden (only because we knew they had stolen our stuff). I managed to hide behind the bonfire, but he caught my friends and gave them a clip around the ear! Liz, whom we had dragged along (because I'd been told by Mum to include her in our games) was so scared she wet herself, and of course I got the blame for that. I also got into BIG trouble when I burned a big hole in my new winter coat carrying chestnuts roasted in the embers of the bonfire. They did taste good though.

Another time I got into trouble was when we had been warned at school about "stranger danger". I think there had been an attempted abduction of a child locally and we were all told to beware of accepting sweets or lifts from strangers. One afternoon we got off the school bus. I was on one side of the road with my friends, Liz was on the opposite side with hers – they were all younger than us. A car pulled up and the driver asked Liz and her friends for directions to "Number 5". I thought he said "Does anyone want a ride", and yelled at the top of my voice "Run for your lives!!!!" All the little kids scattered, screaming and crying for their Mummies. My friend said "Why did you do that?" and told me what had actually been said. The poor driver was sitting there totally perplexed, and once again Mum had to deal with pants wet in fear, so did half the other Mums in the street!

I can still remember so many names and faces. One was Margaret Borrill, who fell off a fence whilst doing acrobatics and cut her leg – she had stitches, really serious stuff! There was Howard – a little boy who was a bit slow, and whose Mum used to invite us all over for the yummiest cakes so we would play with him. Another was Michael Bosky - who always had a green snotty nose. His Mum used to sashay over to the butchers with her curlers in, a fag hanging out of her mouth, and her coat slung around her shoulders. My dad called her "the armless wonder" because she never put her arms in her coat. I think she had something going on with the butcher, because she was always back and forth. I may have remembered something about her from the times when our rent man, Mr. Robinson, came to call. Mum always made him a cup of tea, and as often as I could I joined them as they sat at the kitchen table swopping all the latest scandals and gossip. Sometimes Mum told me to go away – I guess that was when it got a bit too steamy – the gossip I mean, nothing else! He could well have fancied Mum, but I don't think for a minute she fancied him, as he was a grotty, smelly old bloke with a Brylcreemed comb-over, a greasy belted gabardine raincoat, and bicycle clips on his trousers. Next door to us were the Steensons, Paddy and Agnes, and their son George. In Summer Dad, George and Paddy used to go swimming in the deep drainage canal at the other side of the fields. We weren't allowed as it was too dangerous, but we all sat on the bank and watched. Next to them were the Bothams, then Alan and Elsie Stowe lived next door but two. They had two boys, David and Colin. Alan sometimes worked nights, and Elsie hated being on her own, so I would go and stay with her to keep her company. I loved that because they had a telly! It was a tiny little thing – about an 8 inch screen, but it was a miracle to us. I remember watching "Quatermass" and being scared to death. Evening entertainment at home was the radio or reading. We listened to "Journey Into Space" and "The Archers". In the afternoon was "Housewive's Choice" and "Mrs. Dale's Diary". On Sunday lunchtime we always listened to "Family Favourites" followed by "Round the Horne" or "The Navy Lark" and "The Billy Cotton Band Show". Next to the Stowe's was a family with two little kids, Lesley and Tony. I can't remember them as well as the others because they were too young to play with us. Sometimes I used to go to Leeds on the train with Mum to see Auntie Eileen, who was a teacher in Whitkirk. Mum would sometimes leave me there for a couple of nights in the holidays, but all I can remember about that is meeting all sorts of boring old people, visiting boring old Temple Newsam, and feeling desperately homesick.

When we were very little, we only had days out at Hornsea or Withernsea for our summer holiday. Once we had a caravan at Hollym, on the east coast, for a few days, but then as we got older we started going every year to see Dad's relatives in Devon and Cornwall. I can't put into words the excitement of catching the overnight steam train to Plymouth from Paragon Station, and the total joy of waking up as it got light and finding that we were at the Devon Coast near Teignmouth and Dawlish. The train ran alongside the seashore, and we would be glued to the windows gazing at the red cliffs and clear blue sea. The sea on the lower East coast of Yorkshire was muddy and brown from the heavy clay of the Plain of Holderness, so Devon seemed like paradise to us. Our times in Plymouth were wonderful. Auntie Eve lived there. She had married Horace Atrill, who was one of 13 children (surviving – there were 21 pregnancies). His Mum was amazing, she went to the pub every night for her Brandy and Lovage, and swore it's what kept her alive and strong well into her 90s. Usually there was at least one of her many offspring there too! All of Uncle Horace's brothers and sisters had kids our age and lived close by. We would get up at the crack of dawn and help to make mountains of corned beef or spam sandwiches, and hard boiled eggs, then go over to the local shop and buy saffron cakes and jam tarts with traffic light coloured fillings to take for our picnics. Then we would all cram into tatty old cars and drive to

Mothecombe, a magical bay with rock pools and surf and a huge sandy beach, accessed by winding lanes lined with high hedges full of honeysuckle and wild roses, birds and bees. We swam and played all day, there was hardly anyone but us on the beach. There were sea anemones and crabs in the rock pools, and I spent hours searching for fish and popping seaweed, when we weren't in the sea or playing rounders. Plymouth was such a great town too. I remember watching my Dad do perfect Jack-knife dives into the swimming pool on Plymouth Hoe, and climbing Smeaton's Tower, going to the Aquarium, and to Cremyll, where Uncle Horace had an ice-cream van. He was also a bookie, and got himself into trouble with both the police and crooked racehorse owners frequently. Auntie Eve was a bag of nerves, she never knew what was coming next, plus Horace had lots of girl-friends and she knew it. She developed Dementia when only in her 50s, probably as a result of lifelong stress. One of our least favourite trips was to see Minnie, Dad's stepmother. We would sit there bored silly, whilst Minnie criticised everyone – including us – and complained about everything. She had a cousin who lived with her to keep her company, Aunt Nelly. She was really nice to us and always gave us pocket money. I can remember sitting there, counting the whiskers on Nellie's chin whilst Minnie droned on. I was a little bit in love with my cousin Horrie (or "Boy Hor" as the family called him). He was about 5 years older than me and had a record player and some rock'n'roll records. I remember the first time I heard Jerry Lee Lewis singing "Great Balls of Fire" – it was a total revelation to me, I was hooked from day one and have loved Jerry Lee ever since. I can't wait to meet him in heaven and hear him play heavenly music, because I'm sure he will be there. He's a victim of religion, told that he had to choose between his music and God, when in reality God had given him the gift of music to use for letting people know how brilliant He is. Jerry Lee chose music, thinking he had rejected God, and he thinks he's a lost soul, but I know that he only rejected a lie, and anyway, God never lets His children go!

Often we would set out to Cornwall to visit Aunt Bessie in St. Teath, or Dad's cousin, Uncle Owen, and his wife Aunt Lil, at Trebetherick. Aunt Bessie was Dad's Mother's sister. She was married to Uncle Harry, and they had a wonderful old thatched cottage next to a ford in a river. There were gas lights on the walls, and none of the floors were level, we adored it. Uncle Harry was lovely, he said very little but would take us all into the garden to see his chickens and ducks, and let us pick damsons and raspberries. We would wade up and down the river, and make bows and arrows with Uncle Harry's string, always with cousin Gerald in tow. He was Harry and Bessie's grandson, and was profoundly deaf and a bit "slow". Harry looked after Gerald all his life, as his parents, Harry and Bessie's son, Willie, and his wife Ruby, were very busy farming and running a B & B. Gerald could have gone away to a special school but none of the family wanted it, so he stayed home and never really learned to speak properly. I don't know what happened to him when Harry and Bessie died. Aunt Ruby was a very strange woman – Willie was a bit of an enigma too, but I think he was just very shy and didn't mix with many people. The story was that Ruby used to go mad at the full moon, but I never actually saw it! Aunt Bessie was a great cook. We had family banquets there that would put "The Darling Buds of May" to shame. She made her own clotted cream with milk from Willie's herd. On all her kitchen windowsills were wide shallow enamel bowls with thick yellow cream rising to the top and clotting. We ate it with the fresh raspberries from the garden sprinkled with crunchy sugar. Owen and Lil had a B & B at Trebetherick, on the top of the hill between Polzeath and Daymer Bay. Owen was the son of Aunt Sarah Trayes (another sister of my Dad's Mum), who lived in Wadebridge (I think). She was an old grouch and we didn't see much of her. She once told Liz that she wasn't good looking enough to be an Oaten. Quite a nerve, as she was no oil painting herself, and all the Oatens had big noses! We stayed with Owen and Lil a few times too. We loved it there, trekking down the hill to Polzeath one day to do some surfing, and down the other side of the hill the next day to the calmer waters and sand dunes of the River Camel estuary at Daymer Bay. I don't know which I liked best. I loved exploring the dunes and going into St. Enodoc, the church that had been buried in the sand, but I loved surfing the crashing waves of Polzeath, and the dramatic rocks of Pentire Point. Sometimes we used to catch the ferry from Rock over to Padstow, where Mum and Dad got engaged years before. This was also John Betjeman country (he is buried at St. Enodoc), and my incurably romantic nature has been fed by his poetry and writings about this land of my childhood for most of my life! Lil worked so hard, and Mum often helped her when we were there. Owen was a lazy old layabout! He spent most of his time in the pub telling stories to tourists and getting free drinks from them. They had an only son, Bailey, who was a fisherman, and was lost at sea when he was only in his 30s. In later years when we stayed in Trebetherick we used to go to the scout hut down the hill two evenings a week to watch movies. They were almost always corny romantic "weepies", such as "The Wind Cannot Read" starring Dirk Bogarde, whom I adored. I always came out of there with swollen red eyes and nose, desperately in love with the romantic heroes, and with my heart breaking at the terrible tragedy of unfulfilled love (because in those days it never was fulfilled). I remember my disbelief when my hero Dirk eventually "came out". I didn't really understand totally what that meant, but knew that he preferred men to women, so a lot of my romantic illusions were shattered. I can only remember one year when it rained – or drizzled that is, the rest of the time it seemed we had solid sunshine. One year Grandma and Grandad joined us there, I remember Grandad getting the tops of his feet sunburnt, but nowhere else, because he kept all his clothes on! He may even have tied a handkerchief on his head, I'm not sure.

Sometimes Dad's younger sister, Auntie Ethel, and her family, would join us in Plymouth for grand family reunions. She had married Vic Sargeant, from Scunthorpe in Lincolnshire, and they had settled there. I think they met when they were both in the R.A.F. stationed in Lincolnshire. They had 2 sons – Lionel, who was my age, and Barry, who was the same age as Liz. We had great times when we got together, when we were all in Plymouth it was crazy! I remember poor old Auntie Eve twitching constantly- the stress must have been unbearable! When we could, we would go over to Scunthorpe from Hull to see the family there. We caught the ferry from the Pier in Hull, over the Humber to New Holland, and then caught a bus or train to Scunthorpe. I went fishing for the first time with Uncle Vic and Lionel. I loved it and caught 2 roach, but they were so tiny they had to be thrown back. Uncle Vic made his own wine, and the grown ups always got happy and giggly when we went there. I loved the parsnip wine, but of course was only allowed a taste. I can remember he also made potato, rhubarb, and gooseberry wine. Vic's Dad had an amazing garden, really big, and full of lovely fruit trees and vegetable plots. It was the kind of garden you could get lost in, and we had great games of hide and seek there. The only time the Plymouth bunch came north was when Uncle Horace got into trouble with a bunch of crooks who were fixing greyhound races, something to do with dyeing one of the dogs to disguise its identity. He drove the whole family up to Hull in a panic, in an old banger of a car that used as much oil as it did petrol, and I don't think 1st gear worked either! We had a good time though, and the Scunthorpe tribe came over to Hull to join us. I don't know where we all slept, as there were only 2 bedrooms in our prefab.

My first remembered encounters with God were at 682. Mum sent us to Sunday School, which was held in my school, and I loved it. We learned some wonderful children's hymns there – I really enjoyed singing. I remember being very confused because one of the hymns we sang was "Glad that I live am I", and my Sunday School Teacher was called Gladys. I thought it was all about her! She was pretty and chubby with curly blonde hair and wore glasses like Dame Edna Everage, and was engaged to the son of Grandma's next door neighbour, Herbert Sawdon. Herbert was the most miserable bloke you ever saw, he looked like something out of the Addams Family (I think he was probably chronically ill, but to us he just looked awful). They were engaged for about 10 years then she ran off with someone else – no surprise to anyone except poor old Herbert. Mr. Sylvester was the Sunday School Superintendent, he always looked really happy and told us lovely Bible stories. In those days, when grain was harvested, they stood the harvest up in bundles all over the fields to dry in the sun. One day we were playing hide and seek in a wheat field near our house, and I leaned back on the stook I was hiding behind, looked up at the beautiful blue sky, and around me at the golden wheat and red poppies, so thankful for such beauty, and knowing that God was looking down at me and loving me. Another time I had been really naughty and felt very repentant, and sat on my little green trike and promised God I wouldn't be naughty again. I know He heard me too, but of course He knew I'd never keep it up! I also remember, on a walk to Sutton to play on the swings in the park there, sneaking in at the back of St. James Anglican church. There was a service going on, and, thinking I could never remember all the chanting and standing up and kneeling down, I wondered if this was what God was all about. I somehow knew it wasn't.

2 – Bricknell Avenue

In 1955 we moved. I was so sad to leave 682 Sutton Road and all my friends. We moved to Bricknell Avenue, a far more affluent area of Hull. I started at the local Junior School, which was a very good school, and made new friends. I must have adjusted quickly, because I went straight into the top class, and would always come in the top 5 in exams. I also joined the local Girl Guide Troop, held at Bricknell Avenue Methodist Church, and had some fun hiking and camping, as once again we were close to open countryside. I was in the Blackbird patrol. I started to go to the Sunday School there, and as a teenager became a Junior Member of the church, then taught some of the little ones on a Sunday morning. It was just after we moved from Sutton Road that Dad had a really bad nervous breakdown, and for a few years after this he struggled with deep depression and other mental health problems. He was taken into the De La Pole Hospital for a few weeks at first, because he had become almost paranoid, and Mum couldn't cope. After being discharged he had to go back from time to time for "treatment". I found out subsequently that this was E.C.T. – a barbaric process during which the victim was tranquillised, then given a strong electric shock to the brain. I remember Dad sitting and crying because he was so scared of it. It induced convulsions and coma. He eventually did recover from his depression, but I doubt that the E.C.T. did much to help. I'm sure Liz and I were affected by all this, because I have a vivid memory of my Guide Captain coming to our house to ask Mum and Dad if I could go to Guide Camp. I was supposed to have asked them, but I hadn't, because I didn't think we could afford it whilst Dad couldn't work, and I didn't want to burden them with the knowledge that I was suffering any kind of deprivation. I also didn't want anyone else to know about Dad's illness. It was all very emotional, and also humiliating for everyone concerned.

The main attraction to church for me was the Youth Club, we had skiffle bands playing at our dances and socials and, of course, boys! We still lived in a council house, a two storey prefab this time, a lovely, comfy home which was just right for us, but sadly, in some ways, a source of shame to me. I became very conscious of my working class background for the first time, and aware that we did not have much money, or our own house. I guess this was because I was growing up and becoming more self-aware, and because a lot of the kids at my school were from "The Avenues" and had "posh" accents. "The Avenues" was a lovely old Victorian area of Hull, close to Pearson Park, which was full of gorgeous old houses with romantic things like balconies and towers. Incidentally Pearson Park was where one of my favourite poets, Philip Larkin, lived when he was librarian of Hull University, and where his friend (and my hero!) John Betjeman used to visit him. They used to wander around the old areas of Hull, and especially a huge old overgrown cemetery on Chanterlands Avenue, which wasn't far from The Avenues. It was privately owned, and was pretty dangerous because it wasn't maintained, but contained loads of fascinating old mausoleums and tombs with scary old Gothic statues, and even a section of unnamed graves of people who had reputedly died in an epidemic of plague. In later years the council took it over and "manicured" it to look like every other cemetery – tragic!

As well as all my perceived inadequacy (not being posh or rich) and also my romantic aspirations to one day have a big house with a balcony and a tower, and lots of money, Mum and Dad would always be telling me to do my very best at school so that I wouldn't be poor like them. I always had my nose in a book, and dreamed of travelling the world and being rich and famous and beautiful and wise. All these combined influences gave me great incentive to do well, but also sadly to feel that I could never do well enough. If I came 2nd in the class Dad would say "What's wrong with 1st?" I never did come first – or maybe once I was joint first. I think this might have been more to do with my teacher, Mrs. Plumpton, than me. She was a social climber, with her little fan club of Avenues kids, and she really didn't like me (I didn't like her either).

Our new home was 3, Appleton Road (where Mum lived until she had to move into a care home in Spring 2011). This was where I said goodbye to my childhood, but not before I had some great times with my new friends. My best friend was Hilary Mattsson. Her Dad was Swedish and a bit of a nutter, but a kind one! We played dressing up (she had some fantastic old ballgowns) and went for long bike rides. I began to encounter "sex" for the first time (apart from the occasional "Playing doctors" when I was younger!). On one of our bike rides, when we were about 10, we were followed by some pervy biker who stood by the road and waved his willy at us. We took off at top speed and rode into a farmyard, scaring a horse, which nearly knocked the farmer over. When we told him what had happened he said it was a good job we did escape. We didn't know what possible danger we had been in. Around this time we started getting to know a few of the boys in the area. My favourite was Martin Harrison, who lived opposite us and was in my class at school. He was a great artist but was always in trouble, looking back it was because he was creative and different and didn't fit in with the school's sausage factory mentality. I always did go for the bad boys. Hilary liked John Groombridge, who lived 3 doors down from her on Grammar School Road. He once showed us how he could make his willy go stiff if he leaned over backwards, and then demonstrated its efficiency by hanging a swimming flipper off it! The last I heard of him he was a dentist. Martin eventually moved away from the area because his parents got divorced, and I missed him. I also started my first business around that time – breeding rabbits. I used to sell the baby bunnies for 5 shillings each (25p). My first rabbit was Wimpy, he was a "Dutch" and he was amazing, he would answer to his name and follow me when I went for a walk – more like a dog! When he died I got Dinky, she was a crossed English and wild rabbit, and Spotty, a pure English male. They had lovely babies, usually about 6 to 8 at a time, and all kinds of colours and combinations; pure white, pure black, pure grey, white with black spots, grey spots or brown spots, grey with white spots – it was really exciting waiting to see how they would turn out. They were so ugly at first, like little worms, but so cute when they started jumping around and playing. Dinky was a good mother.

In the school holidays Mum looked after 2 kids from round the corner, whose parents both worked full time. They were Robert and Judith Allen, and we had some fun times with them. We used to make huge Bedouin tents in the garden and eat picnics in there. Sometimes we would go to the seaside for the day on the train – usually Hornsea. On the last day of the holidays Mum used to cook us all our favourite meal, and we always chose fried liver and chips followed by chocolate blancmange! What a bunch of weirdos. Another good thing about living at number 3 was that, at that time, Uncle Frank and his new wife, Auntie Mig (Margaret) and their children, Christine and Billy, lived very near by. Frank had left the Navy by this time, and worked in Welfare with Grandad. He eventually became head of Social Services in Middlesbrough, after first moving to Dudley from Hull (where they had another son, Stephen) and then on to Nottingham, before eventually living on Teeside. Liz and I had been "bridesmaids" at their wedding, a very low key affair because Auntie Mig was pregnant with Christine at the time – a big scandal in those days. We had loads of fun with them. We all used to go off on our bikes for picnics at the weekends. Auntie Mig made the best orange fairy cakes in the world. She used National Health orange juice (issued to new mums) for the icing – yummy. I'm sure it wasn't intended for stuff like that. We loved Auntie Mig, and her family. Her Mum was called Violet (Vi) and her Dad was called Gwillam (the Welsh version of Guillaume) – both very exotic names! Vi was a great laugh. Gwillam had dementia, he used to make himself catfood sandwiches when Vi was out playing whist with her many friends, and he regularly went out for walks and got lost. Vi never let it spoil her fun! I swear she used to wear purple dresses, and always had a hat on – I don't think it was red, though. She was probably the original geriatric rebel mentioned in the famous poem by Jenny Joseph. They lived in a big house off Beverley Road opposite St. Mary's Convent and Endsleigh Training College. Mig had an older sister, Betty, who worked in Pathology, and a brother, Tony, who was a real sweetie. He had the biggest ears you ever saw, so we called him Dumbo, but he was far from dumb. Mig had been a Domestic Science teacher before she had the children. Vi's sister, Auntie Grace, lived with them, too. She had studied French at the Sorbonne in Paris, and used to come to our house on the bus and give Liz and I piano lessons on a piano Mum had bought from Gilbert Baitson's auction rooms for £10. Sadly we didn't practice as we should, and eventually gave up. I think Mum was mortified, as Auntie Grace was kindly giving up her time and skill, and we didn't really show any appreciation. There were also some great "School Trips" from Bricknell Avenue School. We went by coach to the Yorkshire Dales and the North Yorkshire Moors, visiting places like Forge Valley (I can still remember the dark, dampness of the place and the overpowering smell of wild garlic), Rievaulx Abbey, Knaresborough, and Robin Hood's Bay, always finishing at Scarborough for a Fish and Chip tea. The trips were punctuated by unplanned stops for kids to throw up or to pee behind a bush (girls one side, boys the other!). They were loads of fun, and there was always one kid who would manage to fall in a river and come home wrapped in teachers' coats and cardigans, nobody drowned though!

I was always in the local library, I read anything and everything. At 11 or 12 I even read the life story of Isaac Semelweiss, who pioneered the treatment of puerperal sepsis, because I had nothing else at hand! My love affair with music continued. We graduated from the old wind-up gramophone I used to play with in the shed to a Dansette record player. I was getting fed up with "Poet and Peasant" and "In a Monastery Garden" - the old 78 rpm stuff I had! It was also getting scratched and broken, and I had pocket money, so started to buy some more records, usually from a shop nearby which sold out of date stuff at cut price. I remember having a couple by Little Richard, and some by Pat Boone, not a very comprehensive selection! There were programmes on the TV like "Juke Box Jury" and "Oh Boy! (forerunners of "Top of the Pops"). I loved Elvis and Cliff Richard. I was heartbroken when Eddie Cochrane was killed. Occasionally I saw Johnny Cash on TV, and liked the "country" sound of his music. Mum had started getting Classical music albums from the record library – mainly opera, I listened to it with her and loved some of it. My favourites were "La Traviata" and "Rigoletto". Dad liked operetta, and had an album of Richard Tauber singing songs from "The Merry Widow" and other Franz Lehar stuff. My tastes were pretty eclectic from necessity, like books, anything was better than nothing! Another LP they had that I loved was by Tom Lehrer, and I still remember all the words to "Poisoning Pigeons in the Park" and most of the other funny songs on that album.

In March 1957 I took my 11+ exam. I'll never forget that day, as I woke up with tummy ache and a strange feeling, to find I had started my periods. In spite of this, I did well and passed the exam with flying colours to go to my first choice of school, the Roman Catholic convent school, St. Mary's Grammar. This was my first choice because Hilary had passed her 11+ the previous year to go there and I wanted to be where my best friend was. My second choice was Newland High School, where Hull actress Maureen Lipman started about the same time. These 2 schools were arch-rivals. I remember my interview with Sister Mary Cyril, St. Mary's headmistress. She read out the letter about me from Mr. Lofthouse, the headmaster at Bricknell School, and mentioned something he had said about my being "scrupulously honest". I was so happy when I heard that, because when I was at Bricknell I had such an overactive conscience I used to blush every time any misdemeanour was read out in assembly! Because of that I was sure everyone must have been looking at me and would think it was me who had done it – whatever it was – even if it was someone peeing over the floor in the boys' toilet! "Cyril" (as we called her) said she was very pleased with what Mr. Lofthouse had said, and I was gratified that he knew I hadn't been the cause of all his school problems. Unfortunately, when I started there, Hilary and I began to grow apart a bit, because it wasn't "cool" for her to mix with the new kids. However, I soon got to know Sue Suddart, who lived on Grammar School Road, and had also passed to St. Mary's. We became good friends. We used to ride our bikes to school together, or got a lift from her Dad in his flashy red Triumph Herald. I can remember being very taken with the nuns at school, and the ritual of crossing ourselves and saying the "Hail Mary" before every lesson. I liked the convent chapel with all the statues, and putting "Holy" water on our foreheads and bowing to the altar when we went in. I can't say I ever felt the presence of God there – just a sense of heavy silence and a fear of offending Him by somehow doing something wrong without knowing it. I quite liked the "God Shop" in the art room, where they sold plastic statues of Mary and various saints, plus medals and pictures of the saints, or of Jesus with a big hole in his chest and a flaming heart leaping out of it. I liked the pink rosaries which I thought were necklaces. They also had crucifixes with Jesus hanging on them dripping with blood, all good material for an impressionable protestant like me.

It was a good school, with plenty of enthusiastic teachers and extra-curricular input. They aimed to turn out well educated, responsible, and well rounded world citizens. Ideally they should be devout Catholics, but sincere Protestants were tolerated! Quite a number of our 6th Formers went to Oxford and Cambridge after leaving us, and University was definitely the preferred goal for all of us. We had four "Houses", Red, Blue, Yellow, and Green. I was "Green". We each had a Latin motto, and a house anthem. Our house motto was "Non sibi, sed alliis" – "Not for self, but for others", and the house song was to the tune of "Men of Harlech". The school motto was "Ad Majorem Dei Gloriam" – "To the Greater Honour and Glory of God". I can remember most of the words of our school song, it was quite inspiring to hear us all singing it with great sincerity and emotion at Speech Days. The first verse was:

"Our gallant ship today we sail with pride,
Upon her decks, we fear nor rock, nor tide.
To her high honour, we our voices raise,
To sing with grateful hearts St, Mary's praise."

We had some famous speakers at our Speech Days. The one who stands out in my mind is Basil Hume. This was before he became a Cardinal, and Bishop of Westminster. When he came to us he was still Abbot of Ampleforth, a Benedictine Monastery in North Yorkshire which had a prestigious college. I can remember him coming into the school hall; very tall with white robes, and the most amazing "presence". You could "feel" that he was a man of true "holiness", and that he had a very special destiny in life. We had other visitors to the school. One of the most inspirational was Gladys Aylward, the missionary to China who was portrayed in the film "The Inn of the Sixth Happiness" starring Ingrid Bergman. She was so tiny and frail, it seemed crazy to have a statuesque actress like Bergman play her character in the film, but when she spoke, and we heard her story, we realised that she was an absolute giant amongst women. Historically significant, but not quite so clear in my mind, was a speaker who came to the school in what must have been 1960 or 61. He had been a photographer on one of Ernest Shackleton's Antarctic expeditions. I can't remember his name, but it could possibly have been Frank Hurley. He was very interesting, and had lots of slides and artefacts.

Some of our teachers were a bit strange. Quite a few of them were nuns, some of whom were lovely, such as Sister Mary Agnes, our art teacher. She later became Mother Superior of the Convent. Another sweet one was Sister Mary Ambrose, who taught us Latin. Others were downright nasty, such as Sister Mary Peter. She had a little bunch of groupies amongst her students, and was quite spiteful to some of the other girls. I heard later that she left the convent, so I'm sure she was a phoney (they would say she didn't have a true vocation!) I had "run-ins" with Nadine Cammish, our French teacher, who was a bit of a psycho, she once screamed at me and kicked me out of a lesson because I translated "Un soupcon de crime" as " A spoonful of cream". Miss O'Rafferty was our Needlework teacher. She was a bitter and twisted old Irish spinster, who delighted in finding minute faults in our work and making us unpick hours worth of stitching, only for us to repeat it and for her to find another reason to unpick it again. It once took me a whole year to make some stupid embroidered half apron, only to realise, when it was done, that it was useless, because the embroidery and smocking she made us do on the top of it narrowed it so much it didn't cover or protect anything. However, it's an ill wind, because fear of her meant I did learn to sew! All of our teachers were women except one, Kevin MacNamara, who taught us History. I think he was only allowed into our testosterone free environment because he was so unattractive! He was a podgy, lily white little man with a silly moustache and hair like an electrocuted brillo pad. He was very interested in Politics, and later became Labour M.P. for Hull North, and a shadow cabinet minister when Neil Kinnock was leader of the Labour Party.

I worked fairly hard at St. Mary's, and did well, but now, increasingly, I was distracted by boys. It was an all girls school, which I'm sure helped feed the obsession. St. Mary's turned out more nympho dropouts than any other school in Hull! Boys were a mystery to me, having no brothers or any male cousins living nearby. Sue and I used to sit on our wall, watching and "grading" the Hull Grammar boys leaving school in the afternoons (we came out of school earlier than them). About once a month Hull Grammar

School held a dance, and when we were in the 3rd year at St. Mary's Sue and I started to go along. We looked forward to these so much. We wore short circular skirts that flared out when we jived/bopped, and underneath them layers and layers of net underskirts to make the skirts stand out like chopped off crinolines! On our feet we wore bobbysox and pumps, tights weren't invented yet and our skirts were too short to wear stockings. The big attraction was the boys of course, and we looked out for the ones we had seen and graded when sitting on our garden wall.

On my 14th birthday there was a Grammar School Dance. I had a lovely new outfit and was really excited about going, I had a feeling it was going to be a special day. It was. Not very far into the evening I was asked to dance by a boy I liked the look of. We danced together for the rest of the night and he walked me home. We got on well, talked and laughed a lot, and he asked if he could take me to the movies the following weekend. I said yes. It was my very first date. We went to see "Psycho", and it was terrifying! His name was Chris Scott. From then on we spent more and more time together, and began to fall deeply in love with one another. I don't think Mum and Dad knew what to do about us. We were certainly spending way too much time together for kids of our age, but Chris's home life was far from ideal. His Mum was divorced, and I think she may have been alcoholic. She was attractive and had plenty of boyfriends, but the main one was married and treated her very badly. Chris used to get really upset about it all. He didn't have much contact with his father, but one of his Mum's ex-boyfriends was a nice guy who would let Chris cry on his shoulder and give him pocket money if he needed it. I think Chris was desperate for some peace and security, and he found it at our house and with me. I was so happy, and Chris was so sweet, he brought me little presents all the time. On Valentine's Day 1961 he brought me a little pot of snowdrops, I planted them at the foot of our garden steps at Number 3. They are still growing there, and I have a clump taken from there growing in my garden now. That February 14th was a significant day for us, but for me in particular, as my period was due, and it didn't come. Enough to say that our love for and intense involvement with one other had inevitably led us a lot further in our physical relationship than either of us intended. I guess I knew deep down that I could be pregnant. We both knew the facts of life, of course, but were young and naïve enough to believe that "this could never happen to us"! I went into major denial, even Chris and I didn't really talk about it, except for him asking if my period had come, and me telling him it hadn't. We joked about it, calling the baby "bugoo" for some reason, but not really believing he (it was always a boy) existed. The enormity of our situation, if I was pregnant, was too much to even contemplate. I was 14, at a convent school, he was 15, it was 1961. This was "News of the World" headline material. So we both carried on as if nothing was wrong. Mum kept asking, but I think she was the same as me – she didn't want to even think about the obvious cause of my lack of periods. She took me to the doctor, an old family friend, who also overlooked the unthinkably obvious and treated me for anaemia. I began to seriously overeat. I was feeling really sick in the mornings by this time, and sugary things seemed to help it, so on the way to school I would stop in at the Cake Shop, buy a bag of meringues, and hide them in my desk, munching on them through the day to alleviate the nausea. I didn't tell any of my friends – that would have been "making it all real". In the evenings Chris would come over, and we would fry up any new potatoes left over from dinner, and sit and eat them in front of our brand new telly. To this day I can't look at a Jersey Royal without thinking of that time. We hardly went out, we had no money, and television was still a novelty to both of us.

In Spring of that year I went on what is still, in spite of the frightening situation I was in at the time, one of the most wonderful and formative trips of my life. I think to compensate me for not being able to afford much when Dad was ill and off work, Mum and Dad had paid a lot of money for me to go to Italy on a school trip. It had been planned for quite a while, and I had been so excited at the prospect of going abroad for the first time, especially to romantic Italy, but when the time actually came I really didn't want to go. I didn't want to leave Chris, I was increasingly lonely and frightened, and one more "unknown" seemed too much to cope with. However, I couldn't get out of it, so just before Easter a bunch of us little Hull convent girls (complete with school uniforms and hats!) set off by train for Rome. What a nightmare journey. I threw up all the way to Dover, then on the boat to Calais, then on the train again all the way to Rome. By the time we got there I was very ill, but didn't realise how bad I must have been until I later studied physiology and biochemistry. I was desperately thirsty all the way but there was hardly any provision for us on the journey. When we pulled into stations there were drinks vendors on the platforms, but we had hardly any time to get out and buy anything, and if we did, the bottled drinks were so expensive I knew I would run out of money very quickly. On top of this we had been indoctrinated by the nuns "not to drink the water or buy food from the locals". Of course the excessive vomiting and lack of water meant that I was seriously dehydrated.

Our first excursion once we got to Rome was to St. Peter's (of course). I can remember being inside the Basilica, feeling as if I was floating around on the ceiling, looking down at everyone. In spite of being so ill, a lasting impression of the beauty and significance of the place dawned on me. At that time Michaelangelo's "Pieta" was at the entrance to the Basilica, and we stood very close to it. It was wonderful. I couldn't believe anyone could create such beauty and pathos from a piece of rock. I was heartbroken when in later years some maniac attacked it with a hammer. Apparently it was repaired, but was then moved to some inaccessible place where it could only be seen from a distance. I feel very privileged to have had the chance to see it at such close quarters. We stayed at the "Foro Italico Della Studente", The Olympic Village. The Olympics had been held in Rome in 1960, and the accommodation was now used for students on trips to the "Eternal City". It was an impressive place. Close to where we stayed there was a small amphitheatre surrounded by statues (all new and pseudo-classical, made for the Olympics) I began to see the difference between true works of art and this cheesy tourist stuff they had cobbled together for the masses of visitors at that time! I gradually recovered from my dehydration, dragging myself on sightseeing trips when all I wanted to do was sleep, but eventually starting to appreciate more and more being in such an amazing place. We went to St. Peter's Square to hear the Pope deliver his Easter message. It was packed, and we were so far back I couldn't see or hear him! At that time the Pope was John 23rd (the Beloved). He was very popular. You can imagine what an impact a bunch of nubile English Convent schoolgirls had on the bottom pinching Italians. Our backsides were black and blue by the time we left the square. I was missing Chris desperately, and reacted very angrily to any approach being made to me by other men. I remember Miss MacAllister, our music teacher, commending me after the trip for what she called my good behaviour, meaning my rejection of all the advances the randy Italians made on us. Not one of the teachers questioned my initial withdrawal and lack of enthusiasm, let alone recognised my illness! Some of the older girls got up to exciting and dangerous stuff. Mary Lord, who was in our 6th Form I think, sneaked out of the window and went to Ostia with some guy on the back of his Lambretta. That was about the worst offence that came to light, but I think there were some pretty serious flirtations with waiters going on all through the trip! After Rome we went South by coach to Naples, past Mount Vesuvius and calling in at Pompeii. I thought Pompeii pretty boring really, apart from the figures of people fossilised by volcanic ash. In later years I realised that we had been carefully shielded from all the interesting stuff! I bought an unmounted cameo there for my Grandma – I still have it, now mounted into a brooch. From there we went to a small town called Vico Equense, not far from Sorrento. We stayed at a little Albergo which looked pretty ordinary when we checked in at about 6pm. We went to our rooms and got ready for dinner, then had our meal in the dining room which had three of its walls covered with bamboo blinds. We were tired, and didn't take in our surroundings too much, so the sight which greeted us when we went down to breakfast in the same room the following day was absolutely overwhelming. The room was really a covered terrace, and the bamboo blinds had been pulled up to reveal the most wonderful vistas of the sun rising through the early morning mist on the Bay of Naples, and of orange groves stretching down steep slopes to the bay. The Island of Capri was just emerging from the milky haze on the still water. That amazing sight has been etched on my memory ever since. Our stay there was marked with trips to Sorrento and Capri – which were lovely – and also by hair-raising journeys around the steep Amalfi coast at breakneck speed, in buses driven by crazy people who thought a car horn was a substitute for careful cornering! It was quite an experience. Our packed lunches from the Albergo consisted of hard dry bread rolls, tiny hard boiled eggs, and greasy chunks of salami or smelly cheese, along with the delicious freshly picked oranges available at every meal. It was all packed into little paper carrier bags, which doubled as "sick bags" on our wild coach trips (especially for me). We just threw them out of the coach windows down the steep cliffs when they were full. My worries had almost receded into the background by this time. The constant pressure of having Mum wondering if my period had come was not there, nobody else knew, and I had started to feel a lot better, with not so many severe attacks of nausea. It was the middle of the holiday, and I came up with the idea of telling Mum when I got back that I had a period whilst I was away. Pressure off, consequences deferred! The beautiful scenery captivated me. I wrote to Chris every day, telling him about the things I was seeing. After Vico Equense we set off in our coach for Florence. This was the most beautiful city I had ever seen. We stayed at a small Albergo in one of the narrow streets leading off from The Duomo. We slept in Dormitories, but ours had a balcony, and from it we could look out on an aspect of the city just like the one in the film "A Room with a View". It was so lovely, and I was totally hooked. The owner of the Albergo was a friendly lady who really took us under her wing. I remember her teaching us how to eat Spaghetti properly by winding it onto a fork held against a spoon to stop it unravelling. We went to The Uffizi Gallery and the Pontevecchio, and to many old churches and museums with famous sculptures, murals and paintings. We stood and gazed in awe at Michaelangelo's "David", both the genuine one in the Accademia and the replica in the Piazza Della Signoria. For once there were no wisecracks from us about "private parts" on display! I think we all recognised another wonderful work of art. We visited a monastery at Fiesole, in the hills above the city. I remember the sight and scent of Wisteria tumbling over an old sun-washed garden wall, and thinking that I must one day have a garden of my own that was full of it. After Florence we again boarded a train and set off for Switzerland through Northern Italy and the Alps. We were headed for Einsiedeln, a little ski resort south of Zurich, and north east of Lucerne. We were to stay at the Hotel Rot Hut, which caused a lot of frivolous speculation about the possible quality of the accommodation (Rot Hut means "Red Hat", so called because a Cardinal had once stayed there). The attraction there was a big old church with a statue of "The Black Madonna". I can't remember her looking very black, I must say, and by that time we'd had just about enough of old churches and religious statues. Einsiedeln was pretty, though, and the mountain scenery on our journey there was awesome. There was not much snow left in the actual village, but we saw avalanches and high waterfalls from the train, as the snow on the mountains melted. The Hotel was really comfortable, and we experienced the bliss of sleeping under down quilts for the first time. The food was pretty good too, lots of Germanic stodge! By this time my appetite was enormous. We visited Lucerne and went for a cruise on the lake, which was beautiful. I bought a pair of white stiletto heels and a bright red lipstick with the money I had left.

But then it was time to come home. Back to awful reality. Mum believed my story about having a period whilst I was away, which gave me time to get my breath. Chris had spent nearly all his spare time whilst I was away working on my Biology project, a pressed flower collection. I had a huge number of specimens, and we worked together on putting them into a file, grouping them in families and species etc. I won a prize for it. We still didn't really talk about my pregnancy. We knew it would mean the end of life as we knew it, and definitely the end of our relationship. The thought of losing each other was unbearable, so we just pretended there was nothing wrong. By this time my breasts were leaking milk, and I had a hard little tummy. I'd always had a podgy belly, so managed to disguise it pretty well, and stuffed tissues inside my bra to soak up the leaks. I was piling on weight, and all my clothes were tight and uncomfortable.

3 – Anthony

The inevitable showdown happened in July, when I was 5 months pregnant. I was a good swimmer, and had been chosen to take part in the school Swimming Gala. Disguising my tummy with clothes was one thing, but in a swimming costume I had nowhere to hide. I was terrified, but couldn't get out of it no matter how I tried. I planned to "go sick" on the day, which I knew would let down all my team mates, but I felt I had no choice. Mum, however, wanted to be proud of me, so went out one day and bought me a new swimming costume. She insisted I try it on, so I took it upstairs, and just as I was taking off my bra she walked into my bedroom. The tissues fell out of my bra onto the floor. She just stood there and looked at me, and saw what she had been denying to herself for months. I remember her walking out of the room and down the stairs. I didn't move for a long time, then heard the most awful sobbing. Mum was sitting at the bottom of the stairs rocking backwards and forwards saying "What shall we do? What shall we do?" I sat at the top of the stairs, also crying. Neither of us made a move to comfort the other. It was terrible. From then on it was a bit of a blur. She told Dad as soon as he came home from work. He was so angry, I think he would have throttled Chris if he had been there. Still no-one showed any kind of comfort to anyone else. I can't remember how I said goodbye to Chris, but we managed to pass a few messages to each other through friends. I missed him so much. His Mum came to see my Mum and Dad – the first time she had shown any real interest in our relationship. It wasn't a very productive encounter. I had a visit from Social Services. Because I was still only 14 there could have been a charge of statutory rape levelled against Chris, until they realised he was just a frightened kid like me. I remember so vividly the humiliation of having to describe our sexual encounters to the social worker – with Mum sitting in the same room. Mum called Sister Mary Cyril, and she asked us to come into school to talk to her. Basically she was very kind, and said that if the pregnancy could be kept secret (to protect the school's reputation) I would be welcome to come back and finish my education. I was so grateful. I think the reason we made public for my not returning to school was that I was going to Leeds to get treatment for my Psoriasis, which had become much worse because of the stress of my situation. By this time all the family knew I was pregnant. Mary and Jim (who were having fertility problems) thought seriously about adopting my baby, but came to the conclusion that it would be impossible for everyone, especially me and the baby, to deal with the resulting family structure. Would they tell him/her? Would anyone guess the truth? Would that result in my having to leave school? (They eventually adopted two children. They were Jonathan, in 1969, and Jane a few years later, both as babies, and neither of whom have ever traced their birth parents). Even Mum and Dad contemplated bringing the baby up as their own, but decided, heartbrokenly, against it for the same reasons.

Auntie Eileen and her husband, another Uncle Harry, said that I could come to Leeds to stay with them until some decisions and arrangements had been made, so after school had broken up for summer in late July, Mum took me on the train to Crossgates, and I moved in with Eileen and Harry, and their children, Jill (aged 4), and Ann (aged 2). They made me very comfortable, fed me well, and did their best to take care of me, but they were very "restrained" people. They had married relatively late in life, everyone thought that Eileen would be the family "old maid". She had been in the RAF, then worked as a Nanny in the South of England before qualifying as a teacher. During this time she had developed a very cultured accent. I thought it sounded a bit affected, and because of that, plus her being away from Hull a lot, and her coolness towards my Grandad, she always seemed a bit aloof to me. She was my Godmother, but I must say that in later years when I tried to bring up the subject of God with her I always got an angry reaction. Apparently when she got the news of my birth she was listening to Rachmaninov's Piano Concerto No. 2, and it was always referred to as "Anne's music" from then on. I do love it actually, and it was one of the first pieces of Classical Music I ever bought. She met Uncle Harry at the school they both worked at in Leeds. Harry had childhood Arthritis, and had suffered all kinds of remedial surgery to his joints. His knees were fixed, and his hands were twisted and painful looking. He was tall and well-built with red hair, and was very kind and cheerful, in spite of being in constant pain. They seemed really old to me, but must only have been in their late 30s or early 40s. I don't think they knew how to relate to me, although I could see that they wanted to do their very best for me, but staying with them for the birth was never an option for some reason. Jill and Ann were sweet. I read stories and played with them, Ann made me laugh with her funny "language". She spoke great long sentences of gobbledegook, absolutely undecipherable even to her Mum. Increasingly, it was becoming obvious that I should have my baby adopted through an adoption society, both to give the baby the best possible future, and for me. I was so desperate for my life to return to "normal" by then that I didn't seriously consider any other course of action. I felt so guilty for bringing such shame on the family, and causing my parents anguish, after all they had been through.

It seemed like the only reasonable decision I could make, and then I could go home and everyone could carry on with their lives. The chance for a good education never seems as precious as when you think it might be taken from you. I never thought deeply about "the baby" as a person with needs and rights, this was too scary for me to consider. Fortunately, others in the family did, and the York Adoption Society seemed like a very good group to consider in looking for parents for my little one. They were a reliable organisation, and matched faiths, backgrounds, education and family likenesses between the adopters and the adoptee, plus carefully vetting them to make sure they would be good parents. I wrote to Chris a couple of times whilst I was at Auntie Eileen's, but when she found a reply from him coming through the letter box she became really indignant and shamed me into stopping writing to him. We agreed to meet on my 21st birthday, when "they" couldn't keep us apart any longer, and that was the last I heard from him until almost a year later.

I guess it was through Social Services that arrangements were made for me to go into St. Monica's Home for Unmarried Mothers, just off Manningham Lane, Bradford. Normally girls would not go there until 6 weeks before the birth, they would give birth in the Home, and then stay for 6 weeks afterwards, until their baby was adopted or taken home. My baby was due on October 24th, but because of my circumstances (unable to stay at my home until then because my pregnancy would be obvious to everyone) they allowed me to move in around the end of August. It was an awful place. The staff were nice enough, but it was a big, empty old Victorian place, with an atmosphere something like what I imagine a Dickensian workhouse would be. There weren't many girls there, and none of them were anything like me. There was Ann, an ex beauty queen who had been abandoned by her rich lover when she got pregnant. Another was Judith, she was in her 30s, and her married boyfriend dumped her for the same reason. Sheila was a Bradford shop assistant who had become pregnant by her Asian boyfriend. There were two West Indian nurses whose boyfriends had deliberately made them pregnant to try and stop them from coming to England, plus a couple more girls that I can't remember very well. We were all there because of our "shameful" condition. In 1961 it was only 50 years or so away from the dark ages when unmarried mothers were locked up in asylums for being "feebleminded" or "sexually delinquent". This was definitely a place not far removed from those days, and in fact, as I discovered later, in Ireland the awful Magdalen Girls Homes were still operating. Miss Stenton was in charge of St. Monica's. She was an ageing spinster with pebble glasses, thick woolly stockings, and heavy lace up shoes, and she was absolutely clueless about the girls in her care. She saw us as moral projects, fallen women who needed to be trained and disciplined. The house was also supposed to be haunted. The ground floor had a day nursery, the kitchen and dining room, and Miss Stenton's office. The laundry was out in the back yard – some of the girls used to go out there for a cigarette, I hadn't started smoking at that point, but used to go out with them for companionship. I heard some strange and puzzling things! I was very naïve. The 1st floor had the common room, the delivery room, a little room for preparing baby food and bottles, a small dormitory for girls almost ready to deliver, and a few rooms for the girls who had given birth and their babies. The second floor and above it, the attic floor, consisted of single bedrooms. These floors were the ones supposedly haunted. Because of this, and because there were so few girls there, everyone was sleeping on the first floor, and there wasn't any room left for me. There was no way I was going to sleep on the haunted second floor on my own, so I made myself "comfortable" on the delivery table in the delivery room! Fortunately a bed became available for me in the first floor dormitory before too long. My lasting memory of that dormitory was lying there wide awake each night with terrible heartburn, and no remedy offered by anyone when I asked. We had to do our own laundry, and took turns to prepare meals and wash up. We were responsible for keeping the house clean and smoothly running. I was useless and clueless. At 14 I had only just learned to make my own bed, so I was well and truly dropped in at the deep end. We had to travel across the city to St. Luke's Hospital for our antenatal care. The first time we were accompanied, but after that we were on our own. It was terrifying. I could cry when I think about the scared girl that I was having to find my way across a completely unfamiliar city, trying to get through the maze of streets and catch the right buses, then to sit in the antenatal clinic with unfriendly women twice my age, being asked about things I had no idea about, treated like an outcast by the staff, stabbed repeatedly in an effort to find my veins, berated for putting on too much weight and for being unable to pee in a bottle for them, all without the loving support that anyone would need in those circumstances. It was a nightmare. The second time I went on my own they took my Blood Pressure several times, and told me it was high. They sent me "home" with instructions to rest, and told me to come back in a couple of days to have it checked again. When I got back to St. Monica's (a miracle in itself) they didn't take much notice. I looked fit and healthy so why should I be allowed to skive whilst all the others did the work? When I went back to the clinic days later they immediately admitted me to the hospital antenatal ward. My BP was even higher. I was put on complete bed rest. I think I actually went back to St. Monica's after a couple of weeks, as I can remember one of the staff at the Home commenting on my "lovely soft hands" – not a compliment – a judgment on my lack of hard manual work! However, I was soon readmitted to St. Luke's when my BP went back up again to dangerous levels. I spent the rest of my pregnancy in the hospital, a child amongst mature, experienced women. The nurses called me "Mrs. Osborne". Only one of them ever called me Anne – once. She was an Irish woman who was about the only one who took time to talk to me and show me some kindness. The hospital ward was one of the old-fashioned ones, a long room with 20 or so beds, divided by curtains, so with very little privacy. The lady in the next bed was nice to me, the others just didn't know how to relate to me, nor me to them. The only other patients I remember, apart from her, were a woman of about 50 who had thought she was menopausal, but found out she was pregnant when her raised Blood Pressure was investigated. She had a big family of grown-up children, who visited her often. She was absolutely distraught and ashamed at the thought of another baby at her age. Another was a woman who had a serious back problem and was kept lying absolutely flat. I can't remember her name, but her husband was Geoffrey, I remember his name because she was always giving detailed accounts of their sex life, supposedly in an effort to understand how she had become pregnant. The thought of either of these old women having a sex life was revolting to me! For the first time I heard the word "abortion". These two women were both possible candidates for this procedure, which was very unusual in those days. If a pregnancy was threatening your life you could be considered, but two senior doctors had to agree, as well as finding someone willing to perform the operation. I don't think the menopausal lady had an abortion, because her pregnancy was too far advanced, but I'm pretty sure Geoffrey's wife had one.

I told everyone I was 17, but my real age was exposed one morning when an arrogant consultant, complete with a bevy of Medical Students, stood at the foot of my bed and asked me, in a loud voice that echoed through the ward, "How old are you, MISS Osborne?" The whole ward became silent, all waiting for my stuttered reply "Sev…Four…Sev…Fourteen". The group then moved on to the next bed, leaving me crying and feeling more desolate than I had ever felt in my life. I still find it very hard to forgive that man, and I'm sure it shaped my critical attitude toward Doctors in later life. Uncle Harry came to visit me a couple of times, and Mum and Dad came most Saturdays on Dad's motorbike, but they had to leave early to get back to Hull in daylight, otherwise I don't think I had any visitors. Goodness knows how I passed the time, it's a blur. I think I was pretty heavily sedated, I had put on 40 lbs, and lying in bed 24/7 did nothing to help my weight. My BP didn't really come down very much, and at the beginning of October there was talk of inducing labour early. Of course, I had already missed a month of school, and even if my due delivery date of 24th was right, I would still be missing another 6 weeks after that, taking me almost to Christmas – a whole term. I think the school sent me some work to do, but I was too scared to do it at hospital – that would be admitting the truth that I was just a schoolgirl. I still kept up pretences, as there were always new women on the ward, but I'm sure all the "old faithfuls" kept them informed about the scandal in their midst. In the end, at about 10 a.m. on Saturday 14th October, I was taken down to an operating theatre and my membranes were ruptured. This was done without any pain relief, and the searing agony of that procedure remains with me to this day. I don't know if I screamed, but I was dazed for a couple of hours afterwards. By 3 p.m. I was having mild contractions. When Mum and Dad came to visit me, I was coping well with the contractions. They just felt like bad period pain at that point, so when Mum and Dad made a move to leave, about 4 p.m., I didn't think about asking anyone to stay with me, nor did anyone offer. To be fair to Mum, there was no tradition of "Birth Partners", either husbands or anyone else, in 1961. You just went in to hospital and got on with it on your own. The image of the chain-smoking expectant father pacing the hospital corridors was the norm then. Mum must have been concerned for Liz, left on her own in Hull, and also for Dad, who had not long recovered from his breakdown, besides the long ride back on the motorbike and the logistics of her staying in Bradford, as they wouldn't have let her stay at the hospital. However, even given all of those circumstances, I can't understand how any woman could leave her 14 year old daughter to give birth to her first child alone. I really think she must have been in major denial of the whole thing. I have never talked to her about what happened to this day. Whenever I try to bring up the subject in any way she makes it obvious she doesn't want to talk about it.

I was put in a room on my own after they left, and my labour progressed. I hadn't had any pain relief so far, and just as the pain was becoming unbearable, the door opened and a nurse came in with a bedpan and an enema. I told her that I needed something for the pain and I was given a shot of something that made me really woozy (didn't help the pain, just half knocked me out!) I then had a tube stuck up my backside and was pumped full of soapy water and left on my own again, perched on a cold steel bedpan on top of my high hospital bed, almost passing out with the pain from the enema combined with my then powerful labour pains, plus the effort of staying on the bloody bedpan because of my semi-conscious state. When I couldn't stand it any longer I tried to get off the bed, almost falling off it, and I spilled the contents of the bedpan all over me, the bed, and the floor. The smell was unspeakable, and I was in a terrible state. I couldn't climb back into bed, even if I had wanted to sit up there amongst the shitty sheets! I think

I just lay on the floor, groaning and screaming for someone to help me. I remember calling for Jesus, Mum, Chris, and the nurse, and seemingly none of them responded. Eventually someone came and cleaned me up. I think they gave me another shot, I can't remember really, but no-one sat with me or reassured me. Nowadays I think it would be considered on a par with torture. By the time I was ready to go to the delivery room I really didn't know what was going on, I was so doped up. When I got there I was greeted by the butcher that had ruptured my membranes. He was very young and geeky, and looking back, I don't think he had a clue about what he was doing.

My little boy was born at about 10 p.m. He weighed 8lbs 13ozs and had beautiful golden-red hair. I was so doped up that I was incapable of holding him properly. I drifted in and out of consciousness as the geek stitched up my episiotomy, making a very bad job of it I might add, to the extent that for a while I could hardly even keep a Tampax in. I was wheeled on a trolley across the hospital, I didn't know where my baby was, and was too dazed to ask. When I woke up in the post-natal ward the next morning he was in a crib at the foot of my bed. I was encouraged to breast feed him, and did so with success for about 3 weeks. I stayed in hospital for about a week I think, and then went "home" to St. Monica's. We were given lessons in changing and bathing the baby, but I didn't really take much in. I can't remember ever feeling confident with the precious little thing, but I did care for him as best I could, and I'm glad I fed him myself for a while, as I feel it gave him the best start. I named him Anthony, because it had a bit of my name in it. I don't know if he kept that name when he went to his adoptive parents. He was pretty placid, and didn't seem to cry as much as the other babies. The clothes we were given to dress the babies in at St. Monica's were horrible. They were grey and worn out, or shrunken and harsh. Mum and

Dad came to see me once after he was born. Dad didn't want to see him at first, but he did eventually, and I could see the tears in his eyes as he looked at him. After a couple of weeks I was told that there was a good chance that he could be adopted sooner than the customary 6 weeks. Suitable parents had been found to take him, and they sounded perfect. They were young University Lecturers, fairly well off, and desperate to have him. I knew by then that there was no way I could keep him, and I longed to get back to school and my friends, and normality. I can't remember exactly, but I think he was about 4 weeks old when I dressed him in the lovely new clothes that had been knitted and crocheted and sewn by Mum and Grandma, and took him to York, to the Adoption Society, where I handed him over to his new family. I didn't meet or see them, nor they me, it wasn't allowed. They were waiting in one room, Mum, Anthony and I were in another. Someone came into the room to get him, and at that point only, when I had to kiss him goodbye for ever, the enormity of what I was doing hit me. I handed him over with a terrible feeling of emptiness and loss inside me, but I daren't say anything. I was so compliant and unquestioning. I dreaded upsetting anyone again, especially Mum. I guess we signed papers after he had gone, I can't remember, but I knew that I must renounce all my rights to my son, and swear never to go looking for him, or ask for any information on him from that time on. I didn't know his new name or address – even the city or country he would be living in, but I think there were regulations forbidding going abroad at first, and the only cities with Universities in that area, at that time, were Hull, Leeds and Sheffield, so the chances are he was brought up in one of the last two. I don't think they would have placed him in Hull because I lived there, but I could be wrong.

Mum and I went home to Hull, and back to my "normal" life, but of course, it was never the same again. I'd had my 15th birthday at St. Monica's, and I was a totally different person then from the girl that had excitedly set out for the Grammar School Dance a year earlier. I don't know how many nights I spent crying in my room, not only for the loss of my child, but for the loss of my girlhood. I had stretch marks everywhere, and a horrible flabby tummy. My breasts, never perky, were droopy and still leaking milk. It seemed as if I bled for weeks. I felt totally "washed up". Nobody knew how to help me, I was just left to sort myself out.

Because I didn't try to find him for many years, it might seem that I just left Anthony at York and let him fade into the past, but that wasn't the case. Once, in the late 80s, I considered putting my name on a register to show that I was willing to be "found", but after I was cautioned about being absolutely sure that I was prepared for the possible consequences of this, I decided against it. I had to consider my husband and children (3 by then, and another on the way). Also, what a terrible thing it would be to reject him for a second time if he was a needy person, and I couldn't cope with helping him. The other awful possibility I didn't want to face was that I would find out that he was dead. Every time I considered looking for him I came to the conclusion that I had to leave it to God, and either let Anthony find me, or wait until I met him in heaven, because I am convinced that I will. I just want to say though, in case he ever reads this story, that there has hardly been a day since he was adopted that I haven't thought of him. He has been part of every prayer for my family. October 14th has been a very special day to me ever since. I longed to know what he looked like, what he was doing, if he was happy and healthy, and, in later years, whether this would be the year he would come looking for me. For the first 9 years, when I was still living at home, I had to seem to forget him, and I never mentioned him to anyone except Chris, on the first occasion we met up. This was a painful meeting. He was totally different, and didn't really seem very interested in me, or in Anthony, or hearing anything about what I'd been through. We had both become different people. We didn't arrange to meet again. I knew that the pain was still too raw for my parents to talk about him, plus we were all so unquestioningly obedient to the "authorities" it would never occur to them that we could try to make some enquiries about him. I missed him terribly at first, but eventually, pain does diminish. They say time brings healing, but often it's the kind of healing that comes after losing a limb. The pain is no longer acute, but your life is permanently changed. I recently read a beautiful poem by Emily Bronte, called "Remembrance". She's actually mourning the death of her lover, but in many ways these verses describe how I feel about Anthony.

> *Sweet Love of youth, forgive, if I forget thee,*
> *While the world's tide is bearing me along;*
> *Other desires and other hopes beset me,*
> *Hopes which obscure, but cannot do thee wrong!*
> *But, when the days of golden dreams had perished,*
> *And even Despair was powerless to destroy,*
> *Then did I learn how existence could be cherished,*
> *Strengthened, and fed without the aid of joy.*
> *Then did I check the tears of useless passion--*
> *Weaned my young soul from yearning after thine;*
> *Sternly denied its burning wish to hasten*
>
> *Down to that tomb already more than mine.*
> *And, even yet, I dare not let it languish,*
> *Dare not indulge in memory's rapturous pain;*
> *Once drinking deep of that divinest anguish,*
> *How could I seek the empty world again?*

4 – The 60s

The highlight of my life was going back to school. I had missed so much, but was able to catch up (with a lot of hard work). The person who helped me most was my biology teacher, Miss Harris. She was so encouraging and helpful, knowing I loved her subject, I think, and she praised me in front of the whole school when I managed to get a 70% mark in the end of term exam. I was really grateful to her. I gradually settled back into a routine, and, after getting weighed and realising I was still about 30lbs overweight, went on a strict diet, losing all of it over a few months. Nobody told me that I could do exercises to flatten my tummy and help my droopy boobs, so I still wasn't a pretty sight naked, and was very much aware of it, but I could wear a "girdle" (most people did in those days!) and awful pointy "Madonna" bras were in fashion, so I started to look pretty good dressed! I took my Maths and English Language "O" Levels (GCSEs) a year early, and passed them both, then in the 5th Form we took the bulk of those most important exams. I had chosen to major on science – mostly because of pressure from Mum and Dad, because I was good at Biology and because "Science was the future" in those days. Mum had ambitions for me to become a Doctor, I think, but I hated Physics, and dropped it not very far into the course. Also, the Chemistry teacher, as well as making the subject totally boring to me, had a very strange attitude towards me personally. I remember her accusing me, in front of the whole class, of bleaching my hair! We did have some fun in the chemistry lab, maybe she found out and was taking it out on me. We would go in there at lunchtime and "experiment", for example, play with mercury and sodium. It's horrifying when you think how toxic they are, we used to drop mercury on the bench and chase it around until it all came together in one blob, and put chunks of sodium into beakers of water to see it burn. Someone must have been watching over us and protecting us! Chemistry was the only subject I failed at first attempt, but I passed it on retake. I did really well in Biology and finished with 9 subjects in all, but definitely didn't want to pursue sciences at "A" Level, and there was no option to "Mix & Match", it was either Sciences or Arts. This caused me a real loss of motivation. I had started to do Calculus after passing my Maths a year early, and I really hated it. I switched off completely during the lessons (I think I read magazines under the desk) and only managed to get 6% in my first exam! The teacher, Miss Thompson, finally got the message and let me give up. She was a funny old thing, little and skinny with straight cropped mousy blonde hair and thick glasses. She was great friends with our other Maths teacher, Miss Normanton, who was huge, with boobs like barrage balloons and black hair cut in a very masculine style. They both wore long skirts and brown lace up shoes. Looking back I think they were probably more than friends, but even at that age we didn't really know about stuff like homosexuality. I can remember someone saying that Princess Margaret was a Lesbian, and when I asked "What's a Lesbian?" nobody seemed to know! I knew that Mum worked with some very effeminate male nurses who used to dress up as women for the hospital Christmas Pantomimes each year. I also knew that Mum and Dad used to laugh privately about them, but how could a man have sex with a man, or a woman with a woman? It seemed obvious to me that the "outy" bits on men fitted with the "inny" bits on women, and that's what it was all about. Shows how much I knew about it all, even after all I'd been through.

In the summer of 1962 we went to Plymouth as a family for the last time, but this time we drove! Dad had bought a second hand Hillman Husky, which was the most uncomfortable old car you ever sat in. Sue Suddart came with us, so the two of us and Liz crammed into the back seat and set off on a 12 hour torture session, eventually arriving in Plymouth, absolutely frazzled. Dad was the only driver, Mum the navigator. He was a man and didn't always listen, and she didn't have a clue about driving. She would bark out orders to Dad, leaving him no time to follow her commands, or else he ignored her, and then there would be a yelling session as we got lost for the umpteenth time. In the back of the car we had 5 lots of luggage, a camping stove and kettle, plus a cage full of young racing pigeons. These belonged to Bobby Tozer, Dad's "moonlighting" partner. Dad had agreed to take them with us and release them around Coventry to see if they could make it home to Hull. We were glad to see them go I must say, but we still had the bloody cage to contend with for the rest of the journey. I remember that road trip as a blur of aching backsides, the smell of pigeons, nausea, desperate tiredness, arguments, and stops by the side of the road to "brew up" on our little primus stove. In later years I watched the TV programme "Till Death us do Part" and cried with laughing at the episode where they all went on a motoring holiday, because it reminded me so much of our trip. The world was "growing" for everyone at that time. Holidays abroad were becoming more commonplace, especially in Spain, which was close and cheap. "The Beatles" burst into our lives – they were radical in those days! Music, which I was hooked on since Jerry Lee Lewis, became even more exciting, as the Liverpool sound took off. I also discovered

James Bond, and we secretly passed paperbacks around at school, even though the nuns banned them! I was so impressionable. For years I was on a search for Balmain's "Vent Vert" perfume (literally translated "Green Wind" but implying "fresh spring breeze") after reading "Casino Royale". Bond had gone into a room, complete with gorgeous seductress lying on the bed of course, and commented that the room smelled of this. I guess I thought it would transform me into a Bond girl! Eventually, years later, I found it in Spain, but could hardly afford it, it was so expensive, but it was gorgeous, and I still love it. I remember a boyfriend asking me what it was at some later date, and when I told him he howled with laughter, telling me that green wind was what they could all smell in the rugby changing room after a curry the night before. He had no romance in his soul!

Whilst I had been away in Bradford Sue Suddart had become more friendly with another girl in our class. Her name was Helena Mudryk. Her parents were Polish, they had come to England and set up a Market Garden in Kirkella, in the suburbs North of Hull. She was a year older than Sue and I, and got her driving license as soon as it was legal – she had been driving trucks around the market garden for years! Her parents had a white Saab coupe, which she would occasionally drive to school. When she did, a bunch of us would cram into it at lunchtime, making sure we had on our school hats, and go joyriding around the town, delighting in the looks of horror we would get from other drivers and passers-by. We only got stopped once by the police, and hadn't committed any offence so were let go with a laugh! She was a lot of fun, and had a boyfriend called Dave who worked at Hawker-Siddeley Aviation at Brough. He had lots of friends, most of whom worked there, and on Fridays they all used to go to the

"Jazz Club" at Windsor Hall on Argyle Street in the centre of Hull. Helena invited Sue and I to go along. We were almost 16 by then, and looked older, so didn't have any problem going to the pub and guzzling beer with them all! Sue immediately got friendly with a boy called George. He was a strange bloke, very serious and intense, I didn't really like him. Helena's Dave was a laugh, he was gorgeous looking and knew it, but he was crazy about Helena, and they eventually got married. I got to know a nice guy called John Cummings. We danced really well together, and had a lot of fun going to parties, and at the Jazz Club, but we were more friends than anything, and found each other quite useful for providing an escort when needed. Some of us used to go to the local "Mecca" dance hall too – but we wouldn't admit it to the Jazz Club crowd! They were all a bit obsessive about being "cool" and would spend hours talking about Charlie Parker, Cannonball Adderley and Miles Davis. I wasn't that keen on most modern jazz, but I liked Miles Davis and bought a couple of his albums when I started work. The Mecca wasn't cool, and actually it was pretty grim, with all the girls, tarted up to the eyeballs, standing around waiting for some spotty creep to ask them for a dance. However, anything was better than staying in on a weekend!

We were by now in the 6th Form at school, I was taking English, Geography and Religious Studies at "A" Level, but didn't have a clue what I would do with it all. Because of this lack of direction, and also because Sue, along with quite a few other friends, had left school to go to work, I started to think about leaving too. Sue had money! She could buy clothes, and records, and cigarettes (by this time we were both smoking). In the end, Mum and Dad allowed me to apply for a job at the local Public Health Laboratory. I know I did really well at the interview, but it was a guy that got the position. I was very disappointed, but the Chief Technician recommended me to his wife, who worked in the Pathology Lab at Kingston General Hospital. They were looking for a student technician in the Haematology section. This also happened to be where Auntie Mig's sister, Betty, worked. She also recommended me, and so I went for an interview there, and got the job. Sister Mary Cyril was really upset that I was leaving. I remember she said "Oh, go and get married and have babies" as if it was the worst thing anyone could do!

So, in early 1964, at 17 years old, off I went, out into the big bad world. I started work in Haematology, earning about £30 a month. I found the job really interesting, and I liked most of the people I was working with. I got friendly with Lynne Bromby, another student. She was quite a character, she had been a scholarship student at a really prestigious local school, Tranby Croft. It was famous, not only as a good school, but because, when it was a private residence, a big gambling scandal happened there involving King Edward VII. Lynne lived in Anlaby, and had a horse called Mickey Mouse which she kept about 3 miles away from home. Every morning she got up at 5 am, rode her push bike up hill all the way to the horse field, fed Mickey and made sure he was OK, and then rode home, got ready for work, and cycled into work, another 5 miles away. I stayed with her a few times (after late nights out together) and went along with her to feed Mickey – I was exhausted all day! In the evening she would do it all in reverse, and exercise him into the bargain. She was super fit, and looked as if she could crack walnuts between her thighs! Her Mum and Dad were older, in their 50s I think. She was very artistic, and decorated her own room regularly. It was turquoise and orange when I first saw it, and she had made a collage of magazine pictures on one wall, stuck on like wallpaper.

I loved it, and immediately copied it (only mine was pink and orange). My wall was a mix of pin-ups, rock stars and models, fashions, adverts, and scenes I liked, and right in the centre of them all was a sort of sunburst with an island set in the middle of a golden sea. I didn't know where it was then, but it was destined to play a very special part in my life. We went to the local Technical College each Monday and one evening a week to study for our Intermediate exam. This exam covered all the Pathology disciplines of that time – Biochemistry, Bacteriology, Histology, Cytology, Virology, Haematology, and Blood Transfusion. This meant we visited other labs in the area, and got to know their students. The guy who got "my" job in Public Health was in the same class at college, too. I really enjoyed work, and it was wonderful to have money – I wasn't very careful with it, and usually had to borrow money from Dad and pay him back at the end of the month!

At some point whilst I was still at school I had become a Junior Member of Bricknell Avenue Methodist Church. I recently read the promise I made at that membership ceremony, and I remember thinking then that I could not make this promise lightly, so I must have been sincere when I actually made it. Could it be because I recognised my need to "repent from my wicked ways"? I don't know, but sadly, like a New Year Resolution, it didn't last long. I had started smoking with a vengeance, and going to the pub was a way of life by then, although I only drank bitter – I couldn't afford anything else! I began to distance myself from the Church crowd, because I seemed to have less and less in common with them, and I also began to view my past "sins" from the "liberated" perspective of the "Swinging 60s". Having money meant my social life was a bit more varied. I still hung around with some of the jazz club crowd, and had a few boyfriends. One of them

I remember was Andrew Drummond. He was really keen on me but I wasn't at all keen on him. I suppose I used him really. He once hitchhiked down to London specially to get me a pair of Levi Cords. Another time he did the same thing to get me a record – "Woolly Bully" by Sam the Sham and the Pharaohs! Hull was such a backwater, we couldn't even get a pair of Levi's there. All of my friends were determined to get out of there as soon as they could, and most of them did. I met Chris once again at a party at Andrew's house. He was at Hull University by then, and had a snooty little girlfriend and a phoney London accent. He was really patronising towards me, I was really disgusted, and think I finally gave up on him at that point, although, even to this day, I remember with sadness the loss of that first love of my life.

Lynne and I decided to go on holiday together, and plumped for St. Ives in Cornwall. She had been there with her parents and we both loved Cornwall, so in June 1964 off we went. We rented a "flat" on Porthmeor Beach. It was just a studio apartment with an en suite bathroom, but we had an amazing view of the sweeping surf and the town in the distance, and it was only a short walk to the beach. We spent 2 weeks surfing and frying ourselves in the sun. Lynne turned a beautiful mahogany brown, I turned salmon pink and peeled! Occasionally we walked through the old town and went to Porthminster Beach, but we had designs on the surfers, the tanned blonde hunks who were based at the Surf Lifesaving Club on Porthmeor Beach, so we mostly hung around there. They never gave us a glance. They were surrounded by women, all bikini clad and gorgeous, I think they took their pick of them. I remember one of the women had a tiny swallow tattooed on her shoulder, and we thought this was so unusual and exotic. Times have changed. We went to "The Lifeboat" pub every night, drank cider, and met a few guys, but nobody special. We cooked our own meals – quick and simple stuff like Sausages in Soup – and we picked up fresh bread, saffron buns and Cornish "Hevva Cake" from the bakery every morning. It was so nice to have our own space, without parents or family pressures, and we both developed an enjoyment of cooking which has carried on all of our lives. We went back again for a week in the September, to a different flat, but the town was very quiet by then, and half the surfers had gone. When we went back to work I found I had been transferred to another hospital – Sutton Annexe. It was a lot further away, and I had no transport but my push-bike, so I had to ride it 6 miles to work every morning (and home at night) whatever the weather. It was a bit quiet over there, and I missed my friends, but it was nice working in a small lab, and in a small hospital. The work was a lot more varied, and I did see my friends at college. I bought a guitar around then, and started playing a few chords, but didn't really press in too much. I enjoyed college, worked fairly hard, and eventually passed my intermediate exam. I then had to choose my speciality subject, and, as I had worked in Haematology, decided to go ahead and specialise in that. I would be working towards a Final exam, and if successful, I would have A.I.M.L.S. after my name – Associate of the Institute of Medical Laboratory Sciences, the equivalent of a Diploma. I could then go on to take a Final exam in another subject and become a Fellow of the Institute, the equivalent of a Degree.

My social life was pretty busy during these years. I dated a student who was working at the hospital as a porter – he wasn't a very nice person, and his mother was a jealous old hag who hated me, so that didn't last long, but through him I met Jill Sizen – who was dating his friend, Nick. Jill worked as a Window Dresser at Carmichael's, a big store in Hull, and she was a great laugh. She joined Lynne and I, plus Wendy Harding, another student at the Lab, and her friend Sue Spafford, a teacher, and we generally hung out together. We went to dances at the Students' Union at the University, and to Art College Balls, as well as pubbing – usually at "The Haworth", or going to concerts. It was an exciting time musically. At Art College Balls we heard bands like "John Mayall's Bluesbreakers", Alexis Korner, and "Zoot Money's Big Roll Band" and at the University I heard "Family" and Sonny Boy Williamson. I went to concerts at the ABC cinema – and saw "The Rolling Stones", Chuck Berry, "The Moody Blues" and Long John Baldry. I saw "The Animals" at Bridlington Spa. "The Beatles" became everybody's favourite so I lost interest in them and started worshipping "The Rolling Stones" because nobody's Mum liked them! My favourite was Charlie Watts. A highlight of my life a bit later on was going to a gig at The Skyline Ballroom in Hull where "Cream" were playing. A couple of us went off to find the loo, and wandered into a room where Eric Clapton and Jack Bruce were sitting at a piano, experimenting with one of their arrangements. They weren't really interested in us country bumpkins, they were trying to sort out their music, but I later saw "Cream" at another gig at Hull Guildhall, and got chatted up by Ginger Baker – the only one I didn't fancy! I also went to a couple of Classical concerts at the Guildhall with Mum around this time. One was to hear Julius Katchen playing Grieg's piano concerto, and the other was Yehudi Menuhin playing either Bruch's or Mendelssohn's Violin Concerto, I can't remember which, both are so beautiful and still favourites of mine.

A few things stand out during this period of my life apart from all this. I went to St Ives again with Lynne, but then she started dating my friend, John Cummings. I was a bit upset, because it meant I didn't have a tame escort when I needed one, but since I had no plans for a future with him felt I couldn't really complain. The following year Jill Sizen and I went on holiday to San Feliu de Guixols on the Costa Brava. I sold my guitar and got an evening job at the Haworth as a barmaid to get some extra money, so I was knackered by the time we went on holiday! I remember getting on a plane for the first time (Manchester airport) and landing in Gerona, where the amazing smell of Spain hit me as we disembarked. It was a mixture of black tobacco, garlic and seafood! I have loved Spain ever since. We had fun, drank a lot of cheap champagne and Cuba Libres, learned how to drink Pernod from special glasses which had a funnel to drip water through a sugar cube onto the absinthe below, turning it a cloudy pale green (we suffered the consequences of all of the above!) I also discovered real coffee, which of course played a leading role in dealing with the "mornings after". I stood on a Sea Urchin whilst we were out swimming one day, which was agony, but the little guy on the beach who rented the deckchairs showed me how to get it all out of my foot. He also showed us how to eat the raw, orange sea urchin roes. We weren't too keen on the taste, but it felt like vengeance! We met some nice English guys, but Jill was very popular with Spanish men, and we had quite a few escapades with the waiters from the hotel. One of them, the "maitre-d'hotel", a greasy, gold-toothed slimeball, was a real pain, and would do things like leaving obscenely carved bananas on Jill's breakfast plate. He also threatened to get his friends to stab Jill's English boyfriend if he ever went down to the town. The morning we left the hotel to go home he was having his photo taken, dressed in his best uniform, next to the pool, so a bunch of us did a massive dive-bomb into the pool right next to him. He got soaked, and I think we would all have been stabbed if we had stayed any longer. I got very friendly with Jill over the next couple of years, and with her family too. Her Dad had been on the North Atlantic Convoys during the 2nd World War, and had spent some time in New York. As a result he had a fabulous record collection. His favourites were Django Reinhardt and Stephane Grapelli – members of the Hot Club de France Quintet, and he also introduced me to Florence Foster Jenkins, who is still a favourite of mine (check her out singing the "Queen of the Night" aria from Mozart's "Magic Flute" – you never heard singing like it!) Jill eventually moved down to London, got engaged to a Hull guy called Howard Godman, and we lost touch.

The following year I went on holiday to Spain again, this time to Lloret de Mar, with Sue Spafford. I made all my clothes for this holiday, and really enjoyed doing it. We had a good time, as well as re-discovering real coffee, Bacardi and Coke, and Pernod. I started smoking Gauloises and Sobranie Black Russian cigarettes. These were gorgeous looking black things with gold filters. What a poser I was! On each trip to Spain I went to the bullfight. Reading Ernest Hemingway had made me curious about bullfighting, and I must say that I loved the atmosphere and ritual of it all, especially the fabulous costumes of the matadors and the parades and music. I can't help thinking that if I was a bull I'd rather die that way, with a chance to fight back, than in some stinking abbatoir with a bunch of other terrified animals. One of the best bullfighters I saw was a "Rejoneador" who fought from horseback. He was nothing like the picadors – who gouged at the bull's shoulders with long lances to weaken the neck muscles so that the matador could make a clean kill more easily at the end of the fight. This was the only bit of the bullfight I felt was unfair. They sat on heavily padded horses (which sometimes were gored because the bull would get its horns under the padding) but this guy was very different and an amazingly skilled horseman. The highlight, however, was going to Barcelona (the year we were at Lloret) to the Plaza De Toros "Monumental" and seeing El Cordobes fight. I had a big poster of him on my wall at home – he was a heart-throb in those days! We were in the cheapest "Sol" seats of the huge bullring there, in the blazing sun right at the top of the steep banks of seats. We couldn't see much detail, but the atmosphere was electric. He fought well, and was awarded both ears and the tail of his second bull, as well as being showered with roses by the rich Senoras in the expensive "Sombra" seats down at the front - unforgettable sights and smells and emotions. My last trip to Spain was again with Sue Spafford, but this time we went to the Costa Del Sol, to Torremolinos. During this trip we went over to Morocco, sailing from Malaga to Tangier. I nearly missed this, because I was really ill with food poisoning after eating some dodgy octopus in a Paella. However, I dragged myself onto the boat, determined not to miss my chance to visit Africa. I was still throwing up and had terrible stomach pains and diarrhoea, so you can imagine what it was like trying to use the loo on the boat. It was typical Moroccan style, a hole in the floor and a strap on the ceiling to hang from whilst aiming. Makes me realise how strong-willed I am! Tangier was a revelation, again the smells of the place were so evocative, and I'll never forget the turquoise sea, and the Casbah, full of little shops selling mounds of brightly coloured spices, exotic fruits, gorgeous carpets, beautiful fabrics, and carved silver and brass ornaments. Tangier was as far as we got, but ever since I've had a yen to go to Marrakech and Casablanca, and to see the Atlas Mountains. Maybe one day!

On the home front, all sorts of things were going on. Hilary, my old friend, had got married to Harry Emerson,

I was her bridesmaid. She eventually divorced him, married a guy called Dave, and moved to Australia. Sue Suddart had dumped George and married a sailor called Keith. Again, I was a bridesmaid. I remember her 21st birthday, she was lying in the local maternity hospital, pregnant with twins and hardly able to walk (she was only small and her twins weighed over 6 lbs each). I was Godmother to Simon and Paul when they were born. She divorced Keith later and ended up teaching in Brunei, married again and now lives in York. We contacted each other again briefly when we were in our 50s, intending to meet up, but I think she thought I was mad when I suggested a bunch of us met up and started a "red hat and purple dress group of "ladies who lunch" (as in Jenny Joseph's poem "Warning"- which I mentioned when talking about Auntie Mig's Mum, Vi) and I didn't hear from her again. Her loss! Wendy Harding was dating a guy called Chris Thomas, whom she eventually married. I dated his friend, John Woodhouse – more of that later. Sue Spafford didn't seem to form many serious relationships, but she later married a guy with lots of money and they eventually moved to Indiana. I can remember a bunch of us girls sitting in the Haworth, agreeing that if we knew we would get married eventually, we wouldn't be too concerned about not having a steady boyfriend! I had plenty of dates, but not with anyone I was very keen on. One guy I do remember, because he gave me the best laugh of my life. I literally could not stop laughing for days, real belly-laughing, with tears pouring out of my eyes every time I thought of him (can't remember his name). I met him at a dance at the university. He was a student there, and I stupidly went back to his room for a "cup of coffee" afterwards. He started getting a bit amorous, and, obviously proud of his physique, ripped off his shirt, threw it over his shoulder, and got on with trying to have his wicked way with me. A couple of minutes later I looked over his shoulder and flames and smoke had started to leap up from his little electric fire! He had thrown his shirt on top of it, and it was well ablaze. That did the trick – he leapt up and threw a coat over it, fortunately remembering to turn it off. I started laughing then, and laughed all the way home on the back of his motor bike. He must have been a nice guy to take me home when I was choking with laughter at the loss of his best shirt and the near inferno in his room, but he never called me after that! What made it worse was that I couldn't tell anyone at home, which made me laugh all the more. I did have fun, but I was getting really fed up with casual relationships. I was longing to love, and be loved in return. I had moved back to Kingston General Hospital by this time, and was working in Blood Transfusion, which I found fascinating. In this department we got to be "on call" for anyone needing emergency transfusions when the lab was closed – nights and weekends. This could be very high-pressured. We had to do a blood grouping on the patient and find compatible blood for them, sometimes there would be two or three patients at the same time. Other nights we would not get one call. We were paid standby, so with this extra money I decided to get some driving lessons. I passed my driving test the second time I took it, and with a small loan from my Grandma I bought myself a car. It was a Green Mini with a white roof. I absolutely loved it, and really enjoyed driving.

About this time a new guy started working in Transfusion. His name was Ian Martin, and as soon as I saw him I fell head over heels in love. He was lovely, tall and blonde and good looking. He didn't seem particularly interested in me, but there was another new guy working in Haematology, the John Woodhouse I mentioned earlier, Chris Thomas's friend. He had just been kicked out of Medical College at

St. Thomas's in London after failing his first year exams. Ian had also just failed his first year exams, but in Pharmacy at Sunderland University. I somehow knew that the kudos of being an ex-St. Thomas's medical student meant that Ian was a bit jealous of John. Added to this, in spite of the fact that John was not a pretty sight, he was terrific fun, and women loved him. I knew that the way to get to Ian was to date John, so I did, and it worked! We dated for quite a while, most of it whilst I was also dating John, but Ian was the one I really loved. He was, however, playing me at my own game, occasionally dating Barbara, a girl from ECG. Probably because he sensed I was so desperately keen on him, our relationship never really became what I wanted it to be, and he eventually married Barbara, telling me that if it wasn't her it would be me. Big deal. I can remember feeling totally numb on the day they got married, I still sometimes feel sad over losing him, but with hindsight I can see that he really didn't care for me.

I carried on dating John, but he didn't want commitment. We had some good times, though. He had left the lab and had started studying psychology at Nottingham University, so I used to go down there at weekends and for big occasions. One visit stands out, when "The Who" were playing at the Graduation Ball. These were the days of Keith Moon drumming and Pete Townshend smashing guitars into amplifiers. They had just written "Tommy" and it was virtually the same concert they recorded "Live at Leeds". It was incredible, I was almost deaf for two days afterwards! The Bonzo Dog Doodah Band were playing in a different room – they were great too, really funny. We also went on holiday together, camping in Cornwall. We began the trip by driving down to the Taunton area in my Mini, to where Lynne and John Cummings now lived. The latter part of the journey was a nightmare, as they lived deep in the wilds of

Somerset where no street lights existed, it was dark, and absolutely chucking down with rain, then my windscreen wipers packed up! However – we survived. After a couple of days with them we carried on to Cornwall. Lynne and John had married in Hull Registry Office, promising to "Love, Honour and Whatever, until something better came along" (literally!) and had moved down to Sampford Arundel. That was 1968 I think, and they are still together as I write, in 2010! We went to Mevagissey, and The Lizard, but the lasting memory of that holiday was that for some reason I could not stop crying. I don't think John knew what to do, he certainly couldn't comfort me. I'm pretty sure a lot of it had to do with Ian getting married, and because I knew that my life had to change. After we came home I began to seriously think about my future. All my friends were getting married or engaged or moving away. Wendy married Chris, John's friend. John was his Best Man, I was John's escort. I had passed my final exam by then, so I started looking for exciting job opportunities abroad. I had often dreamed of working my way around the world, but at the back of my mind was the thought that if I did "threaten" to go abroad, John would beg me to stay and might even ask me to marry him. We had been together on and off for almost two years by then.

5 – My Island in the Sun

One morning in early 1970 I was feeling particularly depressed. I woke up a bit late and couldn't be bothered to hurry to get to work on time. The mail was delivered as I was having my breakfast, and amongst the letters was my Magazine from the Institute of Medical Laboratory Sciences. I opened it up to the "Jobs Abroad" page, and there it was – my dream job! "Wanted – AIMLS/FIMLS to work in a busy Haematology Department at King Edward VII Hospital, Bermuda". My heart literally skipped a beat. I didn't even know where Bermuda was – I thought it was in the Caribbean – but I knew that this was what I had been dreaming of. I immediately wrote out my application and posted it on the way to work. I waltzed in to work on a cloud – soon to be shot down by the rest of the staff. They laughed and said "There will be thousands of applications for a job out there, what makes you think you are so special?" I'd had to give names of people who would provide a reference, and one I chose was my ex-pathologist, Dr. Sacker. He had known me since I was a new student, but he had recently left Hull and was working with the Medical Research Council at St. Stephens Hospital in London. I wrote to him straight away, told him what I had done, and asked if he could help. He certainly did! The Pathologist in Bermuda saw that he was working at St. Stephens with the MRC, and picked me out of 100s of applicants because of his glowing reference. I was shortlisted, and eventually there were two of us. The other applicant was a girl from Liverpool called Isabel. She was older than me, and had worked as a nanny in

Greece before qualifying in Haematology. When Pat Allan, the person in charge of that department, was given the final choice between her and me, she chose Isabel. Pat also was older than me, and she loved Greece, so thought she would have more in common with Isabel. But then came the final twist. Pat was very unpopular with the chief technician and the pathologist at KEMH (I think they had both made passes at her and been rejected) so they decided to overrule her and give the job to me! I can remember when I got the news as clearly as if it was yesterday. Mum phoned me at work, and told me there was a letter from Bermuda. I told her to go ahead and open it, and she read out these words "Dear Miss Osborne, we are pleased to be able to offer you the post of ...." I screamed out "I've got the job!!!!!!" Everyone was gobsmacked. So was I, in a way, but deep down, because I had been so excited ever since I read the advert, I think I had known this was my destiny. I don't remember much about the period in between getting the letter and setting off on my biggest adventure yet. I immediately wrote back and accepted, and was given a starting date of 14th September. The hospital in Bermuda set me a load of tourist literature, and information about the place I would be working. It looked amazing, and for the first time I realised I wasn't going to the Caribbean. On the cover of one of the brochures was a picture which looked very familiar. It was a sort of sunburst, made up of an aerial photo of the island of Bermuda in the middle of a golden sea. It was the very same picture I had pasted in the middle of my bedroom wall collage when I first left school! No coincidence, I know now. My boss had a word with me to make sure I knew what I was doing (getting away from him, the old grouch, but I do think he was genuinely concerned). I got rid of a whole bunch of my "stuff" and packed up the essentials into a big trunk I had bought (Nicky now has it in her living room). Auntie Mary's husband, Jim, worked for a shipping company, so he organised everything, and sent off all my worldly goods ahead of me. I sold my precious mini to "The Rabbit King", a guy who lived around the corner, so called because he bought a lot of my baby rabbits when I used to breed them, and housed them in palatial home-made hutches. John, far from begging me not to go, didn't even show any regret. In fact, when I told him I'd got the job he said "You will give me back my Leonard Cohen album before you go, won't you"! One of the tracks on the album seemed particularly relevant.

"Hey, that's no way to say goodbye"

I loved you in the morning, our kisses deep and warm,
your hair upon the pillow like a sleepy golden storm,
yes, many loved before us, I know that we are not new,
in city and in forest they smiled like me and you,
but now it's come to distances and both of us must try,

> *your eyes are soft with sorrow,*
> *Hey, that's no way to say goodbye.*

I'm not looking for another as I wander in my time,
walk me to the corner, our steps will always rhyme
you know my love goes with you as your love stays with me,
it's just the way it changes, like the shoreline and the sea,
but let's not talk of love or chains and things we can't untie,

> *your eyes are soft with sorrow,*
> *Hey, that's no way to say goodbye.*

I loved you in the morning, our kisses deep and warm,
your hair upon the pillow like a sleepy golden storm,
yes many loved before us, I know that we are not new,
in city and in forest they smiled like me and you,
but let's not talk of love or chains and things we can't untie,

> *your eyes are soft with sorrow,*
> *Hey, that's no way to say goodbye.*

It's a beautiful haunting tune, and the words are very poetic, but it sums up the commitment-shy attitude of many men in the 60s and 70s; "no tears, lets have another quick one before you go, it's been great, but it's getting too serious so we'd better move on". I guess I wasn't really surprised at John's reaction. I knew he was sort of fond of me, but it just confirmed that I needed to get away and make a new start, I was on a road to nowhere with him. I wasn't in love with him, but I was fond of him too, and we'd had lots of fun together, so I was sad to say goodbye to him. He did stay in touch for a year or so, and we met for a drink the first time I came back on holiday, but by then we both had changed, and eventually he married a girl who completely controlled him, which seems strange to me, especially as he was a psychologist and should have recognised emotional blackmail! Looking back on my "misspent youth", I realise I was another female victim of the so called swinging 60s. Women were conned into thinking that freedom was just doing whatever they felt like, or more often what their boyfriends felt like, or even what they thought everyone else was doing, in spite of the inevitable consequences, emotional and otherwise. Many of us dug ourselves into deepening pits of low self-worth by giving ourselves to guys who wouldn't pee on us if we were on fire. We messed ourselves up hormonally taking massive doses of oestrogen in the early forms of "the pill". We screwed ourselves up reproductively and emotionally having abortions when the pill failed us. We gave ourselves psychoses by taking mind-altering drugs. I could go on. It all still does, in fact it's worse now. That's not freedom, it's bondage. What a lie it all is, straight from the pit of hell.

More than ready for my new start, I said goodbye to all my friends and workmates, some of whom I would probably never see again. They gave me a boozy send-off and all signed a big card, writing various things on it, ranging from wishing me well to a joking "good riddance". Ian just wrote "Sail on". I wish I had told him to "sail off" (exchanging the word "sail" for something more expletive) but I didn't. Mum and Dad had mixed feelings about me leaving, of course. I had always told them I would leave Hull at the first opportunity, but this was ridiculous! Three thousand miles away – it seemed almost like the ends of the earth then. They were proud of me though, and told me so, and on Wednesday 9th September they drove me down to "The Pack Horse Inn" in Staines, where we stayed the night. Liz came too, and the next day they took me to Heathrow airport where I boarded a BOAC flight to Bermuda. The three of them then went on to Plymouth for a holiday, and Mum said she cried all the way. I didn't enjoy my flight at all. I had a terrible cold, and my face and ears really hurt. I sat next to a Jamaican woman with a baby that seemed to scream all the way! The flight carried on to Kingston after Bermuda, she was going home for the first time in years and bringing her baby to show to her family. We talked a bit, but she was distracted looking after her little one, so I had plenty of time to wonder what the heck I was doing leaving everything I knew behind me. I felt very lonely, vulnerable, ill, and apprehensive for most of the flight, but then we began the descent to Kindley Field airport. It was incredible. The plane took us over the most amazing turquoise blue sea, interspersed with darker patches of coral reef. My lasting memory is of thinking that all the pictures I had seen were really true, and not touched up, as I had suspected! As we got lower we flew over the island, and I saw crescents of pale pink sand, and gentle surf breaking along the line of coral reef surrounding the coast. Pastel coloured cottages with white roofs were dotted around in a green landscape. It looked like paradise. We landed, and when the door of the plane opened it felt as if I was being smothered by a hot, wet blanket! The temperature was about 86F with a humidity of 90%!

I was met by a friendly chap who was in charge of Biochemistry at the hospital, Vic McKane. He was also acting Chief Technician, a Northern Irish man who had been in Bermuda a couple of years. I was feeling pretty well out of it by then, tired and aching, and overwhelmed by the heat and humidity, but the taxi ride to Paget was beautiful. We drove across the long causeway between the Airport and the main island, then along winding lanes, with high hedges of scarlet Hibiscus. We passed patches of undergrowth smothered with deep purple Morning Glory, tall palm trees bordering pale pink beaches in little bays, and gorgeous flowers everywhere. I saw the pastel coloured houses at close quarters, it was all wonderful. We stopped at a lovely old pink colonial style house with dark green shutters, on Point Finger Road, opposite the Hospital. It was called "Trevelyan", and was to be my home for the next year or so. It had been a guest house, but the Hospital had bought it to house the ex-pat Lab. Technicians and Radiographers who, along with Doctors and Nurses, made up 90% of the staff. It was an amazing house. In the daylight you could tell that it had seen better days, but at night it looked like a mansion (the frayed carpets and tatty furniture weren't so obvious). There was a Grand Piano in the big Drawing Room, a sweeping staircase, a lovely dining room with a huge old table, and a big kitchen. There was also one bedroom on the ground floor, which turned out to be mine. All the rooms had an en suite bathroom, and I was very happy with my new pad (until I saw the ones upstairs!) At the rear of the property were 2 or 3 small cottages. They were occupied by some of the ex-pat Doctors, and one by a physiotherapist, Sue, from the Isle of Wight. More of the hospital staff lived over the road, right next to the hospital, at another old guest house called "Gladwyn". Pat, my immediate boss in Haematology, lived there. Mr. McKane left me to unpack and rest a while. By the time he left me, as well as feeling rotten because of my cold, I was crippled with trapped wind, having been in a crowd for hours, and being too repressed to fart in public. I gratefully sank onto my own private loo, and let go what sounded like the trumpet voluntary. Afterwards I discovered that, behind the closed blinds, my bathroom window was wide open, and was right next to the bike shed, which was full of people at the time. Good start!

After a short rest I went over and met the other lab. staff, and was shown around the hospital. It was very new, and impressive. It was also pink! Everything seemed to be painted pink. It looked out over the lovely Bermuda Botanical Gardens, which became a favourite haunt of mine later. The staff seemed friendly and helpful, and I started to feel less apprehensive about starting my new job. Most of them were Brits, but Kay Kerr, a Canadian, was in charge of Histology and Cytology, and an American, Beverley Perikli, worked in Biochemistry. Bev became a good friend, she was from Boston, the first person in her family to be born in America after they had escaped from Albania. She had started working at KEMH only two weeks before I arrived, and we found out shortly after I started work that we were born on exactly the same day – 2nd November 1946! There was only one Bermudian technician working there, Janet Ingham, and she was only a Bermudian by marriage. She was a very upper class Brit originally (or liked everyone to think so). The pathologist was a little Jamaican guy with links to Bermuda through his wife. In the words of Billy Connolly and my Scottish boss, Pat, he was a "wee nyaff", and made a pass at every woman he met! He dealt with all the pathology problems on the island, including the forensic stuff. He didn't have a clue about the latter, but would get out one of his text books to find out what he should be doing if a job came up, because there was no-one else to do it! I went back to my room at Trevelyan to unpack, and later on met the other girls staying there. There was only one from the lab. Her name was Lynn Juett, who worked in Bacteriology with Janet Ingham. The other three were radiographers. One of them, Liz Penn, was on holiday in Canada, but I met the other two – Jaki Wadham and Mary Button. We went over to the hospital canteen for dinner later. It got dark quite early, and I was overwhelmed by the wonderful feeling of a tropical night. The air was warm and soft, full of the perfume of unknown blossoms, and a totally new sound, a sort of chirping vibration coming from every direction. I asked Jaki what the sound was, and she said "Oh, it's the neighbours". I didn't want to look ignorant, so didn't say anything else, but was at a loss as to what the neighbours could possibly be doing to make such a racket! Eventually I found out that it was the famous Bermuda tree frogs "singing". It's a wonderful sound which starts after dark, and it's very "tropical", but after you have been on the island for a while you don't really hear it, it's so all-pervasive. This is why Jaki had blamed the neighbours. We ate Hamburgers for dinner, and I was so keen to be well mannered and create a good impression, that I ate mine with a knife and fork. They all howled with laughter at me, but it was very good-natured, and I felt quite comfortable with them. They were all really friendly and kind. In fact the ex-pat community on the island was a great support to all the newcomers, I guess because they all knew the feeling of being thousands of miles away from home and not knowing anyone.

I was absolutely horrified when we got back to Trevelyan after dinner and went into the kitchen to make a cup of tea. When the light went on we were greeted by the sight of huge cockroaches (Bombay Runners) scuttling under the fridge and skirting boards. I stepped on one and nearly threw up, it was like standing on a jumbo shrimp, it crunched and squelched, and I was sleeping in the next room to this lot!!! However, I was so tired that I fell into bed, pulled the white cotton sheet over me, and was asleep almost immediately. The next morning I woke up to warmth, bright sunshine filtering through the shutters, and kiskadees (yellow birds) calling from the Pawpaw and Banana trees in the garden. It was magical. I was feeling much better too.

Each girl who lived there had a section of the fridge, and the kitchen cupboards and shelves for our personal food supplies. Mostly we had breakfast at Trevelyan, lunch in the canteen at the hospital, then usually cooked for ourselves in the evening. I went over to the hospital for breakfast that morning, and met Mr. McKane, who then took me into Hamilton so that I could open a bank account and go to the supermarket to buy essentials such as teabags and milk. I opened my account at the Bank of N.T. Butterfield on Front Street. Hamilton was the capital of Bermuda, and the biggest "town". Front Street was where all the major shops were. These were on one side of the street, the other side was the harbour, where all the cruise ships tied up. Shady palm trees lined the waterfront, and under them waited the open topped taxis and the horse and carriages for rent, all with fringed canopies to keep the tourists cool. The harbour was the familiar turquoise blue, and the white cruise ships were dazzling in the bright sunlight. It was the most beautiful vibrant scene. Even the business men dressed in bright colours, they wore Bermuda shorts with matching long socks in reds, yellows, and greens, topped by dark blazers and formal shirts and ties (brightly coloured again!) The policemen wore navy blue Bermuda shorts and long socks, with pale blue shirts, all topped off with a traditional English "Bobby's" helmet. The buildings were lovely, all old colonial style with balconies and shutters, and painted in the usual pastel colours. All that is, except one, which was painted in the most amazing acid shade of chartreuse. This was "Calypso", a gorgeous up market Caribbean dress shop. The walls were covered with Haitian prints and it was full of brilliantly coloured tropical clothes – I loved it, I had never seen anything like it before! We had a quick look at the shops – Triminghams, Smiths, A. S. Coopers, and The Irish Linen Shop, all selling expensive British stuff, geared towards rich American tourists, who flocked to Bermuda for a "little bit of old England". On the junction of Front Street and Reid Street, next to the Irish Linen Shop, was the "Bird Cage", a small metal covered stand from which police would direct traffic. It was completely unnecessary – just a tourist attraction. There were always hordes of them taking photos of the quaint English Bobbies! I also realised that just about every other shop was a Liquor Store! After we had been to the supermarket I realised that I would have to be very careful with what now looked like the small amount of money I brought with me. Everything was very expensive, but I managed to get the essentials, and after a short tour of the central part of the island, headed back for lunch. The island is shaped something like a fish hook, only 1 mile wide at its widest point and 24 miles long from St. Georges at one end to Ireland Island at the other. It is composed of 138 islands, and is about 20 sq. miles in total area. It is divided into "Parishes", almost like small counties. Hamilton sits right in the centre, in Pembroke parish, and the islands curve around it to form a sheltered harbour. At the opposite side of the harbour is Paget parish, which is where the hospital and Trevelyan are.

I wasn't due to start work until the Monday, and everyone else was at work. It was really hot and humid in the afternoon, so, armed with a tourist map, I set out to walk to what looked like the nearest beach. Had I known it, in about 5 minutes I could have walked to the end of Point Finger Road, across South Shore Road, and down to Hungry Bay, where I could have swum and cooled down. However, as well as my being lousy at reading maps, the actual map was lousy, and Hungry Bay wasn't marked on it because it was accessed by a private road (closed to non-resident motor vehicles). I set off, sweltering after only a few minutes, and headed along South Shore Road looking for Ariel Sands, which on the map didn't look far. After about 15 minutes I wondered if I had made a mistake, but thought it couldn't be too much further, and I was desperate for a swim, so carried on. There were no footpaths, because nobody ever walked anywhere, it was too bloody hot! I trekked along the dusty road. A few cars stopped to ask if I was OK, and I wondered why. They must have thought I was deranged or something. Eventually, after about 45 minutes, I arrived at Ariel Sands, only to find it was a private beach, and I couldn't even go for a paddle. I was also really thirsty, (nobody had the revelation of taking a bottle of water with them back then) so by the time I got back to Trevelyan I was half dead, dripping with sweat, dusty and exhausted. Thank God for a shower and good drinking water from the taps. One thing I remember was that the roads were littered with what looked like old dried up leather gloves, and I couldn't figure it out – why would so many people lose their gloves, and why wear them anyway – it was sweltering. They turned out to be squashed toads. At certain times of the year they thronged the roads, were run over and flattened in their hundreds, then dried up in no time because of the heat, yech. Even worse were the big land crabs which crossed the roads at night, the crunch when you ran over one of those was horrendous. Over the weekend I got to know the girls in the house better, and I did get to the beach, on the back of someone's mobylette, which was scary but worth it. We went to Elbow Beach, about 10 minutes away (not walking!) Bermuda has some of the best beaches in the world – they are all absolutely beautiful. The sand is made up of tiny pieces of coral and sea shell, a soft pinkish colour, and really fine and soft. The sea gently laps the beach – a reef further out stops the big waves from getting to the shore, and keeps out most of the sharks. Elbow Beach curves around gently, the famous honeymoon hotel sits at one end, at the other end is a rocky promontory. We parked the bikes and walked down a shady, sandy lane lined with trees and beautiful climbing maidenhair fern. At the bottom of the lane were steps down onto dunes, where Bay Grape bushes grew, and after that was the beach itself. It seemed like heaven to me, and when I walked into the crystal clear warm ocean I was sure it was! I borrowed a mask and snorkel and swam out towards the reef. There were small outcrops of coral scattered all over the area between the beach and the reef, they were great for standing on and resting a while, although they could be sharp and spiky. They were also great for watching the amazing brightly coloured fish which gathered around them. The most common fish were the yellow and black striped "Sergeant Majors", which would come up and have a nibble at anything they could get at, and also the beautiful mauve and pale greenish Parrot Fish, but there were countless others. I loved it all, and to think I might have chickened out of coming!

I met another girl that first weekend, Tina Waldron, who was a secretary in the X-Ray department. She was a lot of fun, and became a good friend. I also got on well with Jaki Wadham, who was one of the Trevelyan girls. She had just got engaged to Vic Wallis, an English guy who worked for the Foreign Office in The Secretariat Building in Hamilton. He was fun, too. Lynn Juett was a Londoner, and very quiet. She didn't socialise much, likewise Mary Button, who came from Todmorden, on the Lancashire/ Yorkshire border. Mary played the piano very well, and was always practising on our grand piano at Trevelyan. She was a bit strange really, one minute friendly and another stroppy and reclusive, but I appreciated the musical background she provided! Liz Penn came back from her holiday later on, and she was really nice, totally dizzy, and kept us all laughing at her hopelessness. She had a cat called Fleabag which we looked after when she was away. Fleabag was always catching lizards and bringing them into the house. One morning Liz put her bread in the toaster, and a lizard shot out of it (it must have escaped from the cat). Her screams woke the whole house! Pat Allan, my "boss" was quite a character. I got on OK with her, but the rest of the lab staff didn't like her. She was a very brusque Scot, from Paisley, near Glasgow. She was a good technician, and wouldn't tolerate shoddy work. If something wasn't quite right she would repeat it over and over again until it was, even if it meant working late, and she insisted that everyone in her department did the same. She had only been there a year, and I think that the rest of the departmental heads had been there long enough to catch the Island's "manyana" attitude. Pat's integrity and diligence got right up their noses and showed them up as lazy and careless, which most of them were! Anyway – I liked her, she was a bit prickly but I knew I could trust her. She had a really nice boyfriend, a Bermudian guy called Barry Hanson. He was an accountant whose family came from Liverpool originally. His Dad had come out to start a cargo shipping company on the Island when Barry was small, and eventually the whole family had joined him and were now naturalised Bermudians. Later on he and Pat split up, but we all had some great times together before he eventually married Liz, a nurse from England.

Everyone agreed that no-one could survive on the island for very long without some form of transport. There were very few cars, most people had mobylettes, and the second favourite way of getting around was by boat! They all told me I had to get a bike, but I didn't have enough money to buy one and also live for the month until my first paycheck. As far as they were all concerned the answer was simple – get a bank loan! I was terrified of getting into debt, and in those days the thought of a Bank Loan was outrageous, but after talking to everyone, and finding out that this was standard practice on arrival in Bermuda, I trotted down to the Bank of Butterfield, and was loaned $100, to be paid back at $20 a month. I went to a little bike rental place in Paget (highly recommended) and became the proud owner of a pale blue ex-rental mobylette and a crash helmet for just $120. I was given a very perfunctory lesson on how to start, accelerate and brake, and off I went. This was the same lesson given to tourists. Only residents were allowed to drive cars, so tourists, some of whom had never even seen a push bike or a road narrower than a freeway, would hire a "pop-pop", and ride off to dice with death on the islands' winding lanes. They were so easy to ride, just like a push bike with a motor. There were no gears, just a throttle on the handlebars which you twisted towards you to go faster, or away from you to slow down. I set off along South Shore towards Elbow Beach, then carried on as far as Horseshoe Beach, which was even lovelier than Elbow. All the way along the road were lovely little bays and gorgeous houses. There were a couple of big hotels, but mostly tourists stayed in Cottage Colonies, groups of small cottages set in lovely gardens, with a central building housing the restaurant and reception. It was all so picturesque, even the garden hedges lining the roads were exotic hibiscus bushes, with red, yellow, peach and pink blossoms. I loved it all, and started to feel so excited about my new life here in paradise! As well as the lovely flowers, I fell in love with the island birds. There were loads of Kiskadees, or Yellow birds, but there were also bright scarlet Red Cardinals and rosy breasted Bluebirds. Everyone knew when spring was here because the "Longtails" arrived. These were dazzling white Long Tailed

Tropic Birds, something like smaller and more delicate seagulls, but with long, white trailing tail feathers.

Work went well, the only thing I found daunting was taking blood from the outpatients who came to the lab for blood tests. We had a nurse who usually took it, but when she was collecting up on the wards the rest of us took in turns. After I had been there a couple of weeks, and (fortunately for them) I was getting better at doing it, a crowd of young guys came into the lab to have their blood taken. They were the latest batch of Police recruits from England. The Red Cross ran the Blood Bank at the hospital, and used the Police Force as a ready made emergency supply, as they were generally strong, healthy and available. To this end, as soon as they arrived on the island, all the new recruits came to get their blood grouped and were then logged in the donor file. It was quite nerve-racking taking their blood. As well as being nervous about actually doing it, all the female lab staff knew that they were being vetted as future dates. Added to this was the strange fact that many big strong guys couldn't stand the sight of their own blood, or needles, and a good many of them fainted. It was always the one you least expected, the biggest, toughest one. The only one of them that stands out in my mind was the first one who fainted when I was taking his blood, but Robbie remembers me taking his.

I started exploring the island on my mobylette, and also to go to some of the parties that seemed to be held every Saturday night. The host would supply mixers (Coke, Ginger Ale etc.) and food, and the guests would bring a bottle of whatever spirit they were going to drink. Booze was very cheap, especially Rum, in fact the local alcoholics were called "Rummies". No cheap old meths drinkers here, there was a better class of bum. Some of the Bacardi family lived on the island, and ran their business from a large office building in Hamilton. It seemed that the national pastime was drinking, and we saw so many tragic accidents in the hospital as a result of people riding their motor bikes whilst drunk, both tourists and residents. I was very nearly one of them. One night a bunch of us, and some nurses, were invited to a party on a Royal Navy Ship which had just arrived in Hamilton. It was a bit boring, so the party moved up to the Police Club at Prospect, in Devonshire Parish. The booze was cheap up there, and there were always plenty of eligible males to chat up, plus the Royal navy were honorary members. That night it was pretty quiet there too, so after an evening of throwing down Bacardi and Coke I decided to go home – on my mobylette. One of the guys from the ship asked if I could give him a lift back to Hamilton, and I said I would. This was common practice even if there was no pillion seat, people still hitched rides and sat on the little metal carrier over the back wheel. It was dangerous, even when the driver was sober (in spite of the 20mph speed limit) but when the driver had consumed a few Caribbean strength Bacardi and Cokes it was suicidal! We headed off down the hill towards Hamilton. As well as my being drunk, the street lights were poor, and I didn't know the road. I saw what I thought was the left turn I needed to make, and headed towards the white line cutting across the turning. Sadly - it wasn't a white line, it was a high kerb, and the turning was actually a gravelled footpath. We hit the kerb and both flew over the handlebars. I skidded along the gravel on my chin, shredding it, my hands, my knees, my beautiful red PVC coat, and my favourite black shoes. My pillion passenger landed in some bushes and only broke his finger. What a horrible shock. When we stood up and pulled ourselves together he decided to walk the rest of the way, as we could see Hamilton and his ship in the distance. I climbed back on my bike and slowly drove the wrong way down a one way street down to the main road. I was stopped halfway down by a police car with siren blasting, but when he saw me with blood dripping from my shredded chin and hands he let me carry on. I got back to Trevelyan, got into the shower, and cleaned myself up as best I could, then was getting myself a glass of water in the kitchen when one of the radiographers came in and insisted on taking me to the Emergency Department to get me checked over. When I got there my ex-passenger was waiting for an X-ray on his finger! I hadn't broken anything, but they put dressings on my injuries and gave me an anti-tetanus shot, then I wobbled home to bed. I woke up the next morning a mass of aches and pains, with chin and knees swelled to twice their size. I couldn't use my hand so I couldn't go in to work, and was a bit apprehensive about their reaction when I phoned in. I needn't have been worried, though. Apparently it was expected that I would come a cropper sooner or later, because that's what just about everyone did on moving to the island and riding a mobylette for the first time. Within a couple of days I was back at work, but didn't look a pretty sight for quite a while. I still have a scar on my chin and a nobbly joint on my left little finger.

Even though summer had come to an end as far as England was concerned, the weather in Bermuda was still warm until November, with the occasional hiccup if a hurricane passed close by, bringing torrential rain, wind and stormy seas. I swam every day, and that, combined with the sunshine, began to clear up my long-standing psoriasis. I had developed this awful skin disease when I was about eight years old, and had suffered with it in varying degrees of severity since then. I had always been very self-conscious about it, but at last it went away, and I had spotless knees and elbows. I felt wonderful, as I had managed to get a gentle tan too, and when my chin healed up I started to feel and look pretty good! I got my first pay packet, and had money, too, so life was good.

6 – Robbie the Bobby

I had made my mind up to break with my past, and stay away from guys who were not interested in commitment. I had a few dates but stayed uninvolved. One of my dates was with one of the new Police recruits, a guy from Liverpool called Harry Parry, whom I met at a party. He was a bit of a nutter, but nice enough. One evening we went out for a drink with a bunch of his Police friends and some of the nurses and hospital staff. We went to a bar in Hamilton called "The Rum-Runners", which was opposite the harbour and had a balcony where you could sit out and watch the boats whilst you ate and drank. We all sat around a big table. I was sitting next to another lab technician called Ann McCullough, and opposite us was a friend of Harry's called Robb Porter. He seemed to be looking at me, and I knew he was interested, but that's as far as it went. It turned out that he was actually eyeing my neighbour, Ann, but he was so drunk that his eyes kept sliding off target! However, Harry told me later that Robb really "fancied" me, and that if Harry and I stopped dating he would gladly step in. My trunk arrived not long after I did, and a guy called Stan Mocklow, who was the Purchasing officer for KEMH, took me to St. Georges to pick it up from the ship. It was good to have more of my stuff, and I began to make myself at home. I bought a radio and a record player, so I had music. I started to do a bit more cooking, and really enjoyed it. Around that time preparations were going on for the hospital ball. This was a grand occasion, held at the Castle Harbour Hotel across the bay from the airport. Dress was formal, so I started looking for something gorgeous to wear. I wanted to look my best, so decided to go for bust and start my search at the best shop in town, Cecile's, which was renowned for being very exclusive and of course, expensive. I tried on loads of gowns, but finished up with a lovely Oscar de La Renta "cheong-sam" in beige with a dark blue border round the neck and hem. It cost me half a month's wages, but it made me feel like a million dollars. It's the only designer dress I ever owned, and I don't even know what happened to it! Harry was my escort, Robb was taking Sue, the Physiotherapist who lived in one of the cottages behind Trevelyan. About eight of us met in my room for drinks before we set off for the ball, then got taxis, as no-one wanted to ride a motor bike in all their finery. Harry got drunk at the ball, as did most of our escorts, which was charming, but the highlight of my evening was when the Chairman of the Hospital Board, Quinton Edness, asked me to dance. He was a light-skinned Bermudian guy, very tall, and striking looking, and had a really bad reputation for womanising. I didn't know this at the time, but was inundated with warnings from all kinds of people after we danced. He called me once after that, but I told him I had a boyfriend, and he didn't persist (he had his pick of the hospital staff I think, so didn't need to pine over what he couldn't have!) The ball passed without any other incident, and I went home, I think Harry passed out and I left him there, but it was the last time we dated. The next morning I was woken up by a knock on my window, then on my door. It was Robb, Harry's friend. He had left his coat in my room the previous evening and wanted it. He brought me a cup of tea, and we sat and chatted. As far as I could tell from what he said, he had failed miserably in his major seduction ploy with Sue, but had passed out in her cottage and been chucked out when he woke up! My gain. I really liked him, and I got a cuppa into the bargain.

It was getting near Christmas by then, and I began to realise that for the first time I wouldn't be spending it with my family. However, there were lots of parties, and, I think because life was so different from home, I wasn't half as homesick as I thought I was going to be. There were so many new experiences and things to see. I realised that the little Poinsettias which appeared on cards and in expensive florists in England, were actually large shrubs! They grew in gardens all over Bermuda, and were in full bloom at Christmas. They looked lovely, and did give the island a seasonal appeal. The other thing I noticed and loved was the smell of cedar logs burning. Most of the bigger houses had lovely open fireplaces, and in winter – especially at Christmas – people would have log fires just for the comfort and cosiness of it. They didn't really need them for warmth as the temperature was still about 60 degrees Fahrenheit! In the 1940s there had been a blight of Bermuda's indigenous cedar trees, and most of them had died. They had been replaced with fast growing Casuarinas, and the dead cedars were chopped down and used to make souvenirs and beautiful furniture, as well as being used as fuel for log fires. The beautiful smell of cedar wood smoke was almost like perfume, and hung in the air all over the island. Another new discovery was the traditional Bermuda Christmas dish – Cassava Pie, which had a sweetish dough made from cassava flour and a filling of chicken and vegetables. It was very different but delicious. As well as parties there was a Carol Concert up at the Police Club. I suppose it was nostalgia that made me want to go there, and it was also a bit of an ex-pat tradition, but none of the other girls wanted to go, so I got on my bike and went on my own. I knew a few of the guys up there through Harry, so wouldn't be lonely, but I was secretly hoping Robb would be there. He was, and we sat together and got to know each other a bit better. We still didn't date, and it's difficult to know when we did actually start to see each other seriously! Most of the girls in Trevelyan and Gladwyn hadn't been in Bermuda very long, and we were all feeling a little bit homesick, so we decided to get together on Christmas Day to cook Christmas Dinner for ourselves. It was a great meal, we all took responsibility for one thing, and there were some good cooks amongst us. The only thing was that none of us was used to cooking for a crowd, so we had mountains of food, ate far too much, and were all groaning by the time we had finished! I phoned home on Christmas Day, but as usual the call was hilarious. Our very occasional and expensive phone calls were saved for when loads of the family were together. They passed the phone round quickly so that everyone got chance to say hello, and as a result I didn't get chance to have a proper conversation with anyone. This call was the same, but fortunately I had drunk half a bottle of wine by then and wasn't feeling much pain. Communication with them was always a bit stilted. We wrote frequently, but this was before computers were available to everyone, so there was no email. We wrote "snail mail", and it was very slow. I got a parcel from Mum just before Christmas with a couple of music albums in it – George Gershwin's "Rhapsody in Blue", and a Yehudi Menuhin recording of Bruch's and Mendelssohn's Violin Concertos. I loved all of the music, but the Gershwin album had on the cover a beautiful picture of Manhattan taken from the air. I longed to go to New York, and it was one of the cheapest "escapes" from Bermuda. People talked about getting "rock happy" – a kind of claustrophobic feeling that crept up on you after you had been on the island for a while – and New York was the easiest place to get to. I determined to get there as soon as I could, and put the album cover on my wall to inspire me.

Just after Christmas, Jaki moved out of Trevelyan into a Studio Apartment on Harbour Road with her fiancé Vic. This meant that one of the upstairs rooms was available, so I grabbed it quickly. It was a lot nicer room with a view over the garden and a lot bigger bathroom. Around then we decided to have a party, and it was very successful. The place looked so good in a subdued light, and since the upkeep of the place wasn't our responsibility we didn't bother too much about the mess, which is probably the best basis for a good party! Robb came along, and afterwards he said he would come back the next day to help us clear up. I was impressed! The only trouble was he didn't turn up until the day after that, and everything was done. I still don't know if he did that on purpose or not, and he can't remember. However, from then on we did start dating. I specially remember one date we had, although not where we went. We went out with Pat and Barry, then back to the apartment Barry shared (with Philip Troake, who worked for British Airways) for a nightcap. Barry had just bought the Woodstock Album, and we were listening to it. I remember Robb sitting in a big recliner chair, with earphones on and eyes closed, playing air guitar whilst listening to Jimi Hendrix's "Star Spangled Banner". What a revelation. I think I started to fall in love with him at that point, he was definitely a "one-off"!

We had some great times. We became very friendly with Pat (my boss) and her boyfriend Barry. We would get together to go out for meals out and barbecues, and occasionally we would go to a Hotel Cabaret. The Hamilton Princess Hotel had some great shows, and we saw quite a few of them. The most popular acts were Bruce Forsyth and Roy Castle, both of whom we didn't really like, but their shows were really entertaining and we enjoyed them. Another person we saw was Tiny Tim – a huge guy who played a tiny banjo and sang "Tiptoe Through the Tulips" in a falsetto voice. We went to some fabulous restaurants, the food was world class, especially the seafood – as we were surrounded by it! The booze flowed like water. Our favourite drink was a "Zombie", made with about 6 kinds of rum, grenadine, and fruit juice. It tasted innocuous, like fruit punch, but the effect crept up on you slowly – it was lethal because by the time the effects were felt you had chugged down quite a few! I had quite a few of these when we saw Tiny Tim, and apparently I staggered out to the stage in the middle of his act to ask him to play something, much to Robb's embarrassment. (He made up for that later by embarrassing me on numerous occasions!).

Bermuda really was an amazing place to be if you were young. Everyone was so laid-back. The island was swarming with celebrities but nobody noticed them, they were common as muck! We went for a walk around Hamilton one Sunday morning and were chatting to Bill Wyman, one of The Rolling Stones, who was fishing from the dock near the Bank of Bermuda. We saw Richie Havens sitting on Elbow Beach one day, and sat next to Frankie Avalon in a restaurant one evening. Life was sun, sea, booze, money, and fun. It was such a beautiful place, too. It seemed that around every corner was a gorgeous sea view, framed by exotic trees and flowers. Lovely white churches nestled in the hollows, with tall spires pointing up into the blue sky. It was so wonderful to wake up to sunshine nearly every morning. I started to find out quaint things about Bermuda, such as the water supply – or lack of it! Everyone collected rainwater on their specially designed white roofs. It was then channelled into a reservoir tank under the house. The history was fascinating too. Shakespeare's "The Tempest" was actually set in Bermuda -"the still vex'd Bermoothes". We were one of only two Crown Colonies in the world – the other was Hong Kong. We had the oldest parliament in the Western hemisphere. Some of the people that lived there were interesting, too, such as the Bacardi's, and the guy who invented Velcro. The only thing I didn't like about the island was that there was quite a bit of racial tension. I had noticed it as soon as I arrived. As

I walked over to work each day I would greet everyone with a smile and a "Good Morning", but quickly found that this provoked looks of hatred from some of the black hospital workers. I had never met with prejudice before, and it is pretty hard to take, I must say. Barry told us that he could remember the Cinema in Hamilton being segregated into blacks and whites, so I guess serious discrimination was a very recent memory. The two political parties were the UBP (United Bermuda Party), who were mostly rich, mostly white, and very influential – and in power. The other was the PLP (Peoples's Labour Party), who were 99% black and not in power! The latter were led by a militant black female lawyer, Lois Browne-Evans, who was deeply influenced by Cuban and Jamaican Communists, and who encouraged the black Bermudians to "go out and fornicate in the bushes" to outbreed the whites! Robb met a lot of prejudice as a Policeman, there were very few Bermudians on the Force, most of the Police were white and from Britain, so they naturally were on the receiving end of a lot of bad attitudes. I was getting very fond of Robb, and, joy of joys, he seemed to be getting very fond of me – in fact he even said he wanted to marry me during a drunken ramble!

We both wanted to see New York, so we booked a trip to go there together in Spring of 1971. I was so excited as we took off from Bermuda, and landing in New York was amazing. We drove by Limo from JFK airport over the Whitestone Bridge and saw the legendary Manhattan skyline, just like my Gershwin Album cover! We were due to stay at a big hotel on Times Square, but when we got there we realised we had made a mistake. We had booked a double room under our real names, and when the heavily made up gay man at the reception desk asked us if we were brother and sister, instead of reading his body language and lying about it, we said we weren't. He had a huge hissy fit and said that America could not possibly condone such immorality! What a joke. We told him to stuff it, and walked out. We found a hotel just around the corner, lied and said we were married, but hadn't got new passports yet, and booked in. I loved New York. I have done ever since. We wandered all over Manhattan, seeing all the famous sights. We ate breakfast at Howard Johnson's in Times Square with all the Hookers finishing the night shift. We tried Japanese food for the first time, took a helicopter ride, and strolled through Central Park. We were starry-eyed tourists, and found everyone friendly and polite – it was far from the dangerous den of iniquity we had been warned about. I bought a load of crappy flower power/ stars and stripes tourist stuff, plus a poster of a white girl with a blonde afro and "White is Beautiful Too" written on it. I was very careful to conceal that as we came back into Bermuda. I used some of the flower power stickers to decorate my bike after painting it luminous green. I thought it looked great, but when I took it for its yearly test at the Dept. of Transport they failed it on the grounds that it needed painting! Basically it didn't fit in with the image the Bermuda government wanted to project to the tourists, so, sadly, I had to take all the stickers off and go back to pale blue.

Jaki and Vic went to England to get married, and when they came back they were offered a bigger apartment by their Landlady. She was an interesting woman who had just married some Norwegian Baron and had properties all over the place. Jaki and Vic asked Robb and I if we were interested in taking over their studio apartment, because they were keen to have someone they knew in there, as they were really fond of it. We had been talking about moving in together since the New York trip. Robb was in Police Barracks, which was a bit Spartan, and had been spending more and more time at Trevelyan. Added to this, the apartment, No. 3 Suntan Studios, was absolutely gorgeous! It was set on a small promontory high above Harbour Road, opposite Hamilton. It had a huge covered verandah which looked out on three sides over the harbour. To the right we could see White's Island, which lay where the harbour started narrowing down towards Crow Lane. Ahead was the dock where all the cruise ships tied up, and Hamilton in the background, and to the left was a wonderful view out over the Great Sound with all its little islands. Below us was the dock where the little ferry stopped, we could catch a boat ride over to Hamilton, or back along Harbour Road towards Warwick and Somerset, from there. The apartment itself was only three rooms, a small kitchen, a good sized bathroom, and a huge living room with patio doors out onto the verandah, plus a big window looking out towards Hamilton. In one corner, facing the patio doors, was a corner seating arrangement which converted to a bed. In another corner was a dining table and chairs, and in another was a bar! There was also a small entrance hall with cupboards for storage and hanging clothes. It was perfect, and we moved in as soon as we could. We had various visitors that summer, one of them was my friend Hilary, who had just divorced her first husband. The sleeping arrangements were a bit difficult, but we managed! My Mum came out, just to see if I was OK. I don't think they could afford for Dad to come too. They were very upset and worried about Robb and I moving in together, but Robb reassured her that we would be getting engaged and married as soon as we could. She made me promise that we would come home for the ceremony.

Summer was wonderful, a blur of sun, sea, parties, barbecues and celebrations. One of the main holidays in Bermuda is Cup Match Weekend, in August. The whole island shuts down for 4 days so that everyone can watch a Cricket match! The weather in August is so hot and humid, even the sea feels warm. It's the only time of year when Bermudians will swim! We weren't interested in Cricket, so 8 of us rented a Houseboat, which was moored amongst some of the little islands in the Sound, and we spent the whole four days on it. As well as Robb and I there were 3 other couples, Pat and Barry, plus two of the guys he worked with – Charlie Kett and his wife Heather – and Doug Tufts with his fiancée Jenny, who was a nurse at KEMH. We had a great time, fishing and sailing and swimming. We cooked the fish we caught on a little Hibachi barbecue. We rowed over to one of the islands one evening and swam from the beach, the phosphorescence in the water as we swam and splashed was absolutely amazing. One evening we were leaning over the side of the boat and saw a "Spanish Dancer" (a type of Nudibranch) swim slowly by. None of us had ever seen anything like it, but it was absolutely beautiful, and we found out afterwards what it was. One of the islands had an empty house on it, and we decided to explore. The island was a bit hostile, covered with sharp coral rocks and Prickly Pear, but we got to the house eventually. It was such a sad place, it had obviously been really beautiful, but was just left standing open and abandoned. All the furniture was rotting and termite ridden. There was a huge picture window looking out over what had once been a terrace, now cracked and overgrown, and then beyond it was the blue ocean and sky, the two blending at the horizon. In later years, when I read in C. S. Lewis' "The Magician's Nephew" about the dying world of Charn this house came into my mind. Back on the houseboat we had run out of water by our third day, so we just swam instead of washing and drank beer to quench our thirst. We cleaned our teeth with champagne! It was such a great time that we decided to hire the boat again as soon as we could. In summer, when we were at home, we spent most of our time on the verandah. We relaxed, ate, slept, and entertained out there. It was lovely, because it was covered and shaded, and also caught all the cool sea breezes blowing over the sound. Life was idyllic. One of the lasting memories I have is of standing there watching rain come in like a gauze curtain sweeping across the sound. We were always prepared, because it usually took about 10 minutes to get to us from when we first saw it! Towards the end of the summer we decided to get engaged, and to go to England for Christmas, so that we could meet each other's families. Robb bought me a lovely diamond solitaire ring from Astwood-Dickinson's on Front Street, I got him a thick silver chain bracelet, engraved with his name, the date, and all my love. We had a lovely party to celebrate. I was so happy.

Suntan Studios was an idyllic start to our life together. We had some very interesting neighbours. On one side was Bill and his fiancée Jeanne. He was a white Bermudian, she was a tall blonde Canadian. She had one of her legs in a plaster cast from hip to ankle, almost all the time we lived there. This was because of a bad bike accident, in which her leg had been shattered. There was talk of amputating it at the time, but against the odds they saved it. Sadly, I think they had to in the end because it had been so badly broken that an infection got into the bone and it wouldn't heal. They did a lot of travelling to really interesting places – a couple of years before we moved in they had been to a big music festival in New York – Woodstock! (The album of that iconic festival almost became the soundtrack to our lives for the first couple of years we were together!) The year we moved in they had gone down to Rio for Carnival, another iconic place that I wanted to visit some time. Our neighbour on the other side was Madame Helene Frith. She was about 60 or so, but such a fascinating person. She had come to Bermuda by flying boat in the 1930s or 40s. She was a Parisienne, working for Guerlain, and had been sent out by them to open the first French perfume shop in

Bermuda. She married into an important Bermuda family of wine merchants, the Friths, and had been widowed quite young, so had decided to use her money to see the world. She had been to some incredible places. Long before flower power, when everyone and his dog set out for Katmandu and Marrakech, she had been there. She had trekked through Tibet to meet the Dalai Llama when he was still holed up in Llhasa – not the media celebrity he is now! All this gave us such a world view of things, and made us realise how tame and provincial our lives had been so far! Travel really does broaden you, but I'm convinced that actually living in another culture is essential for permanent change. The girl had been taken out of Yorkshire, but it took a few years of Bermuda before the Yorkshire came out of the girl (except for the accent that is, which will never go completely).

In December we flew home for Christmas, complete with engagement ring, and were met at the airport by both sets of parents, plus Liz. We all spent some time together at Heathrow before heading off, Robb to Portsmouth, and me to Hull. I met up with lots of old friends, including John Woodhouse, but found that quite a few people had left Hull for greener pastures. John was very "distant", maybe because I was engaged to Robb, I don't know. We each spent Christmas Day with our families, then Robb drove up to Hull on Boxing Day, in time for a family party, when he got to know all the Osbornes and Dawsons. Sadly, this was to be the only time he met my Grandad, who gave him the seal of approval. This was especially after a game of charades, when Robb leapt out of the room, farting loudly as he went, acting out "Gone with the Wind". My Dad always appreciated a good fart, and laughed until he cried. We spent a few days in Hull, making plans for the wedding, choosing a pattern and fabric for my dress and seeing the florist etc. I couldn't find the right colour for my bridesmaids. I wanted a sort of Air Force blue, but finished up with a dark blue-green, which I didn't really like too much, but time was short. The florist persuaded me to go for autumn colours, when what I had wanted was a sort of dusky pink. She said that wouldn't photograph very well, so I followed her suggestion, which probably did look better with the compromised colour for the bridesmaids. These were to be my sister Liz, and my two cousins, Jill and Ann, now teenagers. After a hectic few days I said goodbye to my family and Robb and I drove back to Portsmouth for New Year. I met his family and friends, and had fun, plus everyone seemed to approve of me! I had to be back in Bermuda before Robb, so he took me up to Heathrow before going back to Portsmouth for a boozy week with all his mates. The day he was due back in Bermuda I cooked a special meal – I boned a chicken and stuffed it with pate, which took me ages. I was so pleased with myself, however he was destined not to eat it, because once again (as with our first "date") he didn't turn up – he had missed the plane. How can anyone miss a plane after checking in on time? He can. It was another sign that my dear husband to be was in a different time zone from anyone else on the bloody planet! I think I may have chucked the chicken in the dustbin in a fit of rage, I can't remember. He made it back the next day, to be greeted by a stony silence from me. We must have worked it out in the end, but it did start to change my expectations of him significantly!

We got back into our work routine, and started to organise for the wedding. Mum was making all the dresses, and we had to leave her and Dad to find a venue for the Reception. We didn't really have very much to do, and felt a bit guilty, but they enjoyed themselves I think, urged on by the prospect of seeing Robb make an honest woman out of me (although I'm sure nobody at home knew we were living together)! At some point we had been to see the vicar of St. John's Anglican Church, Newland, in Hull, because we wanted to be married there. This was because it was our traditional "family" church. It was my Grandma and Grandad's parish church, I had been christened there, and most of the Dawsons had been married there. I had also promised Mum that if I got married it would be at St. John's, not 3,000 miles away. This resulted in our being "famous for 15 minutes" (quote from Andy Warhol). This was because Robb's parents told some minor National Newspaper about it, and the story of my "vow" to Mum, and our romance and marriage, was reported both in that Newspaper and the Hull Daily Mail, under the title "Anne Keeps her Wedding Promise" - I still have the cuttings. In those days, someone jetting off to work abroad was News! We may have gone to see the vicar when we came home for the wedding, I'm not sure, but I do remember him challenging us on our decision to be married in church, on the vows we would be making before God, and also on our choice of music, which included Bach's "Jesu, Joy of Man's Desiring". He was right to do so, at that time our choice was total hypocrisy, motivated by tradition, and our parents' expectations, not by any true conviction. Summer came again, and we decided to rent the houseboat again for the May 24th holiday. There were a few problems, and the owner was being a bit elusive, but the weekend came, and we wouldn't take no for an answer. Eventually we borrowed a small dinghy, loaded it up with our stuff, and rowed out to the houseboat in the pitch darkness. It's a miracle we didn't drown, our backsides were in the water all the way because we were so overloaded, and we couldn't see where we were going, but we did get to the boat in the end. It hadn't been prepared for our stay, and in fact was in a pretty poor state, so we spent a very uncomfortable night, and next day we gave up and came home. We then decide to look for another boat to hire, and got a fantastic one, The Valkyrie, for Cup Match weekend that year. We had a great weekend – our last as "singles". Also that summer we added to our household by adopting a psychotic cat. Jaki and Vic had to leave Bermuda as Vic's time there had come to an end. He had been reassigned to Ghana, so we inherited Moolie, their ginger cat, after we had said our sad farewells to our dear friends. Robb and Vic had caused permanent mental damage to the poor creature by teasing it unmercifully when it was a kitten, so it was justice that Robb had to live with the results of his cruelty! Moolie delighted in creeping up on people sitting in the basket chairs we had at Suntan Studios, sitting innocently underneath them, then suddenly leaping up and sticking his claws into their bottoms through the holes in the chairs. He would catch lizards regularly, and bring them into the apartment. I thought this was really sad, they were gorgeous creatures, sort of rainbow coloured, but would turn black as soon as the cat got hold of them. I remember one shedding its tail in an effort to escape from him, and the tail wriggling independently along the runners of our patio doors! Yech!

Another very sad and significant farewell for me came that summer after a call from home to say that my Grandad had been taken into hospital. He was diagnosed with advanced liver cancer. Within a couple of weeks of being admitted he was in a coma, and shortly after that he died. I had all my holidays booked for the wedding in September, and we were saving every penny for then, and no-one realised how soon he would be gone. It all happened so quickly, and I didn't even get to say goodbye to him. He never saw me happily married, or met his great-grandchildren, but I am certain that we will all be together again in eternity, and really look forward to that.

Very reluctantly, we began to see that we needed to start looking for a bigger apartment. Lots of friends and family were asking if they could come out to see us – and see Bermuda too, of course - and we had nowhere to put them up. We realised too, that after the wedding we might need an extra room for any children that came along! We heard about a two bedroom apartment which would soon be available. It was near the hospital, right next to the Botanical gardens in Paget. We went to see it, and liked it, so planned on moving in as soon as we could. We were so sad to say goodbye to Suntan Studios, but it was definitely time to move on. Time to grow up, I guess. The address of our new apartment was "Pitman's Upper Apartment, Garden Lane, South Shore Road, Paget". It was owned by Herbert and Betty Pitman, who lived around the corner on Point Finger Road in the most beautiful old Bermuda house which had the traditional "welcoming arms" steps going up to it. Herbie and his brother, Arthur, had once run one of the island's dairy farms, but Arthur moved to the U.S., so Herbert gave up the dairy and was now the maker of the island's best ice-cream. What's more, the ice-cream factory was below our new apartment! We loved our new landlord and his wife, they were really kind and friendly. I knew Betty already, because she was a member of the Red Cross, who ran the Blood Bank at the hospital. She was from the Turks & Caicos Islands in the Caribbean, and had come to Bermuda to work in the hospital, where she met Herbie. She was a descendant of Captain John Smith (of Pocahontas fame). They had an only son, Lindsay, who spent most of the time we knew him trying unsuccessfully to join various monasteries in England. He died of a heart attack shortly after we left Bermuda, which was so sad. He was only in his late 30s, and I don't think Herbie and Betty ever got over the shock.

7 – Two become Three

We came back to England for the wedding at the beginning of September, which was set for the 23rd. There was still a lot to do, of course. Mum had to make minor alterations to my wedding dress, but it even so I remember it was a bit tight over my boobs! We had a stag and hen night, which I can't remember too much about. Eventually the great day arrived. Robbie and his best man – Ray Lloyd – stayed at Mary and Jim's the night before (and drank all their Ouzo I think). I remember getting into the wedding car with my Dad, who looked lovely in his morning suit. All the neighbours were out watching us, I felt like a million dollars. The ceremony went really well. Robbie looked into my eyes as we made our vows – it was so special, a really wonderful day. The reception was great – all the family were there, including Auntie Eve from Plymouth, who later developed early onset Alzheimer's Disease, but seemed OK then – if still a bit twitchy! Ethel and Vic came from Scunthorpe, Eileen from Leeds, and Uncle Frank from Middlesborough with his new wife, Betty. He and Auntie Mig had divorced by then, because of his affair with Betty. Grandma was there, without Grandad, which was the only sad note to the proceedings. Three of Robbie's fellow Police Officers from Bermuda turned up. They were en route to the Munich Oktoberfest! Lynne and John were there from Taunton, Chris and Wendy came from Doncaster. Sue Suddart who was by then separated from her husband, got very friendly with Ray, the best man. The Bermuda guys were staying in the Hotel Eden, where we held the reception, so afterwards, in the evening, all the young wedding guests stayed on in the bar until it closed. Robbie and I had gone up to change out of our wedding clothes in preparation for going off on our honeymoon. We were to spend our first night at The Beverley Arms Hotel, about 8 miles away in Beverley, planning champagne and oysters in bed. However, when we saw everyone in the bar having fun we decided to join them, and eventually got to our hotel too late for anything except a sandwich and a cup of tea! The Bermuda guys were full of some tragic news. Shortly after we left for England at the beginning of September, Robb's boss, George Duckett, the island's Commissioner of Police, had been assassinated. He had answered a knock at his door and been gunned down. His daughter was also seriously injured in the same attack, but eventually she recovered. This was a great shock to everyone. It was a racial and anti-British rule thing, so we all felt vulnerable. The racism I had noticed was obviously a lot more serious than I had thought. We eventually got to the Beverley Arms after saying farewell to our friends, and fell into bed, exhausted. The next day we were supposed to go to Nottingham. I wanted to take Robbie to some of the old haunts, such as "The Olde Trip to Jerusalem". This was a really old pub which had been the setting off point for Crusaders in the middle ages. It was carved out of a cliff, a unique place. Nottingham also had some great curry restaurants, we had none in Bermuda and Robbie was missing them! We didn't get there for some reason, but went straight to London, and had a few days there, seeing the musical "Jesus Christ, Superstar" and getting a parking ticket in the process! After London we went down to Portsmouth. Robb's parents were away, so we stayed at their house and had days out in the area. Our wedding day had been cloudy and dull, but by the time we got to Hampshire it was Indian Summer. We had a day at Beaulieu in the New Forest, which was absolutely lovely, perfect golden autumn weather. Taunton was our next destination, staying with Lynne and John. We had a great time with them. One place we specially remember was Beer, on the south Devon coast. We sat on the beach and ate fresh crab sandwiches – yummy. Robb's parents were back from their holiday by then, so we went back to Portsmouth for the few days we had left before flying back to Bermuda.

We got back to Bermuda, and moved in to Pitman's Upper Apartment, just in time to get ready for our first Christmas as man and wife. It was a really happy time for us. We had good friends, plenty of money, and a nice apartment, which we were able to decorate to our own taste. Our tastes were pretty grim, looking back! The bathroom was bright yellow and we had purple towels and curtains etc. I also bought some gorgeous yellow and white checked towels from A. S. Cooper's bath store which were soft velour on one side and rougher towelling on the other. They cost the earth, but I loved them – never having seen such luxurious towels before! Our bedroom was pink and orange, the spare room was yellow and orange (those yellow and orange curtains Nanny had upstairs in the twin bedded room at "The Haven" were originally from Pitman's Apartment). At the back of our big living/dining room was a very well stocked bar, above which was a huge wooden "Lowenbrau" sign (probably stolen from somewhere). We put up some shelves, and bought some furniture, a lovely black leather recliner and a white tub chair, plus a brown, black and cream striped sofa. Robb made a folding white screen in a Moroccan pattern which we put behind the sofa to separate the dining area. The other furniture was already there. The kitchen was tiny, but we managed to cook some great food there. We put saloon doors on the entrance. It was all a bit cringeworthy, but we loved it then! We didn't have the spectacular sea views of Suntan Studios, but at the opposite side of Garden Lane was the Bermuda

Botanical Gardens. From our balcony we looked out onto the citrus orchard, which we didn't fully appreciate until the following summer, when the trees were in flower, and the beautiful scent of orange blossom wafted on the breeze, over the hedge and into our open windows. We had a big garden downstairs, with banana, papaya, grapefruit and avocado trees. The grapefruit ripened shortly after we moved in, so we ate them, fresh from the tree, every day, they were so delicious. I bought Robb a Scalextric set for Christmas. He had always wanted one. It was set up in the spare room, Moolie used to go mad chasing the cars. Work was going well for both of us, and we were enjoying ourselves, both smoking and drinking far too much, but so was the rest of the population. In spite of various friends having health scares and bike accidents whilst drunk, we carried on with our over-indulgent lifestyles. Neither of us was giving much thought to the future and we spent every penny we got.

We had talked about having a family, but didn't have a definite plan. However, it was now 1973, and I was 26 years old, so we knew we didn't have that much time to waste. I had come off "the pill" when we got married, as I didn't really like being on it, so it was no surprise, in March of that year, when I found out I was pregnant. I was working in the department of the lab which did pregnancy tests, so knew pretty early that our first baby was on the way. A month or so before that, I had done a sneaky pregnancy test for Sue Headey, who was married to John, another police officer. That test was positive, too – I was the first to know that their daughter, Lena, was on the way! Sue and I became really close as our pregnancies progressed. We were so excited, and told everyone in England almost straight away. They were all over the moon. We were convinced it would be a boy, and decided to call him Sam. However, our sense of excitement was diluted slightly when another terrible thing happened on the island. The new Governor, Sir Richard Sharples, was assassinated, along with his ADC, Captain Hugh Sayers, and his dog, Horsa. They had been walking in the grounds of Government House after a dinner party, and someone shot them. The island was in uproar. The police still hadn't found out who had killed Commissioner Duckett the previous September, so the sense of foreboding and fear amongst them and the ex-pat population in general, was pretty strong. I felt extra vulnerable because I was newly pregnant, and Robbie became very protective. My pregnancy progressed well, after the initial nausea I felt really good, apart from one thing. One evening we had gone to bed early, I had fallen asleep and Robb was watching a movie on our bedroom TV. I woke up suddenly, and didn't know why, I just felt uneasy. The movie was about a family travelling across the US being followed by a gang of Hell's Angels. I watched it for a few minutes but was growing increasingly panicky, so got up and went out on the balcony, feeling as if I needed fresh air. I looked up at the cloudy sky, and realised I didn't feel any better, in fact I felt worse. I was so afraid, but didn't know what of, so couldn't do anything to alleviate it. It was horrible, but it went off eventually, and I went back to bed and slept. A week or so later it happened again, and I became so terrified of it happening yet again I called my doctor and made an appointment. He gave me sleeping pills! No explanation, just drugs! Those were the days – the beginning of the "miracle drug for everything" era. They did give me peace of mind though, and I didn't have another attack during that pregnancy. The thing was, though, that my strong "I can cope with anything" attitude was seriously challenged. If it hadn't been for the sleeping pills I think I would have gone mad with the fear of having another attack. I had to stop drinking, because it gave me terrible heartburn, but I was still smoking, a little less maybe, but still way too much. The summer went by, and being pregnant gave me plenty of excuses to relax on the beach. I can remember, at 20 weeks, lying on Elbow Beach giving my tummy a prod to make the baby move – I still wasn't sure I had felt it move even by then! By the time I was 22 weeks I was sure I felt movement, but I was a bit apprehensive as it was quite late. My doctor had reassured me everything was OK, but I still worried. I was getting bigger, and had to buy some maternity clothes and wear a larger sized lab coat to cover "the bump" at work. We bought a car, realising we couldn't transport a baby on a moped. It was a blue Ford Escort, and we were so proud of it (the only brand new car we ever had!) Robbie already had a Bermuda driver's license, in fact was an advanced Police Driver, but I had to pass my test again. Fortunately I did so at the first attempt, but not without a few rows when Robb tried to give me lessons beforehand. Sue Headey and I went to ante-natal classes together, learning breathing techniques to help with labour pains, exercising to stay supple, and learning about feeding and caring for a baby. On October 3rd Sue and John's daughter, Lena Kathren, was born. She was lovely, with John's dark hair and eyes. Towards the end of October Robbie and I were invited over for a meal at the home of one of the women who worked in Haematology with me, Diana Jack. When we arrived - surprise, surprise - the whole female population of the lab were there, and they had arranged a baby shower for me! This was such a novelty in those days, it was an American custom, no-one in England had heard of it, so I was really excited, and got some lovely things. I was due to finish work only a couple of weeks before my due date – 2nd December – so that I could have most of my maternity leave after the birth to spend with the baby. Sadly, I had to go back to work, we couldn't afford to live in Bermuda on one wage, but I was confident I could cope, and had arranged a child minder who seemed lovely. She was Portuguese – from The Azores – and couldn't speak any English, but her daughter lived in the same house with her family, and she translated for her. Her name was Hortense Lima, but we called her "Tia" (auntie). She loved children and was recommended by Jenny Tufts – who had married Doug (of houseboat fame) and had a little boy, Adam, by that time, who was cared for by Tia when Jenny went back to work as a nurse.

Mum came out to stay in mid November, she would be there to help me with the new baby. I was getting really fed up by the time I finished work, I felt tired and uncomfortable, and couldn't wait to meet Sam! We thought that maybe the baby would arrive on my Dad's birthday, 24th November, but the day came and went with no sign of Sam. On Monday 26th November we had some friends over for dinner. We ate steak and kidney pie and drank Pina Coladas (yech –what a combination!). After they had gone I felt restless and couldn't sleep, so I sat up playing Solitaire after everyone else had gone to bed. Eventually I did sleep, but woke up at about 4.00 am with tummy ache and a "show", I was in labour! I showered and got my stuff together and we drove round to the Hospital around 7.00 am. Mum was in tears as we left, I think a few memories of the last time I was in labour were welling up, as they were in me, of course, but I was so excited. Strangely, in spite of my first awful experience of childbirth, I wasn't in the least apprehensive. After I was examined I was put in the labour room. They said I had a long way to go, and I wasn't in much pain, so was feeling great. Robb, however was in agony. He had terrible griping stomach pains and spent most of the first hour in the loo. In the end he was given pain relief and I wasn't! My Doctor popped in and said he would go back to his office as things were progressing so slowly. At around 10.30 am I decided that I needed something for the pain, and called the nurse. By the time she came in I felt as if I needed to push, and when she examined me there was a huge panic. I was rushed into the delivery room and given a shot of some kind of pain relief, too late, however. They called Dr. McDonald-Smith, who had just arrived at his office in St. Georges – half an hour away at the far end of the island! They managed to find a doctor to replace him, and at around 11.00 am on Tuesday 27th November 1973, I became the proud Mummy of – not Sam – but Nicola Ruth. She arrived so quickly that they had to grab a blue and white gingham tea towel to catch her so she didn't slip out of their grasp! She was absolutely the most beautiful baby I had ever seen. She had strawberry blonde hair, and blue eyes, and was so pretty. She weighed 7lbs 4ozs, and was 21 inches long. We were in love with her immediately, in spite of the shock that she wasn't a Sam! Robbie was bouncing off the walls. He ran over to the lab to tell everyone, and Vic McKane had to give him a shot glass of medicinal brandy to calm him down!

We hadn't definitely decided on our new daughter's name at that point, but Nicola and Ruth were favourites, Nicola because we liked it, and it was trendy, Ruth because we liked it, and for my Grandma. I didn't get very long to cuddle my beautiful new baby before she was swaddled tightly and taken to the nursery. I was given a lovely private room with an en suite bathroom after the birth, and could easily have had her in there with me without disturbing anyone else, but I was quickly confronted with the rigid traditions of KEMH Maternity ward. The Sister in charge was a miserable old battleaxe of a Canadian, who had never had children and had about as much tenderness as a moose. All the babies were kept in the nursery, tightly swaddled, apart from for 30 minutes every 4 hours, when they were wheeled out in a long trolley, separated into 6 compartments, to be fed by their Mums. Last feed was 10.00 p.m. and nothing then until 6.00 a.m. (poor little things)! We weren't supposed to unwrap them or change them, and at the end of the half hour they were taken back to the nursery, whether they had a good feed or not. The little darlings cried most of the time they were in the nursery, and when they were brought out and started feeding, they immediately fell asleep, so never got a decent feed. It was barbaric, as far as I was concerned, but we were all scared stiff of the old battleaxe, so we "toed the line" in spite of all our instincts and exploding boobs! It was a very emotional time, of course. I couldn't help remembering and comparing my two experiences of childbirth, one traumatic and full of loss and confusion, and this one full of love and gratitude and comfort. I can even remember the smell of my lemony talcum powder, I spent 6 days in luxury, pampered and waited on hand and foot! We decided to call our little girl Nicola Ruth. I would have liked her first name to be Ruth, but Robbie said his Dad wouldn't like that because it sounded Jewish! I was learning that "Popsy", as he chose to be called, was a bundle of prejudices and difficult to handle attitudes, but this was his first grandchild, so we didn't want to upset him. Sadly that's the story of his life – someone should have upset him more often – he'd have been a lot happier if they had challenged some of his daft ideas! We had to stay in hospital for 6 days minimum, so by the time I got home with my little bundle I had a problem on my hands, even though I was feeling pretty rested to start with. She wanted to feed all the time, and cried with colic almost non-stop, especially in the evenings. For 9 weeks I didn't get more than 2 hours sleep at a time, and I was so distressed by her pain I was a nervous wreck, and completely exhausted, which probably made her a lot worse. Because I was breast feeding Robbie couldn't really help much. At night he would just roll over and ask sleepily if he could help, knowing he couldn't. I suppose it made him feel better, but it just made me mad! I was such a wreck I was on the phone to Dr. McDonald-Smith every time she sneezed! In the end he gave me some knockout drops for Nicky, which I was to give her before every feed. I'm not sure if they did the trick, or if she was growing out of her colic, but things started to settle down a bit. In spite of all of this I was so happy to be a new Mum. Nicky was a growing miracle, I felt so much love for her I was ready to burst. She grew more beautiful every day. Mum was with us for a week after I came home from the hospital, when she left I had mixed feelings. Robbie hadn't been getting on very well with her, so the atmosphere did improve after her departure, but I was a bit nervous about being totally responsible for the little life we had been blessed with, and I missed having Mum there to talk to and ask questions. I tried to get into a routine, advised by a giant copy of Dr. Spock – but I wasn't very successful. Nicky was happy when we kept her moving, in the car especially, but I would walk for hours around the Botanical Gardens with her in the pram, as the weather was still lovely and warm right up to the end of December. A lasting legacy of those days is my ability to recall Latin names of plants. I used to read all the plant labels as we walked around, and somehow they have all stayed in my memory. In our garden some pretty white flowers were coming into bloom under the banana trees. They were little white "Paperwhite" jonquils, and had a lovely smell. I picked loads of them, and they still always remind me of when Nicky was born.

My sister, Liz, had been engaged to a guy named David Holt for quite a while. I didn't really know him, as she met him after I left for Bermuda, but Mum and Dad liked him, and they had set their wedding date for February 9th 1974. We decided to go over to England for the wedding, and also to show off our lovely daughter – the first Great-Grandchild for both my Grandma Ruth and Robbie's paternal Grandma. We arranged to have Nicky christened the day after the wedding, and Liz and Dave postponed their honeymoon until after the Christening – that really is love! Both ceremonies would be at St. John's Newland, where we were married, and we asked Lynne Cummings, Liz, and Robbie's old school friend Merv Quilter to be Godparents. It shows where we were spiritually, as none of them was a Christian, in fact I think they were all atheists! We were driven purely by tradition. By the time we left for our trip Nicky had "found" her thumb, and as a result of sucking it madly at every opportunity, had settled down to be a perfectly behaved baby, who slept on demand. The night we left for our flight to England she fell asleep in the taxi on the way to Bermuda airport, and woke up as we were walking through the door of "The Haven" – Robbie's Mum and Dad's home in Cosham, Portsmouth, England! Everyone fell in love with her. Nanny and Popsy, Robb's parents, were absolutely in heaven – they just couldn't get enough of her. I'll never forget their faces as we came through Arrivals at Heathrow with Nicky fast asleep in my arms dressed in a little white furry hooded suit. She looked like an angel. She had started smiling and cooing and gurgling by then, a total joy. My Dad couldn't take his eyes off her, he told us that she was the most beautiful thing he had ever seen. The wedding and the christening went off well, and it was great that all the family was together, so we didn't have to do too much travelling around to see everyone, and had a bit of a rest. Wendy Harding, my friend from the lab in Hull, now married to Chris Thomas, had a little girl around the same time as me, and we got together to compare notes! Both of us agreed that if we knew what looking after a baby was going to be like we might have waited a bit longer! I must have been numb after Anthony's birth, I couldn't remember anything about how I had coped with it all. It was a happy trip, but we still missed my Grandad.

As the time approached for us to return to Bermuda, I began to get really apprehensive. I was due to go back to work soon after we got back, and I didn't know how I could bear to leave Nicky in someone else's care. I wanted to work part-time, but that was impossible, they couldn't get someone else out from the UK to work only part-time, so I was told "full time or nothing". I did go back to work, but it almost broke my heart. I missed Nicky so much, and I was exhausted most of the time. I felt I wasn't doing my best either at work or at home, just torn in two, but then a light appeared at the end of the tunnel! I didn't mention earlier that shortly after I started work at KEMH, the other girl who was short-listed with me for my job in Haematology, Isabel, was brought out from England and given a job in Blood Transfusion. She had also married a policeman, and was about 4 months pregnant when I went back to work after having Nicky. We had become quite friendly, and when she saw me struggling to work full time and look after a baby, we began to talk about possible job sharing. We put it to the bosses in the lab and they agreed to let us give it a try after Isabel had her baby. It worked brilliantly! She had her little boy, and from the time she came back to work, we shared her job in Blood Transfusion, which I loved. She worked mornings, and I worked afternoons. This suited me really well. Heather Kett (Charlie's wife) had just had a little girl, Linda, so the 4 of us would go down to the beach in the mornings with a big flask of coffee (and plenty of cigarettes). I would come home in time to plonk Nicky in front of the TV to watch Sesame Street whilst eating her lunch and I got ready for work, and after I dropped her off at Tia's, Nicky would sleep for at least an hour. This meant I didn't miss so much of my baby's waking hours, and also got to spend the best part of the day having fun on the beach with her. We usually went to Elbow Beach, which was often deserted until late morning. It was so beautiful. We were usually on the beach by 9am, and at that time the sea was still calm from the night, with tiny ripples lapping the shore, and the gentle sea breezes meant that the day hadn't become too hot. It was perfect for Nicky, and she became a real "water-baby".

Apart from our beautiful girl growing fast, and fascinating us completely with all her new skills and achievements, one significant thing happened to me during the summer of 1974. I caught Hepatitis. Bermuda was a very small island with limited medical facilities, and one of the things this affected was the Blood Transfusion service. Almost everyone who could gave blood, and as I mentioned, we had an emergency supply in our Police Force. Blood, however, doesn't last very long, and, after being refrigerated in plastic bags for 2 weeks, it had to be disposed of if it wasn't used. In the UK and other countries the expired blood would be sent to a processing plant and used for dried plasma, or processed to extract blood clotting factors for Haemophiliacs, but we had no such facilities, so we would just snip the bags and drain them down the sink, or else the gardeners amongst us took them home to put around their roses or tomatoes! The other problem was that we were a bit behind the rest of the world in testing our donors for transmissible diseases. We were fine for some things, like syphilis and malaria, but there was a growing world concern about Hepatitis B, which was on the increase because of more people using drugs. This was the type of Hepatitis common amongst addicts who shared needles, and could also be transmitted by Blood Transfusions, or by infected blood getting onto a skin cut or deep scratch. KEMH hadn't yet started testing donors for this in 1974, and I was often involved in disposing of expired blood down the sink. I had started to feel very tired and achy, as if I had flu. I also lost my appetite, which was unheard of for me, and I felt nauseous. I was pretty sure I wasn't pregnant again, and wondered what on earth was wrong with me. One morning I was cleaning my teeth and looking in the mirror when I noticed my eyes looked a bit yellow. Robbie confirmed my suspicions. My skin just looked tanned, but my eyes gave it away, and when I was tested the results confirmed I had Hepatitis B. Fortunately, I didn't get much worse than when I was diagnosed, but felt pretty grim and lost loads of weight, and had quite a long time off work, which was lovely, as I could spend it with Nicky and Robb when he wasn't at work. I had to be very careful not to infect them, and thankfully I didn't pass it on to anyone else. The only thing was that I suddenly became aware of my own mortality. Hepatitis can be fatal, not only during the initial infection, but because it can develop into the chronic form of the disease, Hepatitis C, which can cause liver failure, cirrhosis, and liver cancer. Having Nicky had made me appreciate how precious life is, and now I was confronted with the possibility of my own death. I was told to stop drinking alcohol for at least 6 months, and I did manage to cut down a lot, but another significant thing happened to me as a result of not complying with this advice totally. Just before Christmas Robbie and I were invited to a party by one of the guys he worked with, Brian Hanney. He and his wife, Carol, lived in a house which was owned by the police, up at Prospect, in Devonshire parish, number 18 Alexandra Road. This was one of several houses near the Police Club which had originally been built for army personnel stationed there in the early 1900s. Number 18 was a 2 bedroomed bungalow with an enclosed garden. It had a big verandah at both front and back. The walls were thick concrete, which made it really cool in summer, and added to this, the lovely big sash windows extended almost from the floor to the high ceilings, and they opened wide onto the shaded verandahs. The rooms were big and airy. There was a lovely big kitchen with a door surrounded by honeysuckle, which opened onto the garden. There was a utility room outside the kitchen door, plus a substantial shed in the garden which was great for storage, and had electricity too. The garden had allspice, banana and pawpaw trees, pigeon berry bushes, coralita vines, and lots of wild gladioli. In front of the house was a loquat tree, and the tall hedge alongside the car parking space was pink oleander. Prospect was the highest point of the island, so the coolest when breezes blew in summer. As soon as we walked into the party I fell in love with the house. There was something really special about it, and I made a mental note to look into getting one of these Police Houses, if we could, in the future. At this party, for some stupid reason, I started drinking vodka. By the time we went home I was absolutely paralytic. I had drunk almost a full bottle of Black Label Smirnoff. I woke up in the early hours feeling worse than I had ever felt in my life. I couldn't stop vomiting, my head was splitting in agony, and my stomach was so painful. I couldn't even drink water without throwing up for 3 days. I really thought I was going to die, and I think (if not for the grace of God) that was a distinct possibility. I'm pretty sure that I had alcohol poisoning, because of the quantity of spirits I had consumed, and also because my liver was still not working properly, so it took far longer to detoxify my body. This was aversion therapy of an extreme kind, and after I recovered, the thought of ever drinking spirits again made me feel sick. I didn't drink for months afterwards, and since then have, for the most, part stuck to the odd glass or two of wine or beer, although I still love an ice cold, lemony G&T on a hot summer's day in the garden.

We had so many visitors whilst we were at Pitman's Apartment, I can't remember exactly when everyone came, but we had Liz and Dave a couple of times, the first time when she was pregnant with a baby whom we never met, as she had a miscarriage at about 5 months. Apparently that was because of a severe neural tube defect, so even though they were really sad, they were relieved that they hadn't brought a severely handicapped child into the world. Mum and Dad came out twice, I think. Dad loved the place, but really struggled with the humidity, as he had developed Emphysema by this time. Because of this he had stopped plastering and working on building sites, and was driving a supply van for Hull City Council. Of course he had put weight on too, as he didn't get any exercise. He loved the beach, as he had always been a good swimmer, but we teased him unmercifully about his bandy white legs. Usually by the time he left he had started to tan a bit! Playing with Nicky was one of his greatest joys, and she loved him, he was such good fun. Nan and Pops came out to stay at least twice, and they doted on Nicky too. My cousin Jill came out for two weeks. Lynne and John stayed with us a couple of times. They loved it, and the second time they came, as well as bringing their 6 month old son, Daniel, John brought his C.V., and took it around to all the Banks, looking for a possible job on the island. He was successful, and got a position with the Bank of Butterfield. That second visit was when Nicky was about 18 months old, and it was not totally enjoyable! As soon as I saw Dan coming through Immigration in his stroller I had a feeling he was going to be trouble. He was. He had a really sullen, non-responsive look on his face, and when Lynne was around he would get up to all sorts of annoying tricks – yes, even at 6 months. He had a bite like a shark, and delighted in sinking his teeth into Nicky as soon as she came close to him. He even chewed a hole in my carpet!! Lynne refused to restrain him, pointing out that he was only 6 months old. Exactly. Was she blind? Someone needed to try and modify this kid's behaviour quickly, before he grew into a big problem. This drove a bit of a wedge between Lynne and I. When they eventually came out to live in Bermuda, they stayed with us until they found an apartment, and things became pretty tense. We remained friends, but there was a strain in the relationship from then on. One funny thing that happened during their stay with us was when Lynne scoffed a whole bag of my Butterscotch Chips, which had been lovingly imported from Boston (my friend Beverley Perikli had brought them back for me). John got on his moped and scoured every inch of the island trying to replace them, to no avail, because you could only get them in the U.S. In the end they had to confess – which shows the atmosphere was a bit uncomfortable! In later life Dan became the captain of the Cayman Islands Karate team, so happily found a way of channelling his aggression – or whatever it was.

Life was pretty good for us, in spite of my reduction in salary. Robb was working in the Police Parishes Office, and had been made Parish Constable for Paget. He had also been selected to help run an Outward Bound Scheme, so was given time off to teach sailing, kayaking, climbing, abseiling, and survival skills. He would go off to Paget Island in St. Georges Harbour, where there was a young offenders' facility, and teach some of them as well as local schoolchildren. It was just the kind of job he loved, but meant he left me on my own with Nicky quite a bit. He was also sent away on a couple of courses to England and Wales to help with his teaching skills and experience. He was also drinking a lot – I hadn't noticed how much until I stopped. We both smoked a lot, too, me more than Robb. He tried to give it up a few times to try and get fitter but had to give in after a while because I wouldn't even try! He was a lot more physically fit than me, and loved sports. He played soccer for Bermuda Office supplies with Pat's boyfriend, Barry, and a few others we became friends with, such as Philip Pedro, whose wife Barbara also became a friend. They were agents for Saladmaster – a U.S. company which made really good stainless steel cookware. We bought a $600 set of pans from them, guaranteed for life. I am using them to this day (40 years later) and they're as good as ever. One of my grandchildren will probably be using them when I have gone!

We got to know our landlord and landlady well. They were a lovely couple, and were very kind to us. They would invite us all over to their house for meals when family were staying with us. Mum stayed in touch with them for years after we moved out of their apartment. They loved Nicky. She couldn't say "Mr Pitman" and called him "Pippy", a name that we all adopted for him. We were told that we could help ourselves to ice cream whenever we wanted it, but we didn't like to be too greedy, and probably ate far more after we moved out and had to buy it! Herbie kept a few animals, which he would fatten up to eat, and he was also a keen gardener. He exhibited at the Annual Agricultural Show in the Botanical Gardens. We became very interested in all of this, and were inspired to give some of it a try. One of our first ventures was to get some Cochin Bantams. Robbie adapted the hen coop, which was already in our garden, to house them. They were useless as far as eating was concerned (they were all feathers) but the eggs, although tiny, had lovely dark yellow yolks and tasted great. They were really pets, they looked so pretty, with white plumy tails and feathered "gaiters" on their legs. The noise the roosters made was awful, a kind of strangled screech, and they made it frequently, but I must admit I loved the idea of being wakened by our own chickens. I'm not sure what the neighbours thought of it though. Our neighbours were nice. At the end of Garden Lane was the Medeiros family. Dad, Larry, was a lawyer, and they had a lovely big swimming pool which they let us use during the day when they were all at work. Behind us were the Gauntletts, who also used to have a dairy. They had a huge Poinciana Tree in their garden which was covered in scarlet blossom in May. Some of the branches hung just outside the window of Nicky's bedroom, it was beautiful.

Life rushed on. We put Nicky's name down for a Daycare Nursery called "Nambour", which was an Australian aborigine word for "a little more". It was situated just along South Shore Road, on Rural Hill, Paget, and had a wonderful reputation for teaching kids to read before they started school. Lots of police kids went there, and seemed to do very well. The discipline was firm but loving, and the staff seemed lovely. She could start there when she was 2 or potty trained, whichever came first. Our weeks were taken up with work (and mornings on the beach) and weekends with the beach and entertaining or parties. We spent a lot of time with Sue and John Headey, and Nicky (Kicky) and Lena (Lela) became good friends. The Police Club was loaned a small private beach on the North Shore, next to Flatts Inlet, by an old lady who owned the property. In exchange for maintaining it, and the land behind, it Police families could use it. It was a bit of a mess to begin with, but over a couple of weeks everyone worked on clearing the seaweed and flotsam from the beach, and the overgrowth of vegetation behind it, then mowing the grass. It was lovely when we were finished. It had a semicircle of pink sand, with a large grassy area behind it. There was a low headland covered with Bay Grape on the right side, and on the left a small causeway of rocks curving out to Gibbet Island, about 100 yards offshore. This meant that there was a sort of lagoon, protected on 3 sides. The water was crystal clear, shallow and warm, reaching a maximum depth of about 6 feet around the island. It was perfect for children. We started to spend most of our time there, taking our little Hibachi Barbecue with us after work in summer, and cooking supper before heading home to bath Nicky and put her to bed around 7pm. At weekends we did a lot of entertaining. I was getting a bit of a reputation as a cook. Lynne was a really good cook, too. There was a bit of rivalry between us even then I think, but we definitely spurred each other on, making us expand our repertoires. They had found a great place to live, a cottage on South Shore, Warwick, called "French

Leave". It had big open fireplaces and lots of land behind it leading to cliffs overlooking the sea. John had a pretty good job at the bank, but Lynne couldn't work because she had come to Bermuda as John's dependent, so she spent all her time on the beach and she and Dan tanned to a dark mahogany colour. I was jealous!

On Sundays we often went out to Brunch at one of the big hotels. Elbow Beach was one of the favourites, but Castle Harbour was pretty good, plus "The Waterlot", and in later years "The Whaler Inn" were all favourites. We have an oil painting of "The Whaler Inn", which was the Beach House of the Southampton Princess Hotel on South Shore, situated above its own beautiful private beach. These brunches were all absolute feasts. For about $5 you could eat as much as you liked, returning to fill up your plate over and over again with the most delicious food. The hotels in Bermuda were rated 5 star and up – real world-class cuisine – so brunch was a cheap way to sample it all. There would be huge roasts of meats of all kinds, freshly caught fish and shellfish, long tables of hot dishes and cooked vegetables, then another with exotic salads and cold dishes, plus a huge table full of gorgeous desserts. Elbow Beach was famous for its Chocolate Mousse, Nicky loved it! When we had visitors from England, we would always "do Brunch", and they could hardly believe their eyes (or tastebuds). On special occasions a big treat was to eat at one of the top restaurants. Our favourite was "The Newport Room" and we would spend hundreds of dollars eating there. When I look back at our lifestyle and experiences, both in Bermuda and later, there's no wonder that food and drink have been one of our obsessions in life! We were exposed to so many incredible privileges. I also wonder how much money we might have saved if we had lived like "normal" Brits. Actually, I really thank God we didn't, our lives would have been impoverished. As it is, this was part of our learning how to both "abase and abound, and be content in any situation". All this eating and drinking, however, had reinforced my weight problem. I yoyo dieted most of the time I was in Bermuda, putting on weight after I got there, losing it for our wedding, putting it on when I was pregnant with Nicky, losing it again afterwards. It was either feast or famine, moderation seemed impossible to me. In summer of 2005 I was in a slim phase, and decided it was time to get my long hair cut. I went to a trendy new salon in Hamilton and had it cut short and permed into an Afro. I loved it, and so did everyone else. I even modelled at a big Hairdressing Show. There are quite a few photos of me like this, we went ultra fashionable and we both had a wardrobe full of really funny clothes. I wore things like huge wide-legged trousers and boob tubes, Robb had checked trousers and hats to match, and grew a beard. What a pair of posers.

8 – Hellos and Goodbyes

As Nicky was coming up to 2 years old we started to think about having another baby, and in September 1975 I found out I was pregnant again. This time I knew somehow it wasn't a "Sam", and longed for another little girl, deciding even then that she would be called Amy, which meant "Beloved". Before I had Nicky I couldn't imagine ever being the mother of a daughter, but she was such a delight that I then dreaded the thought of having a rowdy boy! There were some mixed feelings, of course, because I knew Robb would like a son – most men do, I think. All the Grandparents were overjoyed. We went to England for Christmas that year. There was a big party at my Mum and Dad's house, I'm not sure but I think it was a late celebration of their 30th wedding anniversary (June 7th). All the family was there, and I can remember everyone dressed up to the eyeballs with long dresses and fancy hairdos. We arranged for Mum and Dad to come out to stay with us in July to see the new baby, and Nan and Pops decided they would come out the following Christmas. We went back to Bermuda, and life went on. My pregnancy went well, apart from the awful night-time panic attacks I had suffered when I was having Nicky – again treated by giving me sleeping pills - and also one incident at about 5 months. I developed and agonising pain in my tummy, which got worse and worse. Robbie took me in to the Emergency department, we had to take Nicky too, as we couldn't get a babysitter quickly enough. They had no idea what was wrong, and by then I was being sick with the pain. I was scared, of course, but knew somehow it wasn't either digestive or a threatened miscarriage. Eventually they had to give me some pethidine, and after about 2 hours the pain began to subside. I still don't know what it could have been. I think they thought it was an ectopic pregnancy, but thankfully, it wasn't. I went home and felt absolutely fine the next day, and the rest of my pregnancy went well, in spite of my still smoking like a chimney and drinking more than when I was having Nicky.

In February 1976 Liz discovered she was pregnant again. We were all so pleased, because she had really grieved over her miscarriage. My Dad was over the moon, he would soon be seeing 2 more grandchildren! That was his biggest desire, lots of grandchildren. However, in late May of 1976, at the age of 57, he had a serious heart attack. We had a call from Mum, saying that he was recovering, but there was a lot of uncertainty about whether he would ever be fit to work again, and of course, whether they would be able to come out see us in July. He was in hospital for a while, but then, as he got better, was transferred to the Nuffield Trust Hospital where Mum was deputy matron. He could finish his recovery in the care of people he knew and under Mum's supervision. They had their Wedding Anniversary on June 7th. I phoned them and they said it had been a lovely warm, sunny day. Mum was at work, so they had spent most of the day together, had a specially prepared lunch, and then walked in the rose garden. I had finished work by this time, as my baby was due around the 25th. On the 9th June, around 3pm, I was working in the kitchen. Robbie was home and watching Nicky play, when Pippy came to the door and asked him to go downstairs to the ice-cream factory. This wasn't unusual because he often asked Robb to help him with heavy work. He was gone quite some time, and when he came back up I could see by his face that there was something wrong. He gently told me that Mum had called the Pitmans and asked them to tell us that Dad had suffered another devastating heart attack, and in spite of everyone desperately trying to resuscitate him, he had died. I can remember sitting on the kitchen floor and sobbing, thinking that now he would never see his 2 new grandchildren. Even then my main focus was the new baby, and looking back I think it was some kind of natural defence against the shock and grief. Poor Dad, he had such a hard life, and only in these last few years had he experienced some of the good things in life that he deserved so much. He never even got the pension he had worked off his butt for all his life! Some might say that it was caused by years of smoking and eating full English breakfasts, or piling butter on his toast. It could be that fighting with us over the crispy fat on roast beef or the golden skin on roast chicken contributed, but I think that severe prolonged stress had far more to do with it. Of course I couldn't go home to be with Mum, or go to the funeral, as I was so close to my delivery date, so in some ways it felt as if it hadn't really happened. I was used to Dad not being around, and I knew that it wouldn't be long before my little Amy arrived, so I was pretty preoccupied. After a few days, Mum called to tell us she had decided to come out to see us and the new baby when the funeral and all the legalities were done with. She booked to fly to Bermuda in mid-July, and we all felt that Dad would have wanted her to do it.

The weather was getting really hot, I felt exhausted and couldn't wait to get rid of my bump, which was pretty big by then, but was really aware of these being the last days I would have with Nicky on her own, so I had a real mixture of feelings. I went into labour in the early morning of Saturday 19th June. We called Lynne, and she came over to babysit Nicky, who was fast asleep. Things progressed fairly slowly, and at some point they tried to speed things up by rupturing my membranes, unsuccessfully because, as I had suspected, I had "sprung a leak" a couple of days before. They managed to dig a small chunk out of Amy's head, so they were able to tell me she was another redhead, long before she was born! I had another easy labour, again with no pain relief, and by 11.45 am Amy Joanna had arrived, 7lbs 2ozs and 20 inches long, with beautiful wavy red hair and lovely blue eyes. I know I would have been just as happy if she was a boy, but my heart's desire had been another little girl to be a companion to my darling Nicky. Dr. MacDonald-Smith was there for the birth, and afterwards he did a great job of stitching me up, reversing the damage done back in 1961 by the guy who delivered Anthony. By the time he had arrived after Nicky was born it was too late to do any fancy stitching, so he had promised me that he would at my next birth, if he could. This time I was determined to do my own thing with my baby, and I flouted all the rules, unwrapping her and snuggling her up in bed with me (shock-horror) regularly. Robbie sneaked up the back stairs of the hospital out of visiting hours with flasks of Campari and soda to keep me going! Sue Headey came to see me and brought me a gorgeous creamy white Magnolia flower. The perfume of it filled my room. Another white flower, this time for my second daughter! I realised even more than when I had been in hospital after having Nicky that the system was totally barbaric, and designed to distress everyone concerned, especially the children. Nicky was not allowed to visit, so the poor little thing was in a terrible state by the time I came home after 6 days, bringing with me a squalling baby who only slept in 5 minute stretches every couple of hours. I had just disappeared in the middle of the night, after being her major carer for all of her little life. Robbie, with the best will in the world, was dropped in at the deep end, and was floundering. Nicky woke up crying every night, and threw up all over whichever bed she was in. Robb spent most of the 6 days in the Kwicky Licky Launderette, washing all the bedding over and over again. The crowning touch was when he nearly lost Nicky. I still feel sick at the thought of this. On Father's Day, 20th June 1976, he took her to Brunch at the Holiday Inn at St. Georges, along with Lynne and John and some others. The Tall Ships race had come to Bermuda that year, and on this day all the ships were leaving for Newport, Rhode Island, and would be passing by the Holiday Inn. Brunch was held on the top floor so it was a perfect place to see this fantastic spectacle. Nicky had on a lovely little pink dress, which was quite distinctive, so Robb allowed her to get down from the table and wander around after she had eaten, whilst he and the others finished their meal. The only problem was that there was another little blonde haired girl with the same dress doing the same thing. It was quite a while before he realised that the child he had been keeping an eye on wasn't Nicky. After about half an hour of frantic praying, searching, crying and enquiring, he went into a loo about 3 floors down, and there she was. I think that may have been our family's first known miracle. I thank God for it, and also that I wasn't there, and didn't know about it until she was safe. I might have killed someone. I may still.

Amy was a really difficult baby. She hardly slept during my waking hours, as I already mentioned, and she cried most of the time she was awake. Her one redeeming feature was that at about 11 pm she fell asleep (probably from exhaustion) until about 7 am. I was so knackered by then that I did the same. Poor little Nicky got hardly any attention, so she started doing naughty things when I was feeding Amy, such as emptying the fridge and dropping eggs on the floor. I was so frazzled and guilty, I was always telling her off, and to top it all, Robb disappeared onto his desert island for a month to run Outward Bound. Mum came out to stay for 3 weeks, and she was in a very vulnerable state after the funeral and winding up all Dad's affairs. To be honest she wasn't much help to me, I felt as if I was looking after her as well as everything else! It was a very low point in my life. I ended up on antidepressants, which helped a bit, but I think a bit of help, support, sleep and understanding would have worked even better. Our friends, Sue and John, had decided they were leaving Bermuda so that John could join the family business in Huddersfield, and I knew I would miss them a lot. Nicky would miss Lena, too. Robb and I weren't getting on very well. He was drinking a lot, when he was home, which wasn't very often, and we argued constantly. Mum went home and we settled into a really stressful period. I went back to work and somehow managed to function. Amy went to Tia, and Nicky started at Nambour, which she loved. There was one teacher in particular that she was fond of, an English lady called Diane Shawyer. She was such fun, and she obviously loved the kids in return. Nicky came home singing little songs she learned there, such as "A B C D E F G, Jesus died for you and me". On my birthday that year, November 2nd, Liz gave birth to a son and called him Richard Alan, after our dad (John Richard) and Dave's dad, Alan. I was an auntie! We spent a lot of time with Lynne and John, and at Christmas that year, when they went home to England for a holiday, we looked after their house. Nan and Pops came out for a holiday, and we had a lovely time there, lighting big cedar fires and seeing our little girls enjoying Christmas. Amy was 6 months old and could almost crawl by then, Nan and Pops loved her to bits. She was pretty, chubby and cheeky, and her hair was a beautiful light red with soft curls. Nicky had Katherine Latter, a friend from Nambour, to sleep over one night, we were surrounded by kids! We got to know Katherine's parents – Ray and Kay – quite well. They were schoolteachers from England. Kay was actually from Fareham, near Portsmouth, and they had a house in the New Forest.

We had 2 beautiful little girls, and were now seriously into parenthood. Sue Headey put it quite well after she had her second child, Tim, when Lena was almost 7 years old and they had gone back to England. She said that with one child she was "A lady with a baby" and could still function as a single person fairly well, but when the second child comes along, that's when you really become a mother. To be honest, as far as I was concerned, Robb didn't let that fact affect his lifestyle very much at all, and I grew increasingly angry and resentful. I was mad when he wasn't there, and even madder when he was, because he was drinking like a fish, refusing to talk about our problems, and acting as if I was the problem because of my attitude! There was talk of having Amy christened whilst Nan and Pops were with us, but we didn't have any church connections, and by that time we had started thinking it would be a bit hypocritical when we weren't sure we believed anything, so decided not to bother. Nan and Pops went back to England, and we went home to Pitman's apartment. I began to feel the lack of a garden. We were on the first floor, and the balcony seemed to be shrinking. We had put a gate up to keep Nicky away from the stairs, but I still had to keep a close eye on her in case she climbed onto the walls. She had a little trike, and would cycle up and down the balcony with her favourite toy "Laow" on the back of it. Laow was a fluffy yellow fur cat which she took with her everywhere. If she had her thumb to suck and Laow to stroke she was happy anywhere, and would sleep to order! Laow was replaced at least 3 times, because his fur would get worn off and he would turn into a nasty looking chunk of dried leather. We went to England in Spring of 1977, and had a lovely holiday in a farmhouse in Wensleydale. Liz, Dave, Richard and Mum came with us, and we had a good time touring the area. I began to appreciate Yorkshire at last, after spending most of my life there itching to get away from it. The countryside was beautiful, and we enjoyed spending some time watching the farmer milk the cows and look after his sheep. Nicky loved it. Robbie enjoyed visiting the Theakston's Brewery, where his favourite beer, "Old Peculier", was made! I didn't get on with Liz very well at all. We had never been very close, and this holiday emphasised our differences. We had a spectacular row over a fish and chip lunch in Richmond. She wanted to sit in the town square and eat out of newspaper, I had to cope with a toddler and a baby, and wanted to sit in a restaurant where I could more easily supervise them. The outcome was me telling her to f... off in front of Mum, who had never heard me use four letter swear words before. (In fact I never did use them, but not because of any moral compunction, but because I didn't like the sound of the word with a Yorkshire accent!) Mum's face was a picture. I think Robb was stifling laughter. We did eventually eat in a fish and chip restaurant, which was truly naff. We even had to ask for ketchup as there was nothing on the tables. When I did ask for some, my Mum said apologetically to the sloppy waitress "Oh, they have ketchup on everything", whilst laughing nervously. I was furious, and said indignantly to the poor waitress "No they bloody-well don't, is it unusual to expect ketchup in a fish and chip restaurant?!" This incident, however, typified the kind of attitude that I was detecting in my Mum and sister. I think they could see that I had changed, and felt threatened by it, so tried to somehow put me down. I think this is something that most people find when they move away from their roots, it's hard to go back.

On our return to Bermuda Amy continued to be a problem as far as her sleep was concerned. She seemed to need very little, and I was getting exhausted, especially when I went back to work. However, I carried on going to the beach with Heather in the mornings. She had another baby now, a little boy called David, so there was quite a crowd of us on Elbow Beach, as Lynne would bring Dan, too. It was a lovely daily respite from all the working and slog. Nicky was doing really well at Nambour. She loved it, and the teachers loved her. I remember one of them rushing out to me one afternoon and telling me what a wonderful vocabulary Nicky had! I was invited to a couple of "Ladies Evenings" at the church that most of them attended by various teachers, but I really didn't think they were my scene. I was touched by their kindness, though.

Around the time that Amy was 6 months old I developed a "crush" on one of Robb's co-workers, Paul Davis. I don't know what it was about him, except that he seemed to be very interested in me. I guess it was because Robb and I weren't getting on, and I was desperate for some affection. It never came to anything, but, looking back on it, it was almost an obsession, and had it gone to its natural conclusion it would have destroyed our marriage. Also around this time we decided to give up smoking. Both Nicky and Amy would get really bad croup every time they had a cold, and the doctor warned me that smoking was not helping them at all. At the hospital there was a new Doctor who was a Seventh Day Adventist. He offered to run a no smoking course "The 5 Day Plan" for any hospital staff who were interested. I decided to join it. Robb had wanted to give it up many times but I had always sabotaged his efforts by refusing to even try. It was a perfect set-up, I couldn't cheat at home because of Robb, or at work because half the lab. staff had joined the course too. On the second night of the course (which called for quitting "cold turkey") I was absolutely craving a cigarette. I got as far as the car, wanting to go out and buy a pack, but somehow I knew that this was now or never. I almost bit chunks out of the car, I was so desperate, but I didn't give in, and from then on it became slightly easier. The worst withdrawal effects for me were that I struggled to concentrate and focus, and felt at a loss as to what I should be doing most of the time – which made things a bit dangerous in Blood Transfusion! Apparently it takes 5 days to rid your body of the physical dependence on nicotine, but the psychological dependence takes as long to get rid of as it did to acquire it, and for months afterwards I would find myself standing next to the bar, where I used to keep my cigarettes, not knowing why I was there. It did work though, and both of us managed to kick the habit completely. We were invited to a big meeting at a local hotel, designed to promote giving up smoking, and they asked us to stand up and tell everyone how we did it. It was a new experience, but one we were designed to repeat many times at later dates, however, we would be promoting something even better! I learnt a few things as part of that course which have helped me since, for example, avoiding situations where I would find the temptation unbearable. We were told to avoid sitting with a coffee after dinner, and instead to get up and go for a walk. We did do this, and of course it helped towards getting fitter generally. We were actually told to avoid coffee completely, because caffeine was strongly linked to nicotine. When I asked if we could drink decaffeinated coffee, as a new brand was being advertised as "97% caffeine free" I found out that regular coffee was 95% caffeine free – it was just a play on words. Looking back on this time, I realise that it was a turning point for me in lots of ways, a real "growing up" type experience once again. I realised that all actions have consequences, and I needed to take responsibility for not only my children's health, but also my own, and that self-discipline could be a reward in itself. I started to feel a lot healthier.

Life rushed by, we had a good social life, and lots of friends. Rocky and Maureen Ironmonger became friends, and we got to know Liz and Tony Smith, and John and Mary van

De Weg. John and Mary had kids at Nambour and John was a police officer with Robb. Some of us loved food and cooking, and would take in turns to put on "Gourmet Feasts" for the whole group of "foodies", as well as eating out from time to time. We had some great meals, but the thing that stands out most to me is when Mary Van De Weg made a potato salad with vanilla yoghourt because she didn't have any mayonnaise. It was truly disgusting, and from then on we realised she wasn't a real dyed in the wool foodie (glutton?) like the rest of us. She was such an airhead, but very nice! One thing that happened to them which was quite formative in my attitude towards medicine and prescribed drugs was what happened to John Van De Weg. There was a world wide "Swine Flu" scare going on in the mid 70s, and all the Police Force were told they must be immunised against it in case of a pandemic. John, like the others, dutifully obeyed, but a couple of days later he was rushed into hospital paralysed from head to toe. He was diagnosed with Guillaume Barre Syndrome, and was seriously ill. He eventually regained movement and sensation everywhere but his feet, but because of that, from then on he shuffled around and tripped frequently because he couldn't tell when his feet were hitting the ground. He was a tall well built guy, and had been a useful member of the Police Rugby team, but of course his Rugby days were over after his illness. I'm not sure whether he ever got compensation from the Bermuda Government, he certainly pursued it, and there has since been a discovery of a definite link between his condition and flu shots. They did pay for him to go through some kind of rehab course in England to assess how much recovery he could expect to make, but this was years later, and he still had the same problems.

I didn't mention before that during the heyday of the Outward Bound programme in Bermuda Robbie had become the Honorary Secretary for an organisation called United World Colleges. He was handed the job by Tony Diggins, who was leaving the island after his marriage to Ann Diggins (nee McCullough, my fellow worker in the hospital lab) had broken up. The organisation seemed as if it was a very creditable one, and by this time both of us were increasingly thinking about doing some good in the world and leaving it a better place as we were getting older. Robbie's job would be to find donors from amongst the mega-rich residents of Bermuda, who would be willing to give money towards scholarships awarded to promising students from the island. The President of United World Colleges was (and is) Prince Charles, and the Hon. Sec. had to maintain a correspondence with him, informing him of any fund-raising or new donors, so Robbie wrote to him regularly. United World Colleges is an organisation which runs a group of Colleges of Higher Education, situated in various places around the world, to which one must be invited to be a student. Basically, what happens is that the top students from the top schools around the world are "head-hunted", and offered scholarships to continue their education at UWC. There they are groomed as future world leaders. When I think about it now, looking at it from any perspective, it is extremely elitist and exclusive, but at the time we thought it was a worthy cause. It was also very hard to find out anything about it, and that rings a lot of alarm bells for me now. However, being Hon. Sec. was a great thing to have on one's CV, and Robb loved writing to Prince Charles! He always was a name-dropper (me too, actually, I'm ashamed to say).

I became an Auntie again in April of 1978. Liz and Dave had a little girl, Rachel Emma. Our girls grew and thrived, and we had some really happy times, with picnics in the Botanical gardens, Friday family junk food nights at Chiquito's on John Smith's Bay, days on the Police Beach,

Easter kite flying and Christmas day swims on Elbow Beach. Most of our celebrations included Lynne, John and Dan. However, Robb and I were gradually drifting further apart. When Amy was about 18 months old we were told we could apply for a Police House. This would really help us financially, as Police rents were less than normal "civilian" ones. However, we were really sorry to be leaving Pitman's Apartment, Herbie and Betty had been really good to us, and I loved the Botanical Gardens. I think that's probably where my love of plants and flowers really started, and the amazing scent of citrus blossom will always take me back to evenings on the balcony of our first little family home there. When we were offered our Police House, imagine my delight when I found out it was 18 Alexandra Road, up at Prospect! It was the house I had fallen in love with when we went to a party there. Brian and Carol and their 2 daughters were emigrating to Calgary, in Alberta, Canada. I was so excited, and couldn't wait to move in, which we did in early 1978, and soon settled in there. It was so lovely to have an enclosed garden for the girls to play in. Our next door neighbours were Steve and Diana "Flip" Petty. Steve was a Bermudian policeman, Flip was a Canadian nurse who worked at KEMH, so we had lots in common. They had 2 daughters, Lisa and Keira, who were about the same age as Nicky and Amy, and they soon all became good friends. There was such a special "feel" to the place. I can remember waking up there early in the mornings, the gauze curtains gently moving in the breeze, dappled sunlight coming in through the windows, the scent of honeysuckle drifting in, and the familiar sound of Kiskadees calling to each other from the Pawpaw trees, reminding me of my first morning in Bermuda – idyllic!

9 – Changes

Nicky was due to start school in the September of that year, and she had a place at Bermuda High School for Girls, a lovely private school in Hamilton. We would struggle to pay the fees, but wanted to build on the really good start she had at Nambour. We also had a problem with my hours at work. Isabel was reluctant to swap our hours around so that I could work mornings and be able to collect Nicky from school at 3 pm, Robb worked shifts, so couldn't be relied on. When I look back on all this I can see the amazing way things worked out for us – and I know who arranged it all! My old boss at KEMH, Pat Allan, had left the hospital and was working for a group of Doctors who shared offices at Woodbourne Hall and had a small private lab. Woodbourne Hall was situated on a road in Hamilton just across from Bermuda High School. Pat was managing the lab and was advertising for a part-time assistant. The assistant's hours would be 9.00am to 3.00pm – Nicky's school hours!

I knew this job was made for me, but it wasn't a foregone conclusion that I would get it. The reason Pat had left the hospital was that she had been "bullied" out. As I mentioned when I talked about how I got to Bermuda in the first place, the other bosses in the lab didn't like Pat because she showed up their laziness and lack of integrity, and eventually they had tried to force her out of her job. Here comes another twist – Bill Cooke – a medical consultant who was in charge of the Woodbourne lab. – knew what a bunch of lying layabouts the other hospital lab bosses were, and was a friend of one of Pat's ex-boyfriends! He also happened to be an important Hospital Board member. Under normal circumstances, if you were an ex-pat and lost your job in Bermuda, there was very little chance of another one, and most people would have to leave the island if it happened to them. Dr. Cooke gave Pat the job at Woodbourne, and because no misconduct or reason for dismissal could be found against her (apart from the dislike of the others), the hospital board ended up paying her $10,000 to leave quietly! I wasn't working with Pat by then, I was in Blood Transfusion, and had tried to stay out of it – which meant not taking sides. A few of us tried to do this, but others joined in her "persecution", which meant Pat was pretty isolated. She was really hurt by the fact that no-one took sides with her, but we were all fearful for our jobs, and to be honest she really wasn't the easiest person to get on with. I think we just wished she would hurry up and leave, as the atmosphere in the lab was awful, and we felt so guilty. Pat and I had naturally grown apart a bit since I got married and had children, but I still felt guilty for not supporting her more, and I still regret that I didn't.

In the light of all this, it was with trepidation I sent in my application for the job as her assistant at Woodbourne. Pat phoned me and asked if I really thought we could work together again. I said I thought we could, and explained my position to her, apologising for my lack of support. Dr. Cooke interviewed me, and seemed to understand what I was saying. I said I thought we had both grown older and wiser, so he decided to give me the job with the proviso that if we didn't get on it would be me that had to leave. I started working there when Nicky started school, and it went like clockwork. I dropped Nicky at Bermuda High, and was at Woodbourne 5 minutes later, ready to start at 9.00am. I loved working there, Pat and I got on really well without the external pressures of the vindictive hospital lab bosses, and I was at school to pick Nicky up at 3.05pm. I learnt a lot of new things, as we had a profit sharing scheme for all employees, did our own book-keeping, ordered all our own supplies, did ECGs, as well as lots of biochemistry testing that I had never done before. We had a lot more to do with patients, and also got to know the doctors well. This was when I began to see that these medical "gods" that my Mum had brought me up to "worship" in fact had feet of clay. Most of them were a bunch of arrogant control freaks with what looked to me suspiciously like contempt for most of their patients, the exceptions being the rich, powerful, famous or beautiful (of which there were plenty in Bermuda)! Some of them were good fun though – we did have some laughs. Bill Cooke was a bit different, he was a one-off! He was rolling in money and spoke at conferences worldwide, but was such a cheapskate! He would recycle any presents he was given to all the Woodbourne staff at Christmas, and once gave me a bottle opener he had nicked from the Hong Kong Hilton. However, he was a good man, and great to work for after all the infighting and back stabbing at KEMH. He was intuitive, honest and fair, and a very good doctor. We had to fight like mad for any salary increases, though!

Home life went on as usual. Mum came out in the summer holidays to look after the girls, so that didn't help with my relationship with Robb. It was great to have her there to look after the girls, but she and Robb clashed constantly, both of them were very unhelpful in their attitudes to one another. Mum also sensed that things were not good in our marriage and, of course, took my side in everything. Around this time our friends, Heather and Charlie, decided to end their marriage, which really saddened us, and made me realise that divorce was a constant possibility. We were having spectacular rows, one of which makes us laugh when we remember it. We had gone out for dinner in Hamilton, drunk too much, and started arguing. I stomped off and started walking home (not too far away, and it was dark, so not too hot either). Robb eventually followed in the car and caught me up about half way home. He got out to talk to me, but I dived into the car and drove off, leaving him to walk the rest of the way. Fair's fair! Not too conducive to making up though. Nicky was doing well at school, she had lovely teachers, and made new friends, as well as having some of the old friends from Nambour there with her. She used to come home exhausted when she first started at the High School, and would fall asleep in the car on the way to pick up Amy, who was at Nambour by this time. I was getting to know the teachers there better, especially Diane Shawyer. I actually did go to a couple of the Ladies evenings at Paget Gospel Chapel with her, and found myself really enjoying some good, clean fun. There would be a silly game, or a competition – such as making an Easter bonnet or a Christmas decoration - with a prize. Someone would sing a solo, or stand up and tell us how they became a Christian or how God got them through a difficult period in their life, as well as tea and coffee and yummy cakes! During one of these evenings Chris Finnegan, one of the Mums from Nambour, was talking about how she had been born-again. She was a beautiful woman, and looked as if she had everything going for her, but she talked about the terrible pain she had experienced through a broken marriage, and drug and alcohol abuse. With nowhere to turn for help, she had spoken to Di, and as a result had given her life to Jesus. She looked radiant, and said that she knew that this was the answer to her problems, and to the world's problems. This was quite a claim, and I was fascinated. Another of the Nambour teachers gave me a book entitled "The Total Woman" by Marabel Morgan. It was really radical to me, and talked about "submitting" to your husband, which I rejected completely at first!

The only person I didn't really warm to at Nambour was the owner, who seemed a bit of a phony to me, always smiling sweetly, but as hard as nails underneath it. We were having a terrible time getting Amy to bed at night. Nicky would be in bed and asleep by 7pm every night, but Amy would still be fighting it at 11pm, and of course this didn't help our marriage either, we didn't get any peaceful time together. We joined a babysitting circle which worked well as far as our nights out were concerned, but evenings at home were a nightmare, and Robb would disappear 9 out of 10, leaving me to cope with everything else. More resentment built up. I tried to talk to the owner about Amy, asking her if it would be possible to exempt her from the "nap" all the children took after lunch. She obviously didn't need it, and getting her to sleep at night might be easier without it. I was pretty desperate by this time, but all I got was a sweet plastic smile and complete indifference to all my explanations and pleadings. I felt like punching out her lights!

We spent a lot of time at the police beach in summer, packing the barbecue and ice chest in the car and heading down there after picking the girls up from school, or from home along with Mum during the holidays. That did help to wear Amy out. However, Lynne had started to come along with us regularly, and I sensed a peculiar change in her attitude towards me. It was something like contempt, if I'm honest, so that didn't exactly add to my enjoyment and relaxation after a hard day. Weekends were great, because we could get down to the beach really early – without Lynne and Dan! I love early mornings anyway – there is such a special feeling when the sun is coming up and everything feels new, but on a beach in Bermuda it feels almost magical. The sea was flat calm, with tiny ripples splashing onto the lovely soft sand. The fish were jumping out towards Gibbet island. The girls played in the shallow, warm water, or climbed along the rocks, whilst I raked up any seaweed or flotsam that had come ashore overnight. If Mum was there she would beachcomb for shells and pieces of coral. No-one else seemed to be around for a couple of hours, it was like our own private place. Robb wasn't always there early, as he was either working, or helping to run the Outward Bound scheme on Paget Island, or teaching Kayaking in Flatts inlet, as well as not being a morning person. However, he would be there later, but I think he missed a lot of the early morning magic. We had one big scare there. One afternoon, when lots of kids were in the water, and most of the parents sitting on the beach keeping watch, I thought I spotted a triangular fin coming around Gibbet Island! As I looked again, in horror, I saw another one!! I screamed to the kids to get out of the water, and there was total confusion as some of the parents dashed in to save their terrified kids. Some of the children managed to climb out onto the little causeway of rocks, but many of them couldn't get to it and stood paralysed with fright, as did a lot of the Mums and Dads. Then, as we watched, the 2 fins turned around and started heading out to sea again, and we realised that they were moving in and out of the water together. Someone shouted "It's not sharks, it's a ray!!" We had seen the "wingtips" of a huge stingray, and mistaken them for the dorsal fins of 2 sharks. The chaos in the water had driven it back out into the safety of the deeper water behind the island. What a relief.

Around this time we added another member to our family. I got to know the pharmacists at Woodbourne, a married couple called John and Frances. One day Frances called to me as I was going into work. She was out walking one morning, and had noticed a paper shopping bag by the side of the road which seemed to be moving. Inside it were 4 tiny kittens, far too young to have left their mother, all crying and wriggling about, full of life. She had picked them up and taken them home, then hand reared them on milk and weetabix! They were now old enough to be found new homes, and Frances wondered if I would have one. We didn't have a cat at the time. Moolie, our adopted ginger psycho-cat, had died before we left Pitman's apartment, so I said I would ask Robb and let her know. He didn't mind, so we became the owners of the sweetest little cat we ever had. Frances brought her to work one day, she was the most pathetic looking little thing you ever saw! Her fur was stuck down to her skinny little body with dried Weetabix, because she had no Mum to clean her up, but I loved her immediately. The best memory of that day was picking Nicky up from school. I drove to school, parked, and walked to her classroom to get her, telling her that there was a surprise waiting for her in the car. As we walked back, I could see the kitten sitting on the back windowsill, and soon Nicky saw her too. She was so excited, her face was pure joy, and she cuddled the little thing all the way home. Amy loved her too, and as soon as we got her home we put her in the bathroom sink to soak off all the caked on food. When we dried her and her fur fluffed up, we realised she was really pretty. She was white, and had a black tail, one black spot on her back, and a black nose and ears. We decided to call her Spot. She was affectionate and full of character, and all of us were really fond of her.

At that time in Bermuda it seemed as if everyone had started running. I'd met a couple of women who had lost weight and "shaped up" through doing it, and I was overweight again. Food was a big comfort and consolation to me, I loved good food, and I was still locked in battle with Lynne over who was the best cook! I was fed up with myself though, and at 32 I was aware of the years creeping up on me, and wanted to get slim and fit before I got old and decrepit, so I decided to try jogging. I started by jogging (very slowly and stopping often for breath) around the block at Prospect. I did it early in the morning, so no-one could see me! I was exhausted afterwards, but decided to keep at it, and soon was running further afield. It gave me the most amazing sense of freedom and potential. Whether that was down to the fact that, as I got fitter and if I had time, I could set out to run anywhere on the island, or because I had really "broken the mould" of my fat couch potato image, I don't know, but it felt really good! I was hooked. I would be out at the crack of dawn every morning, pounding the Bermuda roads, revelling in the beautiful sunrises, the quiet scenery, and the fabulous perfumes of the early morning flowers. Combined with giving up smoking, being a runner made me feel that, for me, the sky was the limit. I wasn't confined by anyone's opinion of me – mine especially – I could do anything I wanted if I really tried. I started to lose weight and get in shape, feeling fit was addictive!

Something else had been happening to me during the course of my marriage. I had started to feel that, in spite of my rejection of church and religion, there must be "something out there". The miracle and wonder of my precious daughters, the beauty of Bermuda, the privilege of living there, the way my employment needs had been met to fit in with bringing up the girls, my complete recovery from Hepatitis, becoming a runner, the fact that I didn't have to stay as I was – many things contributed to this feeling, but there was also a feeling I found very hard to put into words, which made me want to find out about "God". In later years, on reading C. S. Lewis' book "Surprised by Joy", I recognised this feeling I couldn't name as Joy. It was something I had experienced from time to time all my life, a sort of tingling rush of overwhelming "happiness" and gratitude, but now I wanted to find a focus for it. What was the point of it all if appreciation and gratitude couldn't be directed to the source? I looked into yoga and Transcendental Meditation. I had a jumble of half baked Catholic, Methodist, and Anglican ideas hanging around from my youth, but now there was the input from Nambour, the ladies at Paget Gospel Chapel, and the girls. Nicky asked me often if I had Jesus in my heart. I knew I didn't, but would tell her not to be silly. I had also started to occasionally watch a programme on daytime television called "The 700 Club". It was an American Christian chat show, which I wouldn't have watched under normal circumstances, but anything was preferable to Bermuda's home made TV programmes, which were hopeless. My favourite part of the show was when special guests were interviewed by the host, Pat Robertson. To my shame, I would put most of the guests into the category of ignorant rednecks, but then one day I saw that the guest was the super-intellectual, upper class British writer and journalist, Malcolm Muggeridge. I couldn't believe it! He was famous for his atheistic, anti-religious views, and had even gone to live in Russia for a while, because he thought that Communism was the answer to the world's problems. He was obviously still sane and hadn't lost any of his reasoning powers, but was stating, on an international Christian TV programme, that he had been "born again"! This really made me think. What on earth did "born again" mean? Could it happen to anyone? He said that he took a leap of faith and became a Christian when he realised he had to "believe in order to understand, not understand in order to believe", and that's what faith is. It is a blind leap in some ways, because you risk everything you are and have on the chance that Jesus really is the only Way, the ultimate Truth, and the only Life that will be worth living for ever. In other ways, though, He gives you tempting glimpses of His truth, and it begins to dawn on you that this is what you need. However, He won't ever push you. You're the one that has to make that momentous and life-changing decision to jump, and when you do, you land right in His arms. That's when He begins to answer all your questions, and show you that this was the thing you should have done eons ago. Hearing him made me realise that intelligence was no barrier or excuse. During my random church experiences various Bible seeds had been sown, but none of them had sprouted into real faith until now, when with frequent "glimpses" God started to water and nurture them. One glimpse was a remembered a line from the book of Ecclesiastes; "There is nothing new under the sun", and it dawned on me that everything I thought and discovered had been thought and discovered before. I was not in any way more intelligent, and did not have any greater insight, than those who had gone before, and in fact, some of the greatest intellects that the world has ever known were simple believers. The mistaken and patronising conclusion I had come to as I grew up was that religion was all childish fairy tales, which anyone with intelligence ideally grew out of. Another glimpse was when I realised that the only way the world could ever change was if everyone "loved their enemies and did good to those that hated them", as Jesus said we should. Similar words "Thou shalt love the Lord thy God with all thy heart, mind and strength, and thy neighbour as thyself" have been the motivation for 99% of the world's greatest, most selfless, and most effective philanthropists. All this was all contributing to a conviction that I ought to try going to church again. If only I could find the right church. I didn't think I could cope with all the mumbo jumbo of the Catholics, most of the Anglicans I knew were just watered down Catholics, the Methodists didn't drink, the Gospel chapel ladies had to wear head coverings, the black churches were wild and crazy, and I was white anyway! Added to this of course was that I didn't want to give up my Sunday pastimes of jogging, going to the beach, and relaxing on my only real day off (Saturdays were for housework and entertaining). The net result was that I didn't do anything about it, just carried on thinking. We did start occasionally sending the girls to Sunday School at Paget Gospel Chapel, however. It was probably a sop to my conscience at that point, and I could go for a nice long run amongst new scenery after dropping them off! Parents were invited to services at special times of the year, when the children would sing and put on little plays. I specially remember going to an Easter service in the Spring of 1979 and everyone absolutely belting out a hymn with the chorus starting "Up from the grave He arose, with a mighty triumph o'er His foes", and thinking that these people really believed what they were singing. There was none of the polite, silent, "ventriloquistic" mouthing the words that I had experienced in traditional churches, leaving the choir to make a noise. This was real singing, straight from the heart and full of enthusiasm and conviction.

The great "wake-up call" came out of the blue one beautiful day in September of that year. I had gone to work as usual, dropping Amy off at Nambour, and Nicky at the High School. Robb was at work in the Parish Constables' office in Hamilton. About 2 pm I got a phone call from Nambour saying that Amy seemed to be having a fit. They had tried to wake her up after her nap, and she wouldn't respond. They didn't know what to do. I asked how long since they first tried to wake her, and they said "Quite some time". I screamed at them down the phone "Jesus Christ!! Get her to the hospital right now!!!!" I think they phoned Robb at the same time, or else I did, I can't remember – everything was a blur. I drove through Hamilton to the hospital. The traffic was really bad, it seemed like the longest drive I ever made in my life. When I got there Robb was already in the waiting room. We couldn't see Amy, as the doctors were still working on her, trying to stop the fit. We called Flip Petty, our next door neighbour, to ask if she would pick up Nicky from school when she went to get Lisa, and she was more than willing to help by looking after her until we got home. After what seemed like a lifetime a doctor came out to tell us that they had to give Amy a massive dose of Vallium to stop the fit. He said it had worked, but that she was unconscious as a result, and that there was a possibility that she had suffered brain damage because of lack of oxygen during the fit. We would have to wait until she regained consciousness to find out the extent of it. Robb, fighting back tears, told me that he had arrived at A & E before Amy, and that he had seen her being brought in. He said her face had been almost black from lack of oxygen, and that she was foaming at the mouth – he was devastated by the sight. Amy was admitted to the Children's ward. She was totally unconscious, and was put into a cot with sides to prevent her from falling out. Robb went home to look after Nicky, and I stayed, sitting by Amy's cot all of that night, waiting for her to wake up. I tried talking to her at one point, and she opened her eyes, but she looked at me without any spark of recognition before her eyes slid upwards and closed again. Robb put Nicky to bed and came back to the hospital, leaving Flip babysitting. He brought me some needlepoint I was working on to give me something to do during the waiting hours, and to take my mind off the dreadful possibilities of the future. After he had gone home to Nicky, I sat and stitched by the side of Amy's cot. I can still remember those few hours clearly, because it was the first time I experienced what I now know was the presence of God. It felt as if Amy and I were enclosed in a warm golden bubble of peace. Amidst all the stress and desperate worry, I had the incredible feeling that, whatever happened, everything would be OK. I knew that I would be able to cope. In the early hours of the morning Amy regained consciousness, and to my joy and relief, she recognised me. She went back to sleep, and I dozed in the chair. When morning came and she was allowed to get out of bed, we realised that there was some brain damage, but it was only minimal as far as we could see. The left side of her mouth was slightly droopy, she held her left arm in an awkward position, and when she walked she dragged her foot slightly on the same side, but she was fine otherwise – we still had our precious Amy-Jo. She was a bit zomboid from all the drugs for a couple of days, but obviously had the same cheeky little personality. A battery of tests was arranged, including blood tests, EEGs and Brain Scans. The hospital had only just started scanning, and a girl I had worked with in the lab, Susan Mutch, was doing them. The blood tests showed nothing, the EEGs were inconclusive, but the brain scan appeared to show something that shouldn't have been there. Susan told me about it, emphasising that it might not be anything, but said that they would carry on the investigations. She was sent home with a load of appointments to go back to see a paediatrician, and to have repeat EEGs and another scan. She was also sent to an optometrist to check whether there was any evidence at the back of her eyes of a brain problem.

We hardly let Amy out of our sight for a while – I slept next to her, afraid that she might have another fit in her sleep. All of the possible causes of "something that shouldn't be there" in her brain swirled around in my mind. The paediatrician decided to put her on phenobarbitone until they had a diagnosis. This was an anti-convulsant, prescribed in an effort to prevent any possible future fits. It made her sluggish and irritable, and I really didn't like it, because I felt it was changing her personality. Suddenly, life had become a serious business. Could I carry on just having "the good life" as my goal and purpose, when one of the most precious people in my life was suffering, was probably going to suffer even more, and had almost been taken out of it for good?

10 – The Greatest Change

A week or so after Amy's fit Robb and I had our 7th wedding anniversary. We decided to go out for dinner at our favourite Italian restaurant, "La Trattoria", in Hamilton. I felt we needed to get away from the situation for a while and talk. We hadn't dared leave Amy before, and we wouldn't leave her with anyone but a close friend, so Lynne offered to babysit for us. I can remember what I wore that night – it was a lovely cool black linen dress which looked great with my short blonde hair and light tan, and was my favourite thing to wear now that I was slim and fit. I was feeling really good about myself physically, but since Amy's brush with death I was feeling completely at sea emotionally in a way I couldn't describe. I can't remember anything about that meal except for two items of our conversation. One was me telling Robb that the "nicest" diagnosis for Amy was Epilepsy, and the other was him telling me that he was on the brink of an affair with Lynne. To this day I don't know how far things had gone with them – and I don't want to know. The overwhelming sense of betrayal was the same whatever had happened. I felt numb. We went home and I confronted Lynne, who nastily suggested that John and I should get together again and then we could bore each other to death. I wondered how long she had felt like this about me, maybe even going back to the time John was my tame escort when we were students. Incidentally, she's still with "boring" John 34 years later. After she left, Robb explained to me that what happened to Amy had been a special "wake-up call" to him. Since our girls were born he had felt that the consequences of any misbehaviour on his part would be suffered by them, and he almost saw Amy's illness as a direct result of his infidelity, and he had decided to put a stop to it right then. In retrospect, it was a heck of a time to tell me, and I don't think he apologised at that point, but actually, it was the best time to tell me, because it made me realise that I could no longer put off making changes I needed to make to get my life in order. In the space of 2 weeks I had almost lost my little girl and my husband, and my "best friend" definitely no longer fitted that description! My foundations were well and truly shaken, and the consequences of all of this were still playing out. I realised that my family, our friends and social life, our home in Bermuda, maintaining our standard of living, in fact all that I was living for – could go in an instant, and what would I have left?

Amy was back at Nambour, but continued to undergo more tests at the hospital, whilst we thanked "God" for good medical insurance. The EEGs were different every time – they couldn't understand what was going on. The optometrist couldn't see any problems at the back of her eye, but the most wonderful thing was the result of her second brain scan. Again it was Susan who did it, and she told us that there was no trace of whatever it was she had seen in the first one! Our relief and gratitude were overwhelming. We saw the paediatrician, who understood our unhappiness with Phenobarbitone, and prescribed Epanutin instead, which suited Amy far better. She explained that because of the changing EEG results they needed to consider a diagnosis of Epilepsy, and make sure that another fit was prevented. They would review the medication periodically whilst monitoring the EEGs. Amy started to be more like herself again, lively and full of fun and energy. Her lopsided little smile grew less pronounced, and playing and running around strengthened her weak arm and leg. She also started to lose a bit of weight. She had always been podgy, and in fact, when she was a baby, had put on a pound a week on breast milk alone! I had been reprimanded at the baby clinic for overfeeding her and giving her cereal too early in spite of my insistence that she was only having breast milk. Life started to settle down again, in spite of our social life being changed drastically because it no longer included Lynne, John and Dan. There was a knock on effect, too, because our circle of "foodies" was disrupted by this, and I don't think we had any more "Gourmet Feasts" as a group. The only person that I felt was a bit distant with me after Robb's confession was Liz Smith. She was a business consultant and computer expert, whose husband, Tony, was a Police Sergeant. Tony was fine with Robb, but I guess Liz and Lynne were quite close because of their work with computers. Lynne and John had both worked in that field, and, as it was quite uncommon in the 70s, it had drawn Liz to her. I think there was also some common ground in their Bermuda-style drinking habits, and I've since come to feel that Liz had been encouraging Lynne in her bid to steal my husband.

I continued running every day, still loving it and the feeling of strength and freedom it gave me. It also gave me plenty of "thinking time". During Amy's stay in hospital Diane Shawyer had been a real support and encouragement to us. She visited Amy, brought her gifts, called to see how she was, but also called to see how we were. I was starting to get to know her better, and she was such a lovely person. The girls loved her, she was good fun, kind, and understanding, and she listened! My postponed resolve to find a church started to surface again, and I decided that if I was to start really believing in any God, it would have to be a God like the one Diane believed in, because I liked what "he" had made her! Again, I started remembering bits of the Bible, such as "Love your enemies, do good to those who hate you, pray for those who use you spitefully" and

"Love your neighbour as yourself" – words of Jesus that I knew were profoundly wise. The world had become a very different place for me since those weeks around our 7th anniversary. I took more notice of injustice, oppression, violence, and cruelty, and knew that the endless repeating pattern of retaliation in the world could only be broken by someone refusing to "do to others as they had been done by". I also knew that peace on earth had to begin with me. I started remembering people I had known who were like Diane, such as Gwen Poulsom, the Youth Group leader at Bricknell Methodist church. She had been consistently generous, kind and supportive to all of her group, but especially to me when Dad was ill, and, once again, she was someone that was full of fun. Another person was my Sunday School teacher at Bricknell Methodist, Mr. Andrew, who taught me when I was about 12 or 13. He lived locally, and was a Quaker, but wanted to teach young people about Jesus, and there wasn't an opportunity at the Friends' Meeting House. Another was Sister Mary Agnes, my art teacher at St. Mary's. All of these people had a kind of genuine "presence" or inner glow, and a kind of radiant peace, that I wanted. I didn't feel at all drawn towards the Anglican or Catholic churches, because I felt that a lot of what they did was formal, empty ritual, and I instinctively knew that wouldn't meet my need for a real encounter with God. On top of this, I hated the idea of expensive buildings, golden statues and sumptuous robes in countries where people couldn't even get an education, or where children were dying of starvation. I also remembered sneaking in at the back of St. James' Anglican church in Sutton when I was a kid, feeling totally excluded by my lack of knowledge about when to stand up, sit down, or kneel, and hating the tuneless chanting of the psalms and the "churchy" voice of the vicar. I wanted to know God was real, and that He was with me to help me understand and cope with life, not to join some exclusive group or to be hooked on religious practice. Eventually I decided to ask Diane to dinner, on the pretext of thanking her for all her kindness during Amy's illness, but secretly wanting to ask her about her God. Robb had started Woodwork classes on Wednesday evenings, which he really enjoyed and where he made me some lovely things out of Bermuda cedar, including a Jewellery Box, a big Spice Rack and a beautiful tray. I knew he wouldn't want to miss this, so I invited her for Wednesday 28th November, when I knew he would be out. It was the day after Nicky's 7th birthday, but we had already celebrated that with a party the previous weekend.

I put the girls to bed (Amy must have been behaving that night!) cooked a nice meal, and we sat and talked and talked. Diane explained to me that it wasn't a question of finding the right church, but of totally surrendering all I knew of myself to all I knew of Jesus. When I did this I would literally be "inviting Him into my heart", putting Him in control of my life, and trusting Him to lead and guide me for the rest of my life. Somehow I knew that this was "it", the life changing encounter with God I had been looking for. I still had some questions, and didn't really understand the God/Jesus thing, but I knew that I needed God more than anything or anyone else. Diane explained that the first of the 10 commandments was "Love the Lord your God with all your heart, all of your mind and all your strength", but that God knew we would find it hard to love someone if we didn't really know what he was like, so He had sent Jesus to show us. She also told me that we were all sinners, but she explained that sin is not breaking rules or commandments, neither was it sex, which is an idea perpetuated by two mistaken Catholic doctrines (the first being Mary's ongoing virginity after she bore Jesus - when the Bible clearly says that he had brothers and sisters, and the other is that celibacy is a requirement of total devotion to God). Diane said that sin is simply going your own way instead of going God's way, and that this was the problem with the world. Everyone deciding for themselves what is good and what is bad results in chaos, because we are all naturally selfish. The only one who could possibly decide what is ultimately good or bad would be someone who sees the whole picture from beginning to end, whilst caring for even the smallest sparrow. In essence, the sin of Adam and Eve was choosing to go their own way over God's. God told them not to eat the fruit of the tree of the knowledge of good and evil or they would die, the serpent told them not to believe Him, and that eating it meant they would know for themselves and be like God. They decided to do their own thing, and the resulting rift between God and man, spiritual death, was handed down to the human race from then on – original sin. Whilst I thought this was a bit of a fairy story, I could see that symbolically it made a lot of sense. Diane also said that because we are all sinners – instinctively going our own way and not God's – in our own strength we could never be good enough to be "right with God". So Jesus came, not only to be our example of what God was like, but also to pay the penalty of our sinfulness. She explained that God is perfect justice. Our own sense of justice comes from Him (since we are made in his image) and we instinctively know that there should be a penalty for wrongdoing. None of us would feel it right to let a proven child murderer to go unpunished, yet God doesn't "grade" sin. Whenever we are out of line with His perfect plan for the cosmos we are sinners. This world and time and space is just a blink in the context of eternity, which is what we are destined for, and there can be no room for evil there. God is also perfect love, and because He loves us, Jesus came to take the punishment Himself for the sins of the whole world, satisfying justice. He did this on the cross, and in this way God Himself paid our debt, at the same time demonstrating the love He has for us by "giving His only son" for us – which is the ultimate example of human love. The only way to reconciliation with God is through accepting Jesus and His sacrifice. We can't hope to get to Him any other way, because none of us will ever be good enough. Surrender to Jesus, nothing else, allows Him to "move in" by His Holy Spirit, and give us His perspective, His standards, His heart and understanding, and more than this, His power, to do His will, fulfil our destiny on earth and become His representatives, knowing experientially His incredible love for us and for the whole of creation. This was being "born again" – like Malcolm Muggeridge! This was the joyful certainty that enabled early Christians in Rome to be thrown to the lions rather than deny Jesus. Religion is a deadly mockery of this, setting rules for people according to some man-made standard, causing people to either subscribe to a moribund conformity, or give up in despair, or become tools manipulated by some hierarchical organisation or power hungry dictator. It forces external change, when the only thing that will change the world is people with hearts changed by the love of God.

All this rang so true with me. I told Diane that I wanted to be born again. She said I should talk to Robb, tell him what I planned to do, and that if I wanted to go ahead she would come back the next day. She would bring her Bible, and show me what it actually said about what I was planning to do, and then pray with me to be born again. Robb came home from Woodwork, and I told him I was going to give my life to Jesus. I did this with trepidation, thinking that "getting religion", as I had previously thought of it, would probably deal a death blow to my marriage. The consequences for me and the girls could be devastating, because divorce could result in my having to leave Bermuda. If that happened there might even be a remote chance of my losing custody of my beloved daughters. Despite all this, I knew overwhelmingly that I was on the brink of the most important and essential decision of my life, and wild horses couldn't tear me away from it. I had to take that leap of faith, putting everything into the hands of God, trusting Him totally with myself and all I held dear. Robb responded by saying that I could do whatever I liked, as long as I didn't involve him. I hardly slept that night, and at work next day I nearly drove Pat crazy. She thought I had become unhinged by Amy's illness and Robb's confession. I think she was genuinely concerned for me, but she was also a bit disturbed, because her brother, Norman, had recently been born-again too! He had set off on a wild trip by jeep down the length of Africa with a bunch of friends and had got as far as Zimbabwe. Whilst there he met a girl and fell in love, but she wouldn't marry him because she was a Christian and he wasn't. During efforts to persuade her he went to church, heard the same message Diane had given me, fell on his knees, and gave his life to Jesus. He had written to Pat and told her, and I remember her standing in the middle of the lab at KEMH, reading his letter and exclaiming, "Oh my god, Norrie's got religion!"

I couldn't wait for Diane to come over that evening – it seemed like the longest day of my life. I was incredibly excited. Robb went out again, which was a good job, because I would have been too distracted if he was there. Diane came with her Bible, and showed me various verses and passages so that I could see that what she had told me wasn't just her opinion, but that it had been written centuries ago, and, through the disciples, had "turned the world upside down". This was "The Gospel", literally translated as "Good News". It was (and IS) good news – the end of struggling to be good and failing, simply handing everything over to God and asking Him to forgive me and accept me just as I was. The clincher came when she read from the book of Revelation, chapter 3, verse 20 - "Behold, I stand at the door and knock, and if any man hears my voice, and opens the door, I will come in, and dine with him, and he with me". I had a mental image of the famous painting by Holman Hunt, "The Light of the World", which is in St. Paul's Cathedral. In this painting Jesus, carrying a lantern which shines out beams of light into the dark, is seen knocking on a small wooden door, overgrown with weeds and creepers and vines. I felt that this was the door to my heart, and that I knew He had been knocking for years, but I had been standing behind the door pushing against it to keep Him out. In my mind, and with all my heart and will, I opened the door to Him and asked Him to come in. I prayed, with Diane, something like:

"Dear Jesus, I am so sorry. I have been running away from you for most of my life, and I am tired. I have been going my own way, and it is the wrong way. Please forgive me, I want to go your way. I believe, help my unbelief," and then, repeating after Diane, but meaning it with all my heart "Jesus, I know that you are THE way, THE truth, and THE life, the only true God, and that I cannot know your Father as my Father any other way than through faith in You. I believe that you will answer my prayer because you said in the Bible that whoever comes to you will never be turned away. I give my life to you, with all that means. Please help me to live for you, and with you in control, from now on, Amen".

It was about 7.30 pm, Bermuda time, on Thursday 29th November 1979, but as far as God was concerned, he had not only created me, but known me, loved me, chosen me for such a time as this and, most of all, died for me, before the foundation of the earth. I was saved! I had been born again! I had come home. The great adventure had begun. The pain and shock of the past few weeks had resulted in the best thing that had, and ever would, happen to me. I read the following poem, "The Celestial Surgeon" by Robert Louis Stevenson, years later, and it really spoke to me about my experience. I hadn't acknowledged God in all of the many blessings He had poured on me, it had taken bitter pain to make me turn around, acknowledge my need, and truly see Him.

If I have faltered, more or less
In my great task of happiness;
If I have moved among my race
And shown no glorious morning face;
If beams from happy human eyes
Have moved me not; if morning skies,
Books, and my food, and summer rain
Knocked on my sullen heart in vain:
Lord, Thy most pointed pleasure take
And stab my spirit broad awake;
Or, Lord, if too obdurate I,
Choose Thou, before that spirit die,
A piercing pain, a killing sin,
And to my dead heart run them in!

I woke up at 5.00 am the following morning with the most incredible sense of "completeness". I knew that I had discovered the secret of life. I felt totally loved, totally fulfilled. Everyone else was fast asleep, but I got up and made a cup of coffee, then sat on my lovely comfy sofa with the early sun filtering in through the windows, and just basked in God's presence. I didn't say anything, but knew that my innermost being was reaching out to God in thankfulness and joy, true prayer. Running, that morning, was a spiritual experience. Everything around me seemed vibrant and radiant in a way it had never been before. It was as if another dimension had opened up to me, I was seeing in colour instead of black and white, listening to opera at the Met instead of a wind- up gramophone, tasting finest filet mignon after living on porridge all my life — it was wonderful. I ran with tears streaming down my face, pouring out my thanks to God at every step. When the girls woke up I was overwhelmed with a love for them that was totally accepting and understanding. I suddenly realised that I had often made them the focus of my anger and frustration with life in general, and to my shame, they had been an easy target. I thank God that this hadn't resulted in anything other than punishing them for "naughtiness" when they were just "being children", but Dr. Spock reigned supreme in those days, and I had often smacked them when love and a little more attention would have been the best thing. One example of my change in heart came at breakfast that morning, when Nicky spilled her juice over her pancakes (I had cooked their favourite food to show them how much I loved them!) Instead of my usual exasperation and yelling, I gave her a hug, kissed her, and told her how precious she was to me and that I was so sorry for being angry with her over such incidents in the past. I told them that I had Jesus in my heart now, and that I was very happy instead of being "cross". I was aware that Robb was watching me, waiting for me to revert to my old, angry self!

I floated into work that morning, and even my facial expression annoyed Pat! She accused me of looking smug, but I couldn't help it. This made me realise that I had to be careful if I wanted to keep my friends – my enthusiasm had to be tempered with a bit of diplomacy and wisdom. This applied with Robb, too. I had started to see all of the good and lovely things about him, and how fortunate I was to have a husband who provided for his family and had decided to put them first. This resulted in my being very careful not to be too obvious about my new-found excitement with God. I didn't want to alienate him any more, because I wanted our marriage to survive. I realised that I had sometimes put impossible demands on him during our relationship, and that what I expected from him in giving me things like significance, protection, and someone to look up to could never have been met by anyone other than God. I also felt compassion for him, and amazingly, for Lynne, and knew that I wanted to forgive them for hurting me. I had started to love him again, which was a miracle, and sure evidence of a fundamental change in me.

That first Friday lunchtime at work I walked into the main shopping area of Hamilton, to a little Christian Bookshop Diane had told me about, and I bought myself a Bible. I was desperate to read it for myself. I was amazed at how expensive they were, and because we never seemed to have a lot of money to spare, I selected a small, white, old fashioned, King James version, which was designed to be carried by a bride at her wedding, and was the cheapest one in the shop! I didn't care, I just wanted to read it. The significance of even that has only just dawned on me. In the Bible God speaks of His people as being His bride. Maybe I was meant to buy that exact one. Looking back, I can see such significance in so many things that happened. Diane had advised me to start reading at the Gospel of John, so I walked back to work through Par-La-Ville Gardens, where I knew I could find a quiet place under my favourite Jacaranda tree, and I did just that. I had read and heard a lot of the words before, but now it was as if they had been written just for me. It's hard to write about this without using clichés, but as I read, I could feel any lingering doubts about the truth of it all disappearing, and the joy and peace that was filling me kept bubbling up, it was so hard to stop myself from crying! Throughout my school and Sunday School years I had heard many pieces of scripture, and in the following weeks they kept coming back into my mind, but now with a new kind of power and meaning. I started recalling the words of hymns and

Christmas Carols I had once sung mindlessly, and they actually meant something to me. I started singing them in my mind, and out loud when I could! One, which was written by Frances Jane Alstyne, especially ran through my mind during the first few days after my conversion:

> *Blessed assurance, Jesus is mine:*
> *Oh what a foretaste of glory divine!*
> *Heir of salvation, purchase of God;*
> *Born of His Spirit, washed in His blood.*

The chorus was:

> *This is my story,*
> *this is my song,*
> *Praising my Saviour*
> *all the day long.*

I knew that this was about me! I remembered from my Methodist Hymn Book that the note after the chorus was "Repeat", and I did so, loudly, and as often as I could!

11 – A New Life

I had arranged to go to Paget Gospel Chapel with Diane that first Sunday morning, if Robb didn't mind (I was again being careful not to alienate him). He didn't mind, as he was spending his Sunday mornings as a Kayaking instructor for the Bermuda Canoe Association in Flatts Inlet. If I went there I could take the girls to Sunday School and he could be free to "do his own thing". I got up early, giving myself time to fit in a run, and then to get myself and the girls ready. In spite of all my efforts, somehow time rushed by, and we were late. I hurried up the steps into church, after dropping the girls off downstairs in the Sunday School, to find Diane waiting for me at the door, looking relieved to see me. We walked in as the first hymn was just beginning, and imagine my amazement as the words "Blessed assurance, Jesus is mine" rang out. It was my hymn! I knew that God was welcoming me to His appointed place, and that He knew what a hectic morning I'd had, knew exactly what time I would be walking in, knew me personally, loved me and cared about every tiny detail of my life. What a start to my new life, what a morning, what a wonderful God! One of the lines of that hymn, "Washed in His blood", was a bit of a mystery to me, but that morning I had it explained to me through various Bible readings and the "talk". This latter wasn't like the boring old sermons I had heard before, but an explanation of why Jesus came, and why we all need Him. In the Old Testament God had established blood sacrifice, usually a lamb, for the sins of the Israelites. This was to show them the seriousness of sin, their need to acknowledge it, and that there was always a terrible cost to pay. Justice meant that there must be a penalty. They could never clean themselves up, because God's standard is perfection (and nobody's perfect), so the blood of the sacrifices, in effect, "cleansed" the people. The lamb took the penalty. In the New Testament God put an end to this by Himself becoming that sacrifice, through Jesus, "the Lamb of God", once and for all, for the sins of the whole world. Through faith in Jesus, we can be cleansed, and saved forever, from the penalty of sin. It all started to make sense. One of the other hymns that morning had words that spelled out my experience. I want to write it out in full, because a lot of these old Gospel hymns are, sadly, being forgotten, and they can have such significance to someone like me who had just put my life into God's hands.

> *Loved with everlasting love,*
> *Led, by grace, that love to know;*
> *Spirit, breathing from above,*
> *Thou hast taught me it is so.*
> *O this full and perfect peace!*
> *O this transport all divine!*
> *In a love which cannot cease*
> *I am His, and he is mine.*
>
> *Heaven above is softer blue,*
> *Earth around is sweeter green;*
> *Something lives in every hue,*
> *Christless eyes have never seen:*
> *Birds with gladder songs o'erflow,*
> *Flowers with deeper beauties shine,*
> *Since I know, as now I know,*
> *I am His, and he is mine.*
>
> *His forever, only his:*
> *Who the Lord and me shall part?*

> *Ah, with what a rest of bliss*
> *Christ can fill the loving heart!*
> *Heaven and earth may fade and flee,*
> *First-born light in gloom decline;*
> *But while God and I shall be,*
> *I am His, and He is mine.*
>
> George Wade Robinson (1838-1877)

Thank you George!! You died at 39 years old, but this hymn alone has probably given joy and assurance to countless numbers of people since you wrote it, and I'm sure you heard "Well done, good and faithful servant" from your Lord when you went to meet him.

So many things happened around that time to show me that God was with me and for me. One morning I woke feeling a bit depressed. I'd had an argument with Robb the previous evening and felt as if I'd "blown it" completely and that nothing had really changed. I went for my run, as usual, and, as I ran, prayed desperately "Lord, if I didn't really give myself completely then, I really do mean it now, please help me!" I got home, showered, and, as I was sitting at my dressing table putting on my makeup, I suddenly had the sensation of being held and rocked like a little baby, with strong, warm, loving arms cradling me. I burst into tears (again!) I knew God was telling me "Don't worry, you are mine, this is the beginning, you will grow and change, supported and protected by my love and strength".

Another time, whilst sorting out some books, I found a little blue New Testament. I had been given this by Mr. Train, who was our porter in pathology at Kingston General Hospital. He was a strong Christian, and would give a copy to everyone leaving the lab. He had given this to me when I left to go to Bermuda, and I didn't throw it away, in spite of my lack of interest in reading it. This was purely because of superstition, I felt it would be bad luck to throw away a Bible! When I opened it I saw it had been provided by The Pocket Testament League. There was a page at the back paraphrasing John 3: 16

"For God so loved the world, that He gave His only begotten son, so that .... Who believes in Him should not perish, but have everlasting life"

The gap was to be filled in by the reader's name, and I did this gladly. Anne Porter, who believes in Him, shall not perish, but has everlasting life!

When I was at St. Mary's school, one of our set books for Literature was "The Pilgrim's Progress" by John Bunyan. I didn't understand it or enjoy it at the time, but I really wanted to read it again. I can't remember where I found the copy I was to read, but it was a very old one, with loads of footnotes on every page giving scripture references. I decided that if I was going to read it I had to do it properly, and look up all the quotes to help me understand it better. The only problem was that I hadn't a clue whereabouts in the Bible all the quotes were! However, I decided to get on with it. I prayed, jumped in, and started to read, with my Bible next to me. What happened next was incredible. Every time I had to look up a Bible quote my Bible fell open, either at the very page I needed, or at the relevant section. I kept thinking this was a coincidence, and that it would stop any minute, but it carried on until I had finished the book, days later! Little did I know that this sort of thing would go on happening to me over and over again.

Diane told me that she met up with Chris Finnegan on Monday evenings for a Bible Study, and asked if I would like to join in. As they say – "Is the Pope Catholic??" I was mad keen! One of the first things I had decided to do was tell everyone what had happened to me. Every day

I made it a point to tell someone new, and Flip Petty, my next door neighbour was my first. She was very friendly with Hilary Hill, an English nurse who was married to Stan Hill, a Bermudian policeman. They lived just around the corner at Prospect, and Hilary worked as a phlebotomist in the lab at the hospital, so I knew her well. All of us had kids at Nambour and the High School, as well as being ex-pats, living near each other, and having the Police and the Hospital in common. Both Flip and Hilary were also struggling with their marriages, and when I told Flip about being born-again and especially my renewed love for Robb, she went straight round to tell Hilary. They had already been watching my transformation from a depressed, chain-smoking couch potato to a slim, healthy runner, and now this! They both decided they wanted what I had found, and the following Monday there were 5 of us meeting at number 18 Alexandra Road for a Bible Study! I didn't get such a joyful reaction from everyone I told. Liz Smith looked at me as if I was mad, and I don't think she spoke to me at all after that. Other reactions varied from concern that I had been brainwashed, or was cracking up, to the "Whatever turns you on" attitude I'd met from Robb.

Our Bible Studies were such fun. We discovered so much wisdom in our Bibles, had great discussions, poured out our hearts, prayed for and comforted each other. It was a unique situation. We had Di, who had been a Christian for years, Chris, who had been one for about a year, and then Flip, Hilary and me, all new converts. We came from tremendously varied backgrounds. Chris had lived in California during the "Summer of Love" and had been caught up with all the Hippy flower power stuff over there. Hilary was a high Anglican, Flip a Catholic. It made for some interesting opinions! I could tell that Robb was interested in what was going on, but wouldn't admit it. I knew he was still watching me, and still thinking that this couldn't last! I asked his permission to go to church, or to any special meetings, he couldn't believe it, and suspected that something was going on! I think he had been waiting for me to do a bit of "Bible-bashing" or to find tracts stuck to his shaving mirror, but I was careful not to bring up the subject of God, church, or scripture unless he did so first. He admitted to me that he occasionally watched "The 700 Club" and had seen some interesting stuff, specifically George Foreman, the boxer, telling how he had been born-again. I knew he was interested in prophecy and "the end of the world", and in early December I heard, through Di, that there was a special speaker, Dr. Fred Tatford, coming to Bermuda, and he was an expert on the Book of Revelation. I would never have dreamed of inviting Robb to a regular church service, but thought he might be interested in this, so asked if he wanted to come with me to hear it. He did, but fell asleep halfway through it!

By this time it was getting close to Christmas. The girls were getting excited, and so was I. There were lots of activities for them, at school, at Nambour, and of course, at Sunday School. We went to what seemed like endless Nativity plays! That first Christmas as a Christian was so special, and so full of meaning. Birth had always been a most moving event for me, but because I had discovered for myself the love of God that sent Jesus, His only son, as a helpless baby, into this world, to show us the full extent of that love, this birth was absolutely humbling to me. The warm bubble of peace and joy that I had experienced first at Amy's bedside in the hospital, seemed to surround our Christmas. Robb and I went to some of the many parties that were held around that time, and, seeing the changes in me, people were asking "What happened to you?!" I like to think it wasn't just the physical changes, but some inner glow, and capitalised on it anyway, telling them I had been born-again! Some of them were fascinated, some angry, some totally disinterested. One of Robb's bosses, drunk as a skunk, at the Police Commissioner's New Year Cocktail party, mumbled "Wow, you changed from a fat old cow to a gorgeous young girl". The faces of the people around us were hilarious – they didn't know whether to laugh or not. I laughed – I was having a great time.

After all the festivities and spending, I started to think about giving to the church. I was so grateful for what had happened to me, and for Amy's recovering health, and I wanted to give something, somewhere, to show it. At Paget Gospel Chapel they never passed a collection plate around, and this puzzled me, as every other church I had been in expected you to put something in the plate. I talked to Di about it and she told me that the only people expected to give were those who were members of the church. They did so at the "Breaking of Bread" service, which was held early on Sunday before the regular, or Gospel, service. I asked if I could come along, and she explained that it was only for baptised believers. I asked her about baptism, and we studied what the Bible said about it, at our Monday evening get-togethers. I had been Christened as a baby (sprinkled with "Holy Water"), but we saw that, in the Bible, people were baptised by full immersion in water after making an adult decision to become a Christian. This made a lot more sense to me. Also, we learned that it wasn't just symbolic of having your sins washed away, but represented dying with Jesus, being buried with Him, and finally resurrected into a new life with Him. It was a tradition, but one that Jesus Himself had obeyed, and was also a declaration of Christian commitment to the world. We talked about giving, too, and discovered that it was a bit more than putting your loose change in the collection plate! In the Old Testament they gave a "tithe", which meant 10%. Di explained that this was part of "The Law" which was a set of rules which also included blood sacrifices, by which the

Israelites could gain acceptance with God. Jesus brought
the New Testament, Himself becoming our only means of
acceptance with God (the way, the truth, and the life). She
said that, as she understood it, simply giving 10% of ones
income was reverting to the old set of rules, and used the
story of the widow's mite as an illustration. To the poor,
giving 10% could be life threatening, and to the very rich,
wouldn't affect their livelihood at all, but having said that,
she thought 10% was a good guideline. This was radical
to me! I couldn't imagine giving anything like that much
money away – we were always down to nothing at the
end of each month. I couldn't do it anyway, as we pooled
our incomes, and I knew Robb would go ballistic at the
thought! I decided I really wanted to go ahead with getting
baptised, though, and so arranged for one of the church
leaders to come and see me to talk about it. That was
something different about Paget, too. There wasn't a vicar!
The church was led by a "body of elders". I discovered
that, denominationally, Paget was part of the Brethren
movement, which had broken away from the Church of
England because of belief that the Bible says we are all
priests, and that there is only one mediator between men
and God, and that is Jesus. This means we don't have to go
to God through some third party, but can approach Him
ourselves, through Jesus. Some of the Brethren churches
had become exclusive and rigid, but Paget was open and
welcoming. They also taught that Baptism was for mature
adults who had decided to follow Jesus and wanted to
declare it to the world by choosing to be baptised, not just
sprinkled with water as a baby in some sort of ritual which
was a spiritual insurance policy against going to hell, taken
out by the parents. This all made sense to me, too. I had
discovered the Truth, the Gospel. I was angry that in all
my previous church experience I had never heard this.
I had been fed a concoction of powerless rubbish by most
of them. As far as I could see they had been little clubs for

like-minded superstitious people, hoping against hope that when they died their good deeds would outweigh the bad, "believing" in some ineffectual god but never abandoning themselves to the God of heaven and earth who loves us and gave Himself for us. We don't have to settle for some sort of hopeless lifelong struggle to be "good". If that's all Christianity is, we don't have anything more than Moslems, who spend their lives in fear of upsetting Allah, even by inadvertently eating a sausage or something similar! I started to see that religion was the very thing that keeps most people away from God. It means struggling to get up to His standards, when He said "You'll never get there in a million years, but if you trust Jesus you'll see I've done it for you". After some meditation on this I decided to sum up religion by the phrase "Beware of men in dresses and funny hats" perhaps with the addendum "who want you to dress in black and wear veils". Thank God for Jesus!

David Oliviera was the elder chosen to talk to me about Baptism, and he arranged to come over and see me one evening when Robb was around, so as not to appear subversive. After making sure I knew what I would be doing, we set a date for me to be baptised early one Sunday morning at the beginning of February. We would then go on to the Breaking of Bread service at Paget, and then all have breakfast together before the regular service and Sunday School for the children. He then read me some scriptures about baptism. Robb had been going in and out of the room during this time, and came in just before David was leaving. To my great surprise, I heard him asking David to read something from the Bible! The verse chosen was the one that "got" me – Revelation 3:20 – "Behold, I stand at the door and knock............". David then asked if he could pray for us, did so, and left. I could see that Robb had been affected. He told me that when David prayed he felt as if he was talking to someone who was actually in the room. He felt the presence of God, and said that recently he had been thinking seriously about making the same leap of faith as me. In all honesty, I had such mixed feelings about this. I was desperate for others to find what I had found, but, if Robb became a Christian too, it would definitely mean the end of our life as we knew it. I would really have to cut loose and surrender to God, never able to use Robb's unbelief as an excuse to compromise. I talked to Di, and she was so excited. She said that growing in Christian maturity and commitment always meant taking risks that God had something better planned for us, so we arranged for her to come over to dinner the following Monday, 28th January 1980, with Kenny Hayward, a young guy who had recently become a Christian after almost destroying himself with drink and drugs. He was from an important Bermuda family, and had been expected to make a great future for himself, but had crashed and burned before discovering that all he needed was Jesus.

Robb decided to have a last week of "sin" and went out clubbing and partying every night, but I could tell that he wasn't really enjoying it. Monday rolled around, and I cooked a lovely steak meal (we called it Salvation Steak from then on). We had a great discussion, hearing Kenny's testimony of how he had been born-again and set free from his addictions. I think this really spoke to Robb's heart, because he knew that his drinking had become a real problem. I had even seen him putting vodka in his breakfast Orange Juice one morning. At the end of the evening Di asked Robb if he wanted to commit his life to the Lord, and he said yes. He prayed a similar prayer to the one I had prayed 2 months earlier, and we all prayed out loud for him. He had a very physical reaction to all of this, and almost curled up into a foetal position on the sofa, but then we all began laughing and crying, and Robb too, knew he had been born-again. It was such an amazing feeling. We really felt "united in spirit", and I wondered how I could ever have been apprehensive about it. Robb went in to work the next day on the same cloud as I had on my first day as a believer. The Parish Constables' Office was on the top floor of the Hamilton Station, but he met one of his Parish colleagues, Rocky Ironmonger, as he went through the front door. He told Rocky he had been born-again, then went on to speak to someone else. Rocky went on upstairs ahead of him, telling everyone on the way, and when Robb came up the stairs he was greeted by ecstatic Bermudian police-women hugging him and welcoming him to God's family. We found out there were lots of Christian WPCs in Bermuda! My baptism was set for the following Sunday, 3rd February, and Robb asked if he could be baptised too. The elders agreed, so at 7.00 a.m. on a cloudy, cold, Bermuda morning, both dressed in white, we waded into the sea in a little cove near Horseshoe Bay. It seemed as if the whole congregation of Paget Gospel Chapel was on the beach watching! The girls stood with Di, Kenny was there, so were Flip, Hilary, and Chris, with Ashley, her little boy. We sang "Trust and Obey" on the beach before we went into the sea, and the words were so special. David Oliviera baptised us, and I was first. He asked me a few questions to confirm my wholehearted commitment, and then, after I replied "Yes, with all my heart" he gently lowered me completely under the water. The water was so cold that when I came up I couldn't breathe. Eventually I gave a great gasp, and realised I would live after all! It seemed very significant, since I was symbolically being raised to a new life. Robb was next, and then we stood together in the sea, arms around each other, whilst David prayed for us. At that moment, something incredible happened, there was a break in the clouds and a ray of sunlight shone down on us. It was awesome. For us, this was the real beginning of our marriage.

We wrapped up in towels and went to church, changing into warm dry clothes there, then took part for the first time in the Breaking of Bread. There was a crèche for the girls, so we didn't have to worry about them at all, and the service was a total revelation to us. No one person spoke or preached, and there was no list of hymns, people seemed to take in turns to stand and pray, or give a scripture verse and expound on it, or choose a hymn or a song for all of us to sing. All of it was about Jesus and His sacrifice for us, or the last supper and the symbolism of it, or about how wonderful and beautiful He is and how much He loves us. It all seemed to fit together as if pre-arranged, but I later found out that nothing was prearranged, but that the Holy Spirit always brought everything together, co-ordinating themes and feelings, creating a wonderful atmosphere of worship and praise. This was a result of each person praying and preparing themselves to speak before they got there – if so led. It was heaven, and we were able to give to the church for the first time, feeling so privileged to be able to do so. We all had breakfast together afterwards – a "bring and share" meal, which was very special, then the girls went to Sunday School and Robbie and I went upstairs to our first regular Sunday morning service together. The tradition at Paget was that no-one spent Sunday on their own, and we were invited to someone's home for lunch, along with others. We spent the afternoon together and then all went to the 6pm church service together. We got home later, exhausted, but totally happy. We realised that Robb had been saved and baptised before he had even been to church, probably the way it happened in the Book of Acts!

Next came the practical outworking of our new life together. From that time onwards, Robb was never drunk again, and because of that I started to get to know the "real person". We started running together whenever we could, and praying together. We read our Bibles and shared any discoveries we made. Robb still went to the Police Club occasionally, and had a beer or two with his mates. This puzzled everyone, because they associated "getting religion" with giving up everything enjoyable, especially drink. This had been reinforced by the dramatic conversion of Larry Smith, a police colleague, who had immediately gone down to the Club and preached loudly on the evils of drink. As far as we were concerned, moderation and self-control was far better evidence of God's presence than aggressive abstinence – Alcoholics Anonymous could do that! Around the same time as Larry's conversion, another Bermudian cop, Stuart Lambert, a lovely guy who was set for great things, and was actually being groomed to be the first Bermudian Police Commissioner, left the force to become an Anglican vicar. A year or so before this another English cop called Cliff Harries had been converted, felt God was calling him back to England, left the force and moved back to Leicester. Everyone thought he had gone mad, but Robb had noticed a real positive change in him. His party trick had been inviting women to see his family photos and then producing some of the worst pornographic images you could imagine. After his conversion he would even leave the room when the conversation got a bit risqué or a joke was being told. Robb wrote to him later and told him what had happened to us. He wrote back, quoting a hymn, and said "Hallelujah, the blood of Christ can make the foulest clean". He had become a bit "religious" after joining a very strict Baptist church, but we had a good laugh at that. I think everyone wondered what was going on!

One of the first things that happened to Robb was that he was invited to go to Jamaica with the Bermuda Regiment. Every year they went to some jungle area on exercises, and this year they needed someone to teach canoeing. He was so excited, because travel had always been one of his dreams. They were to go very shortly, and he didn't have time to write to his Mum and Dad to tell them what had happened to us, so whilst he was packing we recorded an audio message. We did this often with messages from the girls, but this time it was just us telling them about our new found faith. When his Mum heard it, she knelt down by the side of her bed, prayed, and gave her heart to the Lord, too! Robb went off to Jamaica and had an amazing time. There were one or two strong Christians in the Regiment, and he went with them to some wonderful church services. One was at a little chapel in the middle of nowhere. They walked for miles into the jungle to get there, and didn't get back until 2 a.m. leaving the service still carrying on! Robb couldn't get over the freedom and joyful worship, with everyone included, and children and babies just curling up on the floor and sleeping when they were tired. When they got back – bubbling over with the Holy Spirit – all the others were back in camp after a disappointing night "on the town" in Montego Bay, and were drunk, sick and miserable. What a difference. They went back to the little church a few times, and when Robb left the island the lovely brothers and sisters there gave him presents and prayed for him. He was deeply moved, because they were so poor, yet so generous. The poverty in Jamaica was something that had really struck him. In spite of being a jet set holiday destination, and growing sugar and top grade coffee (and ganja) there was hardly anything on the supermarket shelves for the ordinary citizens.

Back in Bermuda, life carried on. David Oliviera started a men's Bible study, and Robb got some really good teaching from him. Our ladies Monday nights carried on, but we also spent one Saturday at a meeting in Hamilton. To be honest, the name of the group organising it, "Women Aglow", almost made me gag, but Di said that we would really get a lot from it, so we went along. It was very different from Paget! They were a nice friendly bunch of Christian women, and I can't remember anything special about the speaker, but the worship was out of this world. At one point, after we had all finished singing a lovely song, some of the women carried on singing in a kind of improvised harmony with each other. I had never heard anything like it, it was almost like a dawn chorus on an April morning in England, but it was made up of human voices, and absolutely beautiful. Occasionally one voice would rise up above the others, but always in harmony and blending with the others. Di told us that they were "singing in the Spirit", or "singing in tongues". Over lunch she explained that this group were "Charismatic" Christians, who had not only been born-again, but also "Baptised in the Holy Spirit". They had asked God to pour out His Spirit on them, as happened in the book of Acts chapter 2 to the disciples in the upper room at Pentecost. One of the gifts of the Spirit was speaking in tongues, which was "the language of angels" spoken of in I Corinthians 13, and this was the language they had been singing in. It was almost like a hot-line to God, praying from spirit to Spirit. Di said she had been Baptised in the Holy Spirit, Chris likewise, and they both could speak in tongues. They said that praying, understanding the Bible, hearing from God, and knowing His will, had become a delight, and consequently so much easier. Apparently it was not accepted by some Christians, and the Brethren thought speaking in tongues was from the devil. Di actually got into trouble from her boss for "leading us astray", but I couldn't understand why something that made communication with God easier and was the experience of Christians in the New Testament, could be from God's enemy. I decided that I wanted all God had for me, so prayed that God would pour out His Spirit on me, too. Nothing startling happened. I had been warned that this could be a tremendous experience, and that I would spontaneously pray in tongues, but it was a bit of an anticlimax! Chris said that I should just open my mouth and speak whatever came into my head, and I did but it sounded like a load of gobbledegook. However, since this was all a "faith trip", I decided to carry on in private, trusting God that he had given me what I asked for, and that doing it would build up my faith, as the Bible said it would. I never plucked up enough courage to do it in public, though.

We had a wonderful experience that Easter. Even more than Christmas, the significance of it all was overwhelming. At last I understood what it was all about, why Jesus had to die, what He achieved on the cross, why it was called Good Friday, the triumph of His resurrection, and its relevance to me. Good Friday had always been a special day in Bermuda, because of everyone getting together for a Codfish and Potatoes brunch, and then the traditional Kite Flying, but this year it all began with a Church Service to worship and thank God. Even better, on Sunday morning we all got up at dawn, wrapped up warmly, and went down to Elbow Beach for a Sunrise Service. It was so lovely. I was used to the perfection of the beach in the early morning from taking the girls down there before Nicky started school, but there was an extra quality that morning. We sang and prayed and thanked God from our hearts all over again, then huddled around a big urn of coffee and hot cross buns before heading home to get ready for the big Easter celebration at church. Life didn't get much better. This year I found myself singing "Up from the grave He arose" with as much conviction and gusto as I had heard from the others at Paget the previous year. We also sang "Thine be the Glory, risen, conquering son", another old school hymn that suddenly meant something to me.

Not long before Robb had been converted, he had become a Freemason. This was considered a good career move for a cop, and he had been encouraged to ask to join by quite a few of his colleagues, including Tony Smith, Liz's husband. He had progressed quickly up the degrees, but after giving his life to Jesus he started to feel uncomfortable with the Masonic ritual and with some of the members. He asked the elders at Paget what they thought of it all, but they didn't know much about it, and his Masonic colleagues assured him that all the ritual would help him understand the Bible. He continued to go to the lodge, but eventually began feeling almost physically nauseous when there. The thing that most bothered him was that he was forbidden to mention the name of Jesus, even though everything seemed very religious and the Bible was displayed in a prominent position during the meetings. Another thing was that when he had become a Mason he had been pushed, naked and blindfolded, into a coffin in a darkened room, then pulled out, the lights turned on, and told he had been born again! When he was really born again he realised what a mockery this all was. We decided to pray together and ask God to show us clearly how He felt about it, and we had a very clear, quick response from Him. The scripture verse that came into our heads immediately was "You cannot serve two masters, either you will hate the one and love the other, or you will be loyal to the one and despise the other. You cannot serve both God and money." Robb knew that most of the Masons he knew were obsessed with money. I was convinced that God wouldn't be involved in anything exclusive and esoteric. He wants everyone to come into His family, so why would he make it impossible for some to "come to know the truth", as the Masons claimed to have done, whilst excluding women, and, until recently, non-white people, and of course anyone not able to understand all their mumbo-jumbo, such as children and the mentally disabled? God's Truth is simple, attainable, inclusive, and free – just the opposite of Freemasonry. My feelings were reinforced by an incident that summer which demonstrated how being a mason could exempt members from being subject to any other law – especially moral accountability. An ex-pat police sergeant who was a high flying Freemason had been involved in a road accident. He was drunk on duty, in uniform, in a police car, and had knocked someone off a motor bike, severely injuring him. The man lost one of his legs as a result, whilst the police sergeant quietly resigned from the force, and was subsequently given Bermuda status (citizenship), set up in his own successful business, and was never brought to justice. This same guy had once told me that he too was born-again, when I sat next to him at a Masonic dinner and had tried to tell him about what had happened to Robb and I. We began to realise that there were a lot of counterfeits out there, and that Freemasonry was one of the biggest. Robb decide to resign, and sent a letter to his lodge explaining why. The consequences of this weren't immediate, but I think, inevitable.

We were now heading for Summer, and once again we had the problem of the girls being at home whilst both of us had to work. I really wanted to go to England to tell everyone about my conversion, but three return fares was a huge outlay for us. Robbie couldn't go with us as he was once again involved in Outward Bound on Paget Island during the school summer holidays. I prayed about it, as about everything since the previous November. Incidentally, prayer - for me - was never anything like sitting down and verbally reciting lists of requests, it was more an acknowledgement of God's constant presence and involvement in my life, and of His being aware of my every thought. Of course I did ask Him about and for specific things, but mostly it was unspoken, just a constant flow of gratitude and worship to Him from me, and a constant flow of love and comfort to me from Him. I subsequently read a very old book by Brother Lawrence, called "Practicing the

Presence of God", which was wonderful. He was a monk in the Middle Ages, who struggled to feel God's presence in his formal Church rituals, but felt God all around him when he was doing his menial kitchen tasks, or working in the monastery garden. I found it inspiring, and it also confirmed my own experience. My prayer about going to England was answered within weeks, when we came into a small amount of money from a cancelled insurance policy. It was just enough to pay for three air fares to England. More and more I was experiencing such "coincidences", and began to see that they were no such thing, but the result of having the God of the Universe working on my behalf! I wrote to Mum and told her we were coming over, and she decided to come to Bermuda with us when we returned, so the problem of school holidays was solved. I think she was worried about what was happening to us on the church front, and wanted to investigate it for herself! Before we flew off for our trip I was asked to speak at one of the Paget Ladies Evenings, giving my Testimony (telling how I had been born-again) just as I had heard Chris do. Loads of people were invited, Mums from Nambour, friends, and work colleagues. Two friends in particular I know were deeply touched by hearing what I had to say. They were Jenny Tufts, Doug's wife, whom I knew from our houseboat weekends years before, and Liz Hanson, who had married Pat's ex-boyfriend, Barry. Jenny had been suffering from deep depression, and I know she was made aware of her need for God's help through this, but didn't do anything about it. Liz cried all the way through my talk, but at the end, when I asked her if she wanted to pray with me and ask Jesus into her life, she became really angry, told me she was a Catholic and didn't need all this rubbish, and left. Whatever the results right then, I knew that what I had said had an effect, and was like a seed that God would water and nurture over the years, and hopefully would eventually bear the fruit of more joyful surrenders to Him. This had happened with me when I heard Chris and Malcolm Muggeridge speak, so I wasn't discouraged.

Robb had started going to a Bible Study run by a Methodist Minister in Warwick, near where Chris Finnegan lived. Chris and Di were going along, too, and whilst I was in England they were planning to study the three persons of the Trinity, one person per week. The second week, when they were studying the second person, Jesus the Son, Robb had a tremendous experience of the Holy Spirit. While they were singing and worshipping he was suddenly overwhelmed with the love that had sent Jesus to the cross for him, ran out of adequate words to express his gratitude, and began to speak and sing in tongues. The chapel they were using for the study was on the slopes of one side of a valley, and when they were leaving, Robb spotted one of the guys he worked with, a Bermudian called Lynn Hall, driving his distinctive open topped car down the hill at the other side. He ran down, and got to the main road in the middle just as Lynn did, then ran alongside the car telling a very bemused Lynn that Jesus loved him. Lynn replied "Not you too, I'm just getting away from my wife who keeps telling me the same thing!"

I had a good time in England. Everyone was so pleased to see us – fit and in our right minds! Nan, Popsy, and my Mum fussed over us all, but mostly over Amy, aware that they had almost lost her. She was doing really well by then, her medication suited her and she had no remaining symptoms. She had lost loads of weight and was a skinny, wiry little thing, nothing like the chubby baby they all remembered. We still had no diagnosis for her, and her EEGs were still different every time they did one, but I found out that there was epilepsy in the family. Robb's Auntie Vera, Popsy's sister, had severe epilepsy, and still had frequent fits. It was considered a shameful family secret, so no-one had ever mentioned it to us. I also found out that Nanny's brother had died of severe asthma at 27 years old. Amy had started to get really wheezy when she had a cough or cold, so we wondered if she had inherited all the dodgy genes. The best thing that happened whilst we were there was that my Mum was born-again too. As soon as I got to Hull she started asking me loads of questions about what had happened to me, and as I explained, and told her about the things that had led me to the point of giving my heart to Jesus, she cried and prayed that she could have the same experience. Liz and Dave were very cool towards me, and refused to even talk about my conversion, Auntie Eileen (my Godmother!) was positively antagonistic. Most of the others were fairly supportive, but obviously thought I'd had some transatlantic experience that wouldn't fit in with British churchianity. Liz said she would never try to "brainwash" her children, and left them to choose for themselves when old enough (after having them both Christened – just in case). I wondered how they could choose if they didn't know anything about the options. Nanny had started going to a little church in Drayton, close to where they lived in Cosham, with one of her work colleagues. Pops went along occasionally, but with a very patronising attitude, considering himself above all this, but honouring them with his presence. I went to church with Nanny, and discovered it was another Brethren Assembly, and that there were strong links with Paget Gospel Chapel. I began to realise that I really had joined a worldwide family.

When we got back to Bermuda, complete with my newly saved but apprehensive Mum, we found Robb almost swinging from the rafters. He had definitely experienced something powerful, but it scared me, and Mum thought he had gone crazy! He was still involved with the Outward Bound course, so wasn't at home much. It was probably a good job, as Mum got chance to meet Di, Chris, Flip and Hilary, and to join in our Monday Bible Studies and be reassured that we hadn't all gone mad. Flip had just given up smoking, with God's help, and Mum said she would love to give it up but didn't think she ever could. We all prayed with and for her, and she stopped, cold turkey! From smoking at least 40 a day she went to none, with absolutely no withdrawal symptoms. Sadly, when she went home she didn't have any like minded friends to support her, went on holiday to Scotland with Auntie Eileen, and was encouraged to start smoking again. She finally gave up by force when admitted to hospital with a severe chest infection in 2008 – at the age of 85. In the meantime she dyed herself, her house, and everything in it, brown with nicotine. All the family dreaded going to see her because of the choking smoke clouds and stink of cigarettes that soaked into them as they sat with her! I think we enjoyed Mum's visit more that year than any other. She came to church with us and met everyone at Paget, and loved them. She acknowledged that we hadn't gone mad, and began to read her Bible and enjoy it, realising what she had been missing in her occasional formal and superficial forays into the Church. She became a member of Bricknell Avenue Methodist Church when she went home, and made some friends, but never got any good teaching or real heart to heart fellowship, so didn't really grow much spiritually. Maybe she got all she wanted; being radical was perhaps too much of a change for her.

12 – Paradise Lost?

A few things happened that summer to make us start thinking about the future. Amy was coming up to school age, so we faced another lot of school fees. The High School chose this time to put those fees up considerably, and we seriously doubted that we could afford them. The free government schools weren't very good in our area, and I didn't know if I wanted our girls to go there anyway, and not only because of poor education. There was an increasing anti-white feeling on the island, and I felt that they would be multi-disadvantaged. They were white, non-Bermudian, non-rich, and daughters of an ex-pat cop! We were renting a much loved two bed-roomed Police house, but, as the girls were growing fast, we would soon outgrow it, and we had very little prospect of being able to buy our own house on the island, because non-Bermudians were restricted to only buying property valued over $200,000 – an impossible amount of money to us in those days, especially if a good proportion of our income was going in school fees. Across the road from our row of Police Houses on Alexandra Road was "The Ghetto" – the nearest thing to a council estate in Bermuda. It was an area of low cost Government housing, and was a hotbed of racial resentment. The residents were mostly poorer Bermudian blacks, and a lot of them had very bad attitudes towards white ex-pat cops. There had been serious riots over the years, the worst being after they hung Buck Burrows and Larry Tacklin in 1976 (the two men found guilty of assassinating the Governor, Sir Richard Sharples, and of some other race related murders) in Casemates prison.

There were huge protests, in spite of the fact that Buck Burrows, after being born again in prison, had confessed to the murders. He refused to defend himself, saying that he knew he deserved to die and wasn't afraid to do so, as he had repented and made peace with God. There had been others involved, but they escaped the island, notably Ottiwell Simmons Junior, the son of a local Union boss, who escaped dressed as a Moslem woman. In the most recent riots numerous fire bombs had been thrown and people were killed. Our friends Rocky and Maureen had to move out of their house, as it was firebombed when Maureen was alone there with baby Jamie. Nearer home, Flip and Steve, our next door neighbours, had 3 firebombs thrown at their house. The bombs went onto their porch, into their garden, and onto their car, which was parked between our houses. Fortunately the porch and garden ones fizzled out, but their car was torched. I was sitting in our living room the evening it happened, heard a strange "whooshing" sound then turned and saw the flames through my kitchen window. This was getting a bit close for comfort. Rocky and Maureen had decided to leave Bermuda after this, and had gone back to England. Rocky had joined the Hampshire Constabulary, and was doing well. Other things happened which made us start to wonder if it was also time for us to leave. Nan and Pops were having marriage problems, and we were getting heart-breaking letters from Nanny, telling us how lonely she was and how much she missed us – a bit manipulative of course, but still a factor. The main blow, however, was against Robb.

He was totally dedicated to the Outward Bound Scheme in Bermuda, and had seen many local kids given more positive attitudes to life and great opportunities through the courses. He had already poured his heart and soul into the scheme, but after becoming a Christian had also seen another dimension to the experience which increased his commitment to it. Whilst he was on Paget Island in 1980 a group of people made a visit to the Young Offenders Institution there. They were a team of Christians from New York City who were involved in a drug rehabilitation programme called "Teen Challenge". This was a Christian scheme started by Dave Wilkerson, who had written a famous book, later made into a movie, called "The Cross and the Switchblade". It told the true story of a Puerto Rican gang leader called Nicky Cruz who had converted to Christianity, been freed from drug addiction and crime, and had become an international evangelist and preacher. Some of the team were part of the women's branch of Teen Challenge – New Life for Girls, started because the unique and self-destructive lifestyle that most women went into as a result of their drug addiction meant they had many different needs from the guys. Cookie Rodriguez, the founder, and her husband and son, were part of the team that came to Bermuda. Both the men's and the women's schemes were seeing amazing success rates in their efforts to help drug addicts "get clean". They put this down to God, dedicated prayer and Bible Study, discipline, and temporarily removing the addicts from their destructive environments. They were a great bunch of people, all tongues-speaking, full on, gifted of the Holy Spirit, charismatic Christians – a total inspiration to be with. Robb took some of the Outward Bound kids to a meeting they held for the Young Offenders, and got talking to them. He told them what had happened to us, and they asked him to stand up and "give his testimony" (tell everyone about how he had become a Christian) to all the kids. This would show that it was not only criminals and drug addicts that needed Jesus, but also those on the right side of the law! Robb gladly did so, and as part of it he admitted to smoking marijuana, and having a secret "stash" even whilst a Bermuda Policeman. When he came home after the summer he was called up by the deputy Police Commissioner and told he could no longer be involved in Outward Bound. This was because his confession meant he wasn't a good example to the local kids any more. Robb was gutted. A "misdemeanour" like this was also seen as kissing goodbye to any chance of promotion, in spite of the fact that Robb had passed his Sergeant's exam with flying colours. We were pretty sure that there had been some influence from the Masonic hierarchy, too, as Robb had not been quiet about his rejection of Freemasonry, or about Jesus!

This was something like the last straw, and we began to pray about leaving the island. God seemed to be closing many doors for us in Bermuda, so maybe He was leading us back to England. It seemed like a bad time to go back (would there ever be a good time to leave our earthly paradise?) as unemployment was at an all-time high. Margaret Thatcher was Prime Minister, and had confronted the powerful Unions, who had been holding the country to ransom. Things seemed to be chaotic over there, but the conviction that we had to return was growing. So many things had changed for us, not only the Outward Bound incident. Our lives had become centred around Jesus, and our circle of friends had changed radically. Lynne and John were the obvious ones to go, although we did still see them, and we took Dan to Sunday School with Nicky and Amy for a while, but we now had a completely new set of values and priorities, and sadly some relationships just dwindled and eventually fell away. Heather and Charlie had divorced. Pat had long since split up with Barry. Liz and Tony were alienated by our Christianity, our renewed love for each other, and our rejection of Freemasonry. Sue, John, Rocky, and Maureen had all gone back to England. John and Mary Van de Weg's lives had been taken over by coping with John's non-resolving disability. Change was inevitable, and we decided that we should accept it and trust God to provide for us back in England.

That summer now seemed particularly poignant. A really special thing for me was running in the Bermuda 10K road race. The best woman runner in the world at that time, Grete Waitz, was running in it too. My time was nothing like as fast as hers, of course, I did it in just under an hour, but I felt such a sense of achievement. Robb ran it too, and when he finished, ahead of me, he ran back to meet me and we ran my last few hundred yards together. We spent wonderful weekends camping at the beach. It wasn't really permitted to camp at the Police Beach but we had managed to get around this in previous years by "testing out camping equipment for Outward Bound" so nobody challenged us. Typically, we would take the girls down to the beach on a Friday evening, have a barbecue, then put up the tent when everyone else had gone home. We would build a driftwood fire, and after the girls fell asleep on their little camp beds Robb and I sat by the fire, talking and praying and listening to the fish splashing around in the water, full of wonder at the amazing sky full of stars above us, and the privilege and blessings God had poured on us. We woke early on the Saturday mornings, before anyone else arrived, and it really felt like our own private, wonderful little world. We ate breakfast, did a bit of beach-combing and clearing weed and debris that had washed up overnight, then spent the day swimming and lazing around, chatting to friends and colleagues, then going home for baths, showers and comfy beds, ready for Church on Sunday morning.

Robb was by this time working at Government House, where extra security had been provided since the assassinations and riots. The police had a regular, armed presence there, and he was part of the team. As I mentioned before, as a spin off from Outward Bound Robb had also become the local representative for United World Colleges, an organisation seeking to train future world leaders from every country by "creaming off" the local students showing the greatest potential for success and leadership, and giving them a scholarship to one of several special Colleges worldwide. I have strong reservations about it all now, and see it not only as elitism, but a new age preparation for a one-world government. When Robb was first involved, however, it seemed like a good thing. Part of the duties of local reps was to canvass for the colleges and solicit contributions from some of the rich local businessmen. Robb did well at this, and as a result got to know some very influential people, including the ex-governor, Sir Ted Leather. This, combined with working at Government House and getting to know Sir Peter Ramsbotham, who was the Governor at that time, counteracted some of the negative effects of leaving the Freemasons, and he was encouraged to apply for Bermuda status (citizenship). We were so torn, but in the end felt that God really was calling us back to England.

So many people were upset by our planned departure, particularly our new friends at Paget Gospel Chapel and in the wider Christian community. One very special comment came from the father of Carol and Carla Ming, a black Bermudian Salvationist. Nicky and Amy had made friends with his girls at Nambour, and we got to know the family slightly through this. When he found out we were leaving he said "Please don't leave, Bermuda needs people like you". I was very moved by this, after being on the receiving end of a lot of painful racial and national prejudice. We started to organise the move back to England. Robb wrote to Hampshire Constabulary to ask about returning to work for them, and was told that he was too old! However, we really didn't want to look anywhere else, because we felt his Mum and Dad needed us nearby at that time. They were overjoyed at the thought of having us "back home" and seeing their grandchildren grow up. We started getting rid of unwanted accumulated "stuff" by holding yard sales, however, some of the things we got rid of we didn't sell, but destroyed. As we learnt more about the Bible it became clear to us that various things we had in our home weren't really compatible with true Christianity and needed to be chucked out. For example, Jaki and Vic had given us a Fertility Idol from Ghana, and we were uncomfortable with some of our music albums. The 60s and 70s produced some great rock music, but a lot of it was fuelled by drugs and some of it was downright satanic! The biggest thing we got rid of was a statue of Bacchus which my Grandma had given to me. I had loved this since I was a little girl and had asked her if I could have it when she died, but she gave it to me when I got married. It was worth quite a bit of money, but I didn't want a reminder of the god of booze sitting in my home, so I gritted my teeth and smashed it, not wanting to knowingly pass on such a symbol of hopelessness to anyone else. Auntie Eileen (my Godmother!) went ape when she found this out. Apparently she had thought it was to be hers, and was angry when Grandma gave it to me. She would probably never have found out, but when she asked me if it had survived the move back to England later on I told her (perhaps foolishly – I'm not sure) what I had done. I was accused of being "like Hitler, burning books he didn't agree with". I never did find out how she stood with God. She went to church occasionally, and said she could never have coped with losing Uncle Harry if God hadn't helped her, but she always became angry if I tried to talk about the God I knew, even if I was just answering her questions. Theoretically, the God I worshipped was the same one she did, but you would never guess it. I also got rid of a statue of Michaelangelo's David. This wasn't so much because we worshipped it, but because we could see that a lot of the Christians who came to our home weren't really comfortable with having a bloke's privates on full view in front of them! The statue also reminded us of a pre-Christian massive booze fuelled argument we had which had ended in me chucking a pint of Planters Punch in Robb's face. We were having a Quiz on one of our houseboat weekends and Robb had asked me where the original "David" was. I, smugly, gave the answer (having actually seen it on my school trip to Florence) and he said he needed the latitude and longitude. And that's when the fight started, as they say! We did have some memorable and spectacular rows, good job God stepped in or we might have both been on death row.

It was really hard to start packing up our home and selling things off, and I wasn't very good at it, but Robb kept focussed and got us organised whilst I got on with our necessary day to day stuff. He made a big packing case at his woodwork class, and we started putting in it all the things we needed to keep or couldn't bear to part with. During this time Diane left Bermuda and went back to England. She was given some money by a rich Bermudian Christian to start a Day Nursery of her own, and she found a property in Worthing on the South coast. Rocky and Maureen were based in Whitehill, just north of Portsmouth, so we knew we would have friends nearby if we settled there. Robb found out from Sir Peter Ramsbotham that his home in England was in the same village as John Duke, who was then Chief Constable of Hampshire Police, and that he knew him well. Sir Peter wrote to him, giving Robb a glowing reference, and we were really grateful for that. Ted Leather gave him a reference, too. We gave in our notices at work, and started on a round of farewell parties. We were given two beautiful Bermuda oil paintings by our friends at Paget Gospel Chapel, one was of the little bay where we had been baptised, and the other of The

Whaler Inn, which was one of our favourite places to eat and take visitors. The food wasn't anything too special, but the setting was one of the loveliest on the island, set on the cliffs above a little cove – the private beach of the Southampton Princess Hotel – with a big terrace where you could sit and eat under umbrellas; listening to the sea and looking out over the bay. As a result, eating there, especially Sunday Brunch, was a special treat, and was one of the things I knew we would miss a lot. The ladies at the chapel gave me a gold necklace with a Longtail bird pendant. We had Books about the island given, and loads of lovely cedar things. Liz and Steve Peterson (Liz Penn of Trevelyan fame) gave us a model of a Bermuda cottage with a piece of local coral rock inside it. Flip and Hilary gave us a cedar Friendship Goblet. I still treasure all of these.

One gift that puzzled me, and I must say disappointed me, was from a lady I had befriended at work. She was suffering from severe emphysema and used to come in for blood tests regularly. She could hardly breathe, and looked so scared, and I felt so sorry for her. I remembered her from the Hospital, she was one of the "Pink Ladies" who ran the coffee and gift shop, and she was a miserable, stroppy old thing that nobody liked! She was married to the owner of a shipping line, so was rolling in money, but it obviously hadn't made her happy, and now she was dying a really distressing death. I started praying for her, and in the end, when Pat wasn't around, I asked her if she had any religious faith. It was as if a flood gate had opened, she started talking, and it was clear that she had absolutely no confidence that she was going somewhere better when she died, which would probably be fairly soon! I arranged to go and see her, and did so on most Mondays from then on, in spite of being really busy, as this was only about 3 months from our departure date. I would read the Bible to her and pray for her, but I was never clear on whether she actually gave her heart to the Lord. When I asked her I would get a muddled answer. I think she was just very lonely and scared and needed some company. I wrote out a prayer for her that would ask Jesus in to take control of her life if she meant it with all her heart, but I never knew if she actually prayed it. Her home was gorgeous, she had amazing Chinese porcelain table lamps with silk shades painted to match the decorations on the bases, but she also had hundreds of nasty little Dachsund dogs that smelt awful and sat on the furniture shedding horrible little sharp brown hairs over everything, so I didn't really enjoy being with her, and often felt inadequate because I couldn't seem to give her what she obviously needed, a relationship with God. I got a phone call from her a week or so before we left asking me to go and see her because she really wanted to see me, and had something for me. We didn't have a car by then, so I ran all the way to her home near Gibbs Hill Lighthouse, thinking that she had "prayed the prayer" and wanted to tell me – and to be honest I speculated about the super leaving gift she would give me in gratitude! When I got there she was in bed, not well at all. She had nothing "spiritual" to tell me, and just gestured to a soft package on her bed. It was a pink knitted bed-jacket, obviously something she had been given and didn't want! Why the heck would she think I would want such a thing? I prayed for her, said goodbye, and ran all the way back – getting home exhausted, sweaty, disappointed and sad. I wondered if all my efforts had been wasted. Who knows? I do hope not, and that I will meet her again in Heaven (will there be Dachsunds there? Maybe, but with no hairs or stink!!)

On our last night at 18 Alexandra Road we slept in camp cots, in a row in our bedroom. Our furniture had all been sold, dumped or given away, and our remaining possessions shipped off back to England. All we had left were our suitcases. We took our lovely little cat, Spot, round the corner to the Dunlcavy's house. They were another police family who had children at Nambour, and they had offered to 'adopt' her. We were really sad about leaving her, but knew they would love and care for her. I slept next to Amy, and in the small hours was wakened by a strange noise. I looked over at Amy, and saw that her eyes were open, but they were rolled up as if she was looking into a corner of the ceiling, and she was obviously "not with us". I woke Robbie, we picked her up, and within a couple of minutes she was looking at us and wondering what was going on. We saw that she was fine, and eventually we all went back to sleep. As far as we know, that was the only other near seizure she ever had. We called the Paediatrician the next day and she just told us to watch her, and make sure we saw another specialist when we got back to England. We spent our last few days in Bermuda staying at Nambour as a guest of the Olivieras. It was so kind of them, but we felt so restricted. David was a good man, if a little repressed, but I found Lydia pretty hard work. Meals were eaten in total silence. It took a few evenings around the table, with Robb and I chattering away and getting no response except a sort of "smile", with mouth clamped shut, from everyone else, before we realised that no-one was supposed to speak! After meals Lydia would wash the dishes in hot soapy water before loading them into the dishwasher. When I asked her why she did both she gave me a sort of smug, pitying look, and explained to me that it was more hygienic. Thank God we didn't get sucked into that awful lifestyle. I feel so sorry for them. Jesus loved a good party, all the sinners invited Him to their houses. He turned water into top class wine when his friends ran out at their wedding. He was accused of being a "wine bibber and a glutton" and said that He came to give us Life in all its abundance. I couldn't see much evidence of that in the Olivieras' lives, and it made me realise afresh that man-made religious rules rob us of something very precious – the overflowing, genuine, joie-de-vivre that Jesus brings.

13 – This Sceptred Isle

We left Bermuda at the beginning of April 1981. Only Pat came to see us off. We didn't want any tearful airport farewells, and knew she wouldn't crack emotionally! We were feeling pretty fragile and having last minute doubts about the sanity of exchanging a much loved home in such an amazing place, and our secure, well paid jobs, for dull rainy old England, probable unemployment, and life with (very!) doting parents – albeit temporarily. We had so much to thank Bermuda for. Much of it is so important and intrinsic to our characters and behaviour that we don't recognise it, but I can see that in many small ways I do things the way I learned to there. For example, I never leave food uncovered or unrefrigerated, because if we did that in Bermuda it would either be carried off by an army of ants or overrun by cockroaches. The memories of the mistakes that taught me this are still vivid! We never waste water. We couldn't in Bermuda because it was so precious. We had to buy it if there wasn't much rain and our tanks ran dry. To this day I still feel guilty flushing the loo after only one pee! Living there had stretched us and taught us in so many ways. We met each other there, our first home had been there, our beloved girls had been born there, but, most importantly of all, we found Jesus there, and because of Him, our very reason for living.

We had a small reprieve as we were flying first to Florida to take the girls to the new Walt Disney World in Orlando. We had a great holiday there, and visited as many attractions as we could. We watched Shamu the Killer Whale perform at Seaworld, and saw pearl divers diving for oysters we had "bought", bringing them to the surface and opening them to see if there were any pearls inside. Nicky's contained a small pearl, but I don't know what happened to it since! We loved "Wet and Wild", a theme park with every water attraction you could think of – flumes, surfing, tubing, swimming – you name it. I think that was our favourite. Disney World was amazing, but the queues were endless, and that spoilt our enjoyment a bit. We had also booked into a hotel at Cocoa Beach, just across from Cape Canaveral. We found out that the first ever Space Shuttle, Columbia, was due to be launched from there on the day we had booked in, and after initial excitement about this we wondered how easy it was going to be to get there! After some thought we decided not to go, and were very glad about that decision when we watched the TV news that night. All the roads around Cape Canaveral and Cocoa Beach had been gridlocked most of the day, and in the end the shuttle wasn't launched because of unfavourable weather. It was actually launched on 12th April, the day we landed in England. After Disney World we went to Palm Beach and Miami, loving the relaxed lifestyle and the fantastic food, especially the roadside vegetable and fruit stalls selling wonderful, fresh produce at a ridiculously cheap price. Our favourite place was Tarpon Springs, on the Gulf Coast. We only had a couple of days there and wished we could stay longer. It was like a Greek fishing village, with sponge diving boats and little Tavernas, and Pelicans sitting around the docks. The people were lovely, and many of them were actual Greek immigrants. Our time in Florida came to an end, but it cemented a love for America and its people that has grown stronger over the years.

We had a 9 hour overnight flight from Miami, and landed at Heathrow on Sunday morning 12th April 1981, Palm

Sunday. Rocky and Maureen came to meet us, along with Nan and Pops. It was so lovely to see them again, but we were all shattered, and it wasn't long before we said a fond farewell and were heading back to "The Haven", Nan and Pops' home, for a real cup of English tea and some much needed sleep. The countryside looked beautiful. The drive from Heathrow to Portsmouth is through typical English countryside, and there was blossom everywhere. The cherry trees were in full bloom, and pink and white petals were showering down in the breeze. We felt so glad to be back. We soon adjusted to the time change, and went about the business of finding a school for both of the girls, as Amy was just coming up to 5 years old. We got them into Court Lane School, which seemed really nice. We liked the headmistress, and she seemed to like the girls, which is a good sign! The girls were desperate to see snow, and had been praying for it, but as the weeks went by and May began we tried to tell them, gently, that there wouldn't be any until winter, but they wouldn't give up. Pops got a new car and gave us his old one, a blue Ford Cortina. We went up to Hull in it to see everyone, and almost didn't get back – because snow blocked every lane but one on the M1 as we came back to Portsmouth! It was mid-May!! The heater on the car packed up too, and we were absolutely freezing, but the girls were overjoyed.

Robb reapplied for the Hampshire Police, but was turned down again on the basis of his age, and we then found out that we weren't eligible for any benefits as we had been out of the country for so long. This wasn't too much of a problem right then, as we were living with Nan and Pops, but it meant that things could get pretty serious before too long. After about 3 weeks Robb had a phone call from the Police, saying that they were reviewing their recruiting policy, and had decided to look for some older, experienced men! We just laughed, and knew God was behind it. He passed his interview with flying colours, the decision influenced by Sir Peter's character reference we were sure. He was told that he would have to retrain, as he had been away so long, and also that his years of service would not be counted, either for seniority or for his pension, which was a blow, but we felt that God had opened this door and we shouldn't refuse to go ahead. In Summer of that year he went off to the Police Training College at Chantmarle in Dorset. It was the most beautiful place, set in a valley halfway between Dorchester and Yeovil, just around the corner from the famous Cerne Abbas Giant. Robb did really well there, and when he finished was awarded the Commandant's Cup, given to the most outstanding student, and never before to an experienced Police Officer. He felt that it was because he had decided that if he could help any other student on the course, he would, because that's what Jesus would do. I went down to Chantmarle for Robb's Passing Out Parade, which was to be followed by a formal dinner. Because we had been used to formal dining in Bermuda, I chose to wear a favourite long evening dress, but I was horrified, when we went down for drinks, to find all the other women in short day dresses. However, I was proved to have chosen well when we were invited to join the officers and their wives for drinks in the Officers' Mess, and saw that they all had on long evening dresses like me. God is good, and he's in the small stuff (not so small to a woman who feels she sticks out like a sore thumb!)

The girls were doing well at Court Lane School, but when Robb came back from Dorset he was posted to Havant, and we started looking around for a home of our own. It was definitely time for us to move out of 'The Haven'. Popsy enjoyed having the girls there for a while, but he wanted his own space back. The girls loved him, he was so good with them. He would do silly tricks, such as producing polo mints from behind his ear, or finding bags of crisps growing on trees in the garden, but his good will was starting to wear thin. We had managed to bring some money back with us, enough to put a deposit on a small house, and we found one we liked in Purbrook – 8 Craigwell Road. It was a 2 bedroomed semi, nothing special at all, and needed some TLC and updating. It had been owned by an old couple, Mr. & Mrs. Sparkes, who hadn't moved with the times, but I knew it was "the one". It had a lovely long garden, which backed onto, and was surrounded by, other long gardens. Along the side of our next door neighbour's garden was a row of Beech trees, in between us was a hedge of fragrant Jasmine and little pink Rambling Roses. At the end of the garden were Sweet Chestnut and Walnut Trees. We moved in August of 1981 and started setting up our new home. Our belongings had arrived from Bermuda, we bought some furniture from the Sparkes, and "made do" with a lot of things because money was so tight. Nanny helped us a lot. For months she had been buying extra stuff when she did her shopping, like cleaning equipment and larder basics, and that was such a blessing. We got a little white kitten, and called him Sam. We missed Spot, and Sam looked just like her, but he was never a real replacement in our affections. Our neighbours were nice. Dick and Doris Jones lived one side, and Doris's Dad, Mr. Blake, lived at the other. Doris was always singing, and she had a lovely voice. At the end of our garden our neighbour was a local GP, Dr. Morgan, who was really friendly. Across the road was a family with 2 sons the same age as the girls, and they all played together. It was a quiet, friendly neighbourhood and we loved it. We bought it for £22,200!

Robb had been started on basic pay, and it was nothing like as much as we needed, with a mortgage to pay, and 2 growing daughters. I looked into getting a part-time job in the local Hospital Labs, but the only vacancy was in Cytology, which I knew nothing about. I even started doing a cleaning job, but soon gave up because it was so soul-destroying. Anyway, we had both felt that I should stay at home, if possible, until the girls adjusted to being in England, so we lived on soup, home-made bread, and vegetables grown in our garden. An apple tree overhung our fence and I collected windfalls, cooking and freezing them. I got a bike, and rode off to Purbrook Heath to gather Blackberries and wild plums. We loved it! It gave us such a desire to be self-sufficient. The girls had moved to Morelands School in Crookhorn nearby, and settled in, doing well and making friends. I had carried on with my daily running as soon as we got over the jet-lag from the flight back to England, and had built up a lot more stamina, running up Portsdown Hill every morning after dropping the girls off at school. When we moved to Purbrook I started running with one of Amy's teachers, Susan Spencer. She was an American from Fort Bragg, in Northern California, who was in England on a teaching exchange programme, along with her husband David and their two children, Holly and Devon. We jogged around Purbrook Heath early in the mornings, and I got to know her well. She had been baptised as a teenager after attending a Baptist Church all her life, but she didn't have any vital faith at all, just tradition, and we had some interesting conversations as we ran. One morning we rounded a corner and came face to face with a young deer, which was lovely. We got to know Purbrook Heath well, and I have appreciated the area ever since. It's so close to "civilisation", but feels as if it's in the depths of the countryside, with little fords and streams, and woods full of sweet chestnut trees and bluebells, and amazing wildlife. Susan and I stayed in touch for years after they went back to the States, and they came to visit us once, but unfortunately we never got to Fort Bragg. Robb and I painted and wallpapered and dug and planted. It was a really happy time for us. We took Amy to see a consultant paediatrician at St. Mary's Hospital, he was arrogant and uncommunicative, and we realised what a blessing private medical care had been – we certainly got what we paid for! He kept Amy on her medication for the time being, with periodic reviews, and had no further information for us on her diagnosis. By this time she was a skinny little thing, full of energy. Her hair was a nightmare to brush, it was a mass of red curls, and we looked on her hair care as pure torture for both of us! Even when she was podgy she had been very energetic, always turning cartwheels and standing on her head, so we decided to channel it through dance classes. She joined Miss Hapgood's school of dance in Southsea, and took part in the yearly revues. Nicky had gone to ballet classes in Bermuda and appeared in their yearly "spectaculars" at Hamilton City Hall. I can still see her in her little ballet costumes, posing with Catherine Latter in front of the big pond full of water lilies in front of the building. She had lost interest in it by the time we came back to England, so Amy went on her own. She enjoyed it for a while, but didn't like Miss Hapgood, who was a bit of a tartar, especially if you weren't Royal Ballet material!

Our first winter there was a bit of an awakening. The girls hadn't given up on praying for snow, and they certainly got it that year. It snowed heavily for days, and stayed for 3 weeks. We could hardly get out of our road because it had a small incline and was covered with packed snow and ice. I pulled the girls to school on a sled every day. It was quite an adventure, added to by the fact that we didn't have central heating. It was freezing. Our bathroom had a gas powered Flatley clothes drier in the corner, and a grille fixed into the wall through which we could see daylight, presumably to deal with the fumes from the drier. Having a bath was an ordeal to be overcome with the greatest speed, before being overcome with hypothermia or carbon monoxide poisoning. Oh, for the warmth of Bermuda. By the following winter we had the comfort of central heating and cavity wall insulation, but in a way we missed the fun of living in the dark ages before English houses were warm. Spring, when it came, was so special, bringing colour after the drab browns and greys of winter. Snowdrops and crocuses were the first flowers to come through, then blackthorn started to blossom in the hedges, and the daffodils slowly appeared. I really enjoyed having seasons again. In Bermuda they just seemed to merge, without any being distinctive, and I had dreamt then of some day living in a place with "real" seasons; golden autumns, snowy winters, colour exploding springs, and hot summers. After being back in England for a few years, however, I realised that it didn't fully meet those criteria! One of the best things about being in that house was the spring dawn chorus. It was extra special, because it seemed to echo around all the surrounding trees. I would wake up at 4.30 a.m. deliberately to hear it, it was so beautiful. I particularly remember one Easter Sunday Morning, getting up before dawn and walking in the woods nearby. I stopped and sat on a tree stump to listen to the magical sounds, and thank God for the Resurrection, and for the ability to see and hear, and to thank Him for, whilst actually surrounded by it, the beauty He created. I felt as if Jesus was there with me, as He was with Mary Magdalene in the garden that first resurrection morning. It was as if I could see a miracle in every dewdrop on every tiny blade of grass. It was all for me. I think it was a taste of heaven.

We had started to attend South Road Church, where Nanny worshipped, and they asked us to take over running the Youth Group. We enjoyed doing this, and they were a great bunch of kids. Our little house was always full of them. We liked the people at South Road, but we often disagreed with some of the "old guard". They seemed to set great store in "doing things correctly and in order", sacrificing spontaneity and flexibility. This became more apparent to us as time went on, and we found one lovely man, who read the notices each week, worrying over making small mistakes in front of Christian "brethren" he had known for years, because he knew he would "get it in the neck" afterwards! In the Breaking of Bread meeting, when all the men were free to stand up and speak about things they felt God had spoken to them, Robb and I were consistently touched by what a man called Kevin shared. He was educationally subnormal, after having an accident as a child which had caused brain damage, but he spoke from the heart. It was always something simple and beautiful, but often very radical and thought provoking. He definitely had a great relationship with the Lord. However, his father, who was one of the elders, would stand up immediately after Kevin had spoken, and do a bit of damage control, contradicting anything that didn't fit in with the "party manifesto"! Another thing that bothered me particularly was the fact that women had to keep silence. At Paget women couldn't even attend the Breaking of Bread without a head covering, and of course it was a given that they would keep quiet. It wasn't quite so strict at South Road, but we were still supposed to sit down and shut up, even if we didn't have to put our hat on. When we were first saved we didn't question things, because we didn't know much, and I would dutifully put on my hat before going to the meetings, but we were beginning to see that religious rules reared their ugly heads in all kinds of ways. I had no problem with not standing up and "preaching", that definitely wasn't my forte, but sometimes I was bursting to pray, or read out an appropriate verse of scripture, or choose a hymn that fitted in with what people had spoken about. Looking back, this was genuinely Biblical. In one of Paul's epistles he states that everyone had a psalm, a hymn or a spiritual song to share when the believers got together. Very often my heart would be beating frantically – which I had learned was a sign that the Holy Spirit was prompting me to do or say something. Sadly, at South Road I almost always resisted out of fear of being rebuked by the elders, and eventually I stopped getting these prompts.

Popsy started to come along to church with us sometimes, and on a couple of occasions he responded to a challenge from the speaker to come forward and give his life to Jesus. I think he did it to keep everyone happy, and didn't have a real life-changing conversion experience. Whatever he did do when he went forward, it didn't seem to make any difference in him. However, he got on well with some of the people there, albeit in his "I'm honouring you peasants with my presence" way, and so continued to put in an appearance occasionally. He was friendly with an old ex-Navy man, Wilf Lakeman, in particular. Wilf was a lovely man, who loved the Lord with all his heart. Charles Savage was another, and we really respected them because of that. Wilf had some funny ideas, however, and I remember being very distressed by a story he told me from his Navy days. He had been answering questions from someone who wanted to find peace with God after leading a very self-indulgent life. Apparently he cried and cried, thinking he could never be saved, because Wilf told him that he had to feel that he was a miserable sinner first. From what I understood, the guy knew he wasn't going God's way and wanted to change, but was stopped by Wilf's terminology! How tragic – I still think of him and pray he eventually heard about God's love from someone else. I challenged Wilf, telling him Robb and I didn't really know what sin was until after we surrendered to Jesus, and pointing out that the Prodigal Son only came back to his father because he was starving and destitute, not out of any deep conviction of sin, but Wilf thought we were being heretical! I wonder how many people have been kept away from God by Christians?

Some really good things happened whilst we were at South Road, but some bad ones too. Amy was eventually taken off her Epanutin because she had no further problems with fits or strange episodes. I began to wonder whether the reason she had been such a bad sleeper and so difficult to get to bed as a baby and toddler was because she had been having fits in her sleep which we didn't know about. The downside was that as soon as she came off it she started to put on weight again, with no change in her diet or activity level. I wondered if there wasn't some underlying metabolic problem which had been affected by the drugs. Nicky stopped sucking her thumb! I actually had mixed feelings about this as it meant she was growing up, but I guess it had to happen. We got into gardening in a bigger way, and grew some lovely vegetables. I loved being frugal, and carried on with my blackberrying and sloe picking. I made some awesome sloe gin! I scrounged quince from neighbours' hedges and made quince and rosehip jelly to give to teachers for Christmas. It was so nice to be a stay-home Mum, and not have to rush around with divided loyalties to be at work. We had numerous visits from Jehovah's Witnesses whilst at Purbrook. We always tried to reason with them and tell them what had happened to us, but generally didn't feel we made an impression on their blinkered, scripture quoting responses. One time, however, we started discussing the Gifts of the Holy Spirit, which they said were not for the present day. Robbie replied that we had both received the gift of praying in tongues, and when he gave them a demonstration they shot away up the drive as fast as they could. The amazing thing, though, was that it was the first time I had heard him pray out loud, and he sounded exactly like I did! From then on I didn't doubt that my "prayer language" was genuine, and not something I had made up.

We didn't have much money for holidays and days out, but we did go to some great Christian events, notably "Spring Harvest" and "Royal Week". Spring Harvest was held at the Butlins Holiday Camp at Prestatyn in North Wales, and Royal Week was held in Cornwall. It was in fact held at Wadebridge, the area my Dad's family came from, and the area where I'd had so many wonderful times as a child, so it was a great blessing to go back there and show the girls some of my favourite spots. We went to Prestatyn a few times, and heard some great speakers, but the best part (at Royal Week too) was the morning worship in the huge marquee, when everyone got together to start the day with God. I love singing hymns anyway, but singing them with hundreds of other like-minded Christians was absolutely wonderful – a taste of heaven. Robbie had also joined the Christian Police Association, and we went to a few of their meetings, including an important one that gave us a favourite family memory. The meeting was to be held in central London, at a big church not far away from the Natural History Museum, so we decided to make it a day out for us all. I could take the girls to the Museum whilst Robb was in the meeting. We finished early, so went to the church and crept in at the back, just as some Archbishop was closing in prayer. The place was big and sepulchral, and every little sound echoed around and was magnified. It was also full of VIPs, so I was doing my best to keep the girls quiet, when little Amy suddenly sneezed violently and farted loudly at the same time! Nicky and I almost died laughing – and we couldn't keep it quiet – we totally lost it. Amy then got really angry with us and started telling us to shut up – and trying to hit Nicky, which made things even worse, so I laughed even more! The noises echoed round and round, and everyone turned around to see what was going on. In the end I just dragged the girls out and tried to find somewhere to hide and wait for Robb where he wouldn't be seen associating with us! Looking back, I can even see God in things like this, because He's never let us get so "religious" that we can't have a good laugh at something like a loud fart in church! In fact, on some occasions it may have been a fair comment on the proceedings.

We were learning to trust the "leading of the Holy Spirit" in many ways, and one incident showed us that that we were right in doing so. Amy had started having bad nightmares, and even thought she could hear "voices". We prayed and prayed with no results, and eventually decided to fast, asking God to show us what was wrong. After a day or so, whilst we were praying together, Robb reluctantly told me that he felt God was telling him to get rid of a music album he had brought back to England from Bermuda. It was rare and worth quite a bit of money, which was why he kept it. It was produced by Frank Zappa, and featured a sad man who called himself Wild Man Fischer. He wrote his own material and then sang it, and it was weird and crazy. Apparently Frank Zappa was his "mentor", making money out of the poor guy's mental disintegration. I too felt that we should get rid of it, so we broke it up and chucked it out. Immediately, and independently, we both started thinking about Amy's "induction" into the Brownies! We had gone to the ceremony, which we later realised was around the time she started getting nightmares, and we had both been very uncomfortable about it. There had been a lot of candles and a circle of Brownies which Amy had been brought into. They sang a song "I've got that B.P. (Baden Powell I presume) spirit down in my heart", which we really didn't like. Robb had wanted to stop the whole thing, telling me it was just like his induction into the Freemasons! We felt that Amy should stop going to Brownies, and that we should get rid of her uniform. This seemed so ridiculous, we were talking about the Brownies, for goodness sake! A bunch of little girls doing a good deed every day and earning badges for learning interesting stuff! However, we were also learning that God's ways weren't our ways, and finding out that we really could hear from Him, plus Amy was getting really distressed by the nightmares and voices, and we were very concerned. Added to this, she wasn't enjoying Brownies that much, and had started to find excuses not to go. We decided to trust that God was leading us, took her out of the Brownies, and burned her uniform (as we had done with Robb's Freemasonry regalia). She never had another nightmare or heard voices from that time on. This strengthened our faith tremendously. We had discovered a strong principle with God, which is that obedience leads to revelation (and, conversely, disobedience leads to deception). Robbie got rid of his Wild Man Fischer record in obedience, and immediately God revealed the key to Amy's problem. I prayed a lot about this, because I realised that it wasn't something we could tell many people. Most people would think we had lost our minds! I realised also that this wasn't a blanket condemnation of the Scouting and Guiding movement. Nicky had joined the Girl Guides and didn't have any problems apart from once catching head lice at camp! This was an example of why Christians need to be led by the Holy Spirit, and not just follow a set of rules. This was for Amy, not a doctrine for anyone else to comply with. I did think a lot about the link between Amy's induction ceremony and Freemasonry, and I came to see that the "British" concept of Christianity is very much one of doing good works, which is the essence of religion. Most of my generation, and those before, were brought up with "be a good girl/boy or you won't go to heaven", literally encouraging us to score "Brownie Points" with God. Freemasonry is, at best, a religion of performing charitable works to get into God's good books, maybe the scouting movement started as a Junior branch of Freemasonry! Lord Baden Powell, who started it all, was certainly a high flying Freemason, and the "good works" concept would predispose Boy Scouts to rely on the charitable aspect of Freemasonry, as well as giving them membership of another elite group. Robb had not been a scout, but had joined the Boy's Brigade, which gave boys all the fun and adventure of scouting, but which also taught them the Gospel. He hadn't responded to it as a boy, but we wondered if some seed had been sown then which had grown and contributed to his salvation experience later in life.

One day we were at church when a young woman walked in with her little girl. She had been cycling by and heard the singing, and decided to check us out. We sat and talked for ages and eventually she prayed and gave her life to Jesus. Her name was Jane, and we became good friends. She'd had a really hard childhood, her mother was a witch (a real one) and Jane had been experiencing some disturbing things which she felt were occult in origin, but we would pray and she felt a lot safer. I used to take her and the children out for picnics, because she didn't drive, and one day we went over towards Hambledon. We found a suitable spot and set up our picnic, and had just started eating when we noticed a herd of about 20 cows coming over the hill up in the far corner of the field we were in. Before we knew it they were stampeding towards us, so we frantically grabbed the kids and made it over the gate just before the cows thundered up to it. I'm sure we would have been killed if we hadn't got out of their way. I knew it was a blatant attack from the devil, however, because earlier, as we were driving, Jane had been asking me if demons could live in animals. I answered yes, because of the story in the Bible of Jesus casting out a legion of demons from the possessed man in Gadara and sending them into a herd of pigs, which then stampeded over a cliff. I think this was the first time I really knew experientially that we have an enemy that hates us and wants us dead. Jane and her husband John moved up to Derbyshire eventually, with their 3 little ones, and we lost touch, but I knew she had God's protection so I look forward to seeing her again in eternity!

We had one good holiday whilst we were living in Purbrook, paid for by Mum with some of the money Dad had left her. She took us to Greece, and we stayed near Corinth on the Saronic Gulf. We had an interesting time, with plenty of laughs, but also clashes between Mum and Robb, which really amused the girls. I clashed with her quite a bit too, especially when she wanted to force some massive pills down Nicky's throat to counteract some tummy bug she had picked up! Amy was a great source of amusement to all the hotel guests. She was a bundle of energy, jumping in and out of the swimming pool and making people laugh – she always had a gift for that. The pool attendant loved her. He was an Egyptian who diligently emptied the seawater pool every other day and filled it with fresh water from the Gulf. We had a very nice tour guide who stayed in our hotel. He got a new puppy, and ran a competition to give it a name. Robb and I won, with the name "Metro". Little did anyone know that "Metro" was short for "Metro de merde" – our giggling, Retsina fuelled attempt at a French translation of "tube of poop", which summed up our attitude to the canine species generally! We had some lovely meals on the terrace overlooking the Gulf, although it seemed that chips came with everything. At one meal we ended up getting about seven servings of chips with only 5 meals. The girls enjoyed the holiday, apart from being dragged for a long walk along the road into Corinth under a broiling sun to get to the local museum and see some old lumps of marble. Another unpopular event was sitting on Mars Hill, "watching" some obscure display on the Acropolis which we needed telescopes to see, but we had a lovely cruise around some of the islands nearest to Athens (during which Amy lost a shoe overboard coming into Aegina), a great feast in a local village (which we stumbled on by accident and were invited to join by the villagers), plenty of Retsina and Ouzo, and Robb and I had some memorable runs through the pine forests. Whenever I smell pine trees on a hot day I remember Greece.

Soon after that my Grandma Ruth moved in with my Mum, because she had a suspected stroke in 1982 and couldn't look after herself any more. She was an amazing woman, she was still climbing a ladder to wash her own windows until a few days before the stroke! Number 98 was sold, and all Grandma's stuff shared out or disposed of. It was so sad to say goodbye to that house, for all of us. It had so many happy memories and lasting impressions for us. Each spring, when I see Grape Hyacinths, I think of the garden path at 98, which was lined with them. I loved them as a child and still do now – so does Nicky. In January 1983 I had a call from Mum and had to rush up to Hull. Grandma hadn't been eating properly for over 6 weeks, she just refused food and only had the odd cup of tea with maybe a little dry toast or a rich tea biscuit. She had been taken ill and rushed into hospital, but had died soon afterwards. I think she just decided she'd had enough, and stopped eating to hurry the departure process! Mum was on her own and very upset, so I went up to be with her for a few days, and to help with the arrangements for the funeral. We sat and talked about Grandma and all she had meant to us, it was a very special time. The minister came to ask about the hymns for the funeral service, and I helped choose them. One of the hymns I chose was "Oh Love that will not let me go" which is still one of my special favourites.

> *Oh, Love that will not let me go,*
> *I rest my weary soul in Thee:*
> *I give Thee back the life I owe,*
> *That in Thine ocean depths its flow*
> *May richer, fuller be.*
>
> *O Light that followest all my way,*
> *I yield my flickering torch to Thee:*
> *My heart restores its borrowed ray,*
> *That in Thy sunshine's blaze its day*
> *May brighter, fairer be.*
>
> *O Joy that seekest me through pain,*
> *I cannot close my heart to Thee:*
> *I trace the rainbow through the rain*
> *And feel the promise is not vain,*
> *That morn shall tearless be.*
>
> *O cross that liftest up my head*
> *I dare not ask to fly from Thee:*
> *I lay in dust life's glory dead,*
> *And from the ground there blossoms red*
> *Life that shall endless be.*

Sadly, I knew I couldn't be there, as Robb was back at work after some days off and I had to go back to the girls. Once again, I was to miss the funeral of someone near and dear to me – Dad, Grandad, and now Grandma, but I was certain that these also were people I would be with again in eternity. I felt, in retrospect, that it was more important for me to be with my Mum whilst she coped with everything she had to do in the immediate aftermath of losing her own Mum.

The Headeys had come down to see us when we were still living at "The Haven" after we came back from Bermuda, and it had been great to see them all again and renew our friendship. They had their son, Tim, by then and he was a little sweetie. We called in and stayed with them at Burnham-on-Sea on our way back from a Cornish holiday, and Lena came to stay with us at Craigwell Road. John was the southern rep. for Habasco, his brother Geoff's company, and as such he visited the Carrefours Supermarket at Chandler's Ford, so it was easy to meet with him there and pick up Lena. James, one of the boys from across the road, fell madly in love with her, and after she went home he was constantly asking when she would be coming back to stay. I wonder if he remembers her now! One day we were driving along and she started asking us about church and God. We explained the Gospel simply to her, and she sat in the back of the car and gave her life to Jesus. I don't think she ever got to follow it up with any church experience after going home, but I believe she made a sincere, if child-like, commitment, and I know God will never leave her or forsake her. Sue and John moved back to Huddersfield, their home town, shortly after that, to start their own business, Helensgate, selling glass and interior design pieces from all over the world. It became very successful, but they had to work really hard. We stayed with them in Huddersfield too, and had great discussions about what had happened to us, because we hadn't become Christians until after they left Bermuda. Sue was really touched by what we had to say, and was also being dragged into every passing church by Tim when they were out walking! She called me late one night after I lent her a book about someone's path to Jesus. She had really connected with the story, and called to tell me she had "entered in" to a new life with Christ (which is the way conversion was described in the book). She tried a couple of churches after that but didn't settle in any, and pretty much gave up on formal religion, but she's another person I'm pretty sure I will be with for ever! A lasting memory of one of our visits, which I'm sure God used, was of 2 year old Tim climbing into bed with Robb and I one morning to get us to read stories to him. It was so lovely to have that little person snuggling up to us and chattering away, we had forgotten what a joy it was!

We saw quite a bit of Rocky and Maureen. They had another son now, David, as well as Jamie, who was born in Bermuda. Together with John McPhee, a solicitor from the Winchester Police HQ, Robb and Rocky managed to get Bermuda Police Service recognised, as far as experience and related salary was concerned, nationally. They didn't manage to get it recognised as far as pensions were concerned, but it was still a great breakthrough, although it took quite a while before we saw it in Robb's pay packet. John McPhee became a Christian too! He had just become involved in Christian Science, and we managed to show him that it was neither Christian nor Scientific, and soon, he too made a commitment to Jesus. Rocky and Maureen were another thing completely. They loved hearing about our faith but definitely kept God at arms' length!

14 – In Pastures Green

Something very significant happened around that time. We decided to take our Youth Group away for a "retreat", and one of them, Ross Roseveare, told us about a suitable place he had been to with his previous church. It was called "Green Pastures", and was situated in a lovely little village a few miles from us. It was a typically English village, reportedly the home of the very English game of Cricket, the first ever game of which had been played near there. Robb and I went to visit Green Pastures to see if it would be possible to take our group for a weekend, and we were bowled over by it! It was a farm, which had been jointly owned by Lizzie and Stuart, a sister and brother who had been left it by their father. He had been a vicar of the village, and had owned a considerable chunk of it. The family originally lived in a big house on the outskirts of the village, and the land between it and the local church was theirs, but on their father's death it had been split up between three children. The house and some of the land was sold, and the rest of the land was shared by Lizzie and Stuart, as their older brother had sold them his share and gone up to Scotland to buy a farm there. The house's new owner's wife was the High Sheriff of Hampshire for a while, and had a mention in "Debrett's Peerage". I don't know who or what he was, but he was very autocratic. By the time we visited the place, Lizzie and Stuart were in their late 60s, and Stuart had sold most of his share of the land around the farm to Lizzie, who had made it into a Christian Trust. Lizzie lived in an old stone farmhouse with Bee, a friend she had met a few years before at a Christian conference. Bee's real name was Beatrice, but she didn't like it, and had started to call herself Diana when she was in the army, posted to the Far East during the 2nd world war. Diana had then become "Bee" when she was staying in America in the 70s. Bee was a divorcee, and had a son, who I think was in his early 30s at that time. She had lived near Chichester, and was part of the Bosham Fellowship, where she had been given a word from the Lord that she should "Go out, not knowing where" like Abraham. She sold her house and went off to join Ruth Heflin's Mount Zion Fellowship in Jerusalem, then after that she went to America, staying with some people she had met in Israel. On her return to England she met Lizzie, who offered her a temporary home at Green Pastures. As soon as Bee arrived there she said that God told her that this was the place He wanted her permanently. Between them Bee and Lizzie ran Green Pastures as a retreat centre. As well as the farmhouse there was a cottage, "Bethel", where George and Win Davidson lived. George was a trustee, and both he and Win helped Bee and Lizzie with the running of the place. There were also two beautiful old flint walled listed buildings, a hay barn (named "The Ark") and a cow shed. The hay barn was used for storing junk, and Lizzie and Stuart used the cow shed for Vanessa, their milk cow, plus Lizzie's little flock of Jacob sheep, and the donkeys which Stuart used to breed. Another building, which had been a stables block, was rented by a local potter, who had set up his workshop and studio there. He made some lovely stuff, mostly in browns and blues, really rustic and very trendy at that time. The other significant building was a turkey barn which had been converted into a sort of chapel, and named "Beulah". It had a large meeting room, lined with old sofas and chairs, a smaller room separated from the meeting room by large sliding doors, a large kitchen, and some washrooms and toilets. It was perfect for the Youth Group, and we booked it for a weekend in late May.

The weekend was a great success. The weather was beautiful, and I think everyone was touched by God in some way. One of the group, Gordon Rea, who had only recently become a Christian, was very deeply touched. One of the best things was a wonderful communion service in one of the fields, during which everyone was encouraged to take part by praying or speaking or choosing a song – even the women! We had group discussions and wandered off for quiet times in the lovely countryside, but we had plenty of fun, too, including a great game of rounders at the nearby Cricket Club. Having freedom to worship God without any rules and regulations in such a lovely place was a life changing experience. We found out that there was a small group of people who met there on Sunday afternoons for worship, followed by a "bring and share" tea together. They came from various churches in the area, and everyone was invited to participate, so there was a great variety of contribution. The meetings were led by Bee, and were "Charismatic" in essence, with the gifts of the Holy Spirit (mainly prophecy, speaking in tongues with interpretation, prayer for healing, and deliverance from demonic influence) being much in evidence. Bee had a prophetic gift, and would use it during the meetings to "give a word from the Lord" to the others. She also had the gift of discerning demonic influence, and would use this on people frequently, praying for deliverance in a sometimes spectacular way. After being in a church which denied that the gifts of the Spirit were for the present, and which said that women should "sit down, shut up, and put your hat on", this was exciting stuff. I went to their "Ploughwomen's Lunches", simple women's lunches of bread, cheese, and fruit, which were followed by a speaker and with prayer for anyone who wanted it. I loved these lunches and started to go over to help set up. We made the place look beautiful, with little arrangements of fresh wild flowers on each table, delicious rolls from the village bakery, and a selection of cheeses and fruit, which often included Lizzie's home made Coulommiers cheese. We had some inspiring and interesting speakers, not all women, and I often took some of the women from South Road with me. Some didn't like the Charismatic emphasis, but some did, and one, Ruth Myers, loved it. She and her husband eventually became part of the Fellowship there.

We also began to go over to help Lizzie with her sheep, and she taught me to milk the cow and to make cheese, which we did in the large kitchen in "Beulah". We helped her around the farm generally, and began to fall in love with the place. We got to know Bee and Lizzie, and grew really fond of them. They were so wholehearted for the Lord, and didn't seem to put any restrictions on the Holy Spirit, in spite of their age and conservative upbringing. They often did street evangelism, and had even gone over to the Isle of Wight Festival one year to be part of an evangelism team. We loved the idea of two old ladies preaching to all the kids and druggies at the festival! Putting my initial reaction of disliking Bee behind me, I got to know her and started to like her. She was so outspoken, and often very funny, and she was so encouraging to us in our faith adventure, inspiring us to trust God more and more in everything, for which I will always be grateful. Eventually Robb was asked to become an "elder" in the little fellowship that met there, and we started to think about leaving South Road Church. Our little Youth Group was dwindling, due to various factors, such as members going off to university or moving away for work, some were simply outgrowing the group or getting married, and many other reasons. Added to this was a hardening of the rigid "Brethren" stance at the church. There was a big children's ministry there, which was not just the Sunday School, but also mid-week "Crusaders" and other groups, and the church was offered the chance of a Youth pastor to co-ordinate it all. It was all becoming too much for volunteers to cope with, we really needed a full time worker, but the old guard insisted that there was no New Testament Biblical endorsement of the role of a paid "pastor". The origin of the Brethren movement was based on a revelation of the priesthood of all believers, and consequently employing some specially ordained person to do the job that any believer could do went totally against the ethos of the church. This was very commendable, but who was actually going to do all the work? David and Joan Roseveare, two great people who had worked themselves almost to a standstill over the years by doing the majority of it, decided they'd had enough, and left the church. For us it spelled out the writing on the wall, and we decided to have a day together, fasting and praying to know where God wanted us. Almost as soon as we started to pray, the feeling that our time at South Road was over became overwhelming, and the thought of having more time for Green Pastures gave us such a sense of inner peace, combined with excitement at the prospect. We had started to go to the leaders meetings at GP, and found it so exciting to be part of a team that was seeking to be "cutting edge" in the lead up to Christ's return. The emphasis was on this being "the end times", and that Green Pastures was a very special place in God's plan for this. There were many prophecies, from many people, about the significance of GP, and it did seem that a lot of scriptures were relevant to it. As well as this, the fact that one of the most successful and established English vineyards was right next door seemed particularly significant, as God uses vineyards and the care of them many times in the Bible to symbolise his people and His dealings with them. This was a typical English village, peopled by retired Admirals, pillars of the Women's Institute, and country people, plus it was the home of the game of cricket – you couldn't get more English than that! Was God going to do something there that was a microcosm of his end-time plan for England? Was this the reason He had clearly led us back from Bermuda? We felt it was, whatever that might mean, or might cost us. We all felt that God was going to add to the land – maybe we would even be running the vineyard!

I had been praying, too, about our financial situation. Robbie was still on minimum salary, and whilst we enjoyed "making do" we never had any money to spare for travel or holidays, or even for entertaining, and we loved to use our gift of hospitality. Our mortgage was crippling us, and we wondered if this was the way to go on. Shortly after the time we had prayed and fasted for direction, Bee and Lizzie told us that George and Win were moving into Portsmouth, as they had been asked to join the leadership of Langstone Fellowship on Eastern Road, and the long journeys to and from there were growing tedious as they were getting older. This meant that Bethel would be empty, would Robb consider becoming a Trustee, and would we like to move into Bethel? We felt that this, along with our decision to leave South Road, was such an answer to prayer, in fact, it was like a dream come true. The scripture "Delight yourself in the Lord, and He will give you the desires of your heart", from Psalm 37, became our experience. Before we left Bermuda I had dreamed of living in the English countryside, in a lovely cottage, growing our own vegetables, having a few chickens, living in wellies and jeans! We were so excited. We had thought that God was going to answer our financial prayers by giving us extra money to pay off the mortgage, but instead, here was a chance to get rid of it completely. Moving back to England and seeing God provide for us had built up our faith tremendously, and this seemed like another chance to see His promises being fulfilled in our lives.

George and Win graciously showed us around Bethel, and we realised that we would need to make a few changes to the place to accommodate us and our two growing girls. In spite of this we were all sure that this was to be our future home. The girls couldn't wait to be more involved with looking after the animals, especially the lambs. After more prayer we decided to sell our lovely little house in Purbrook and use some of the money to update and expand Bethel. There were always visiting speakers at Green Pastures, and we wanted to do our part in making them welcome and comfortable. In our daily Bible readings we read the Old Testament story about the woman who added "a room for the prophet" to her house so that Elijah could stay there when he was in the area. We both felt that we should extend Bethel to provide a spare room for any future visitors if needed, and to give us extra space from day to day. We had become friendly with a few people from The Church of the Good Shepherd (COGS for short) the local Anglican church in Crookhorn, just down the road. It was a lively, modern church, only recently built (and designed by Marcus Pegg, a friend of Popsy from the Coop) with young families who had children at Morelands school with Nicky and Amy. Some of the Mums, plus other ladies from COGS, came to the Ploughwomen's Lunches at my invitation, and one of them was a German lady called Margot Parkes. She and her husband, Jim, had recently moved from our area to buy a corner shop in Havant, but were struggling to "stay afloat" and wanted to sell up and move back to Purbrook, to be near their church again. When they found out that we might be selling our house they came to see it and loved it, and we really felt they were the ones to have it. We didn't want to just put it on the market for any old person to buy, and have everything orchestrated by an Estate Agent, we wanted to ask God to send the right people and give us the right selling price, as well as arranging the timing of it all. This, we felt, was another answered prayer, and Margot and Jim put their shop on the market.

Eventually we moved into Bethel at the beginning of March 1985. I remember the last night at 8 Craigwell. I cried and cried. Even though moving to Bethel was our "dream come true" I was so sad to leave the first home we actually owned. We had such happy times there, and we loved the house and garden and our neighbours. We had also come under a lot of pressure from Bee to move, delivered in irritable tones. She seemed to be in a great rush to get us over to Green Pastures. I was a bit puzzled, as she was supposedly to be our "spiritual leader" and didn't seem to have any patience at all with our desire to wait for God's timing, house price, and buyers. Was I beginning to see a bit of inconsistency in her character? I remembered the feeling I'd had when we first met her, that I didn't really like her, and that she had very cold eyes. I had immediately "repented of my nasty attitude towards her" and eventually became very fond of her, but this old feeling came back to me as we spent our last night in Purbrook. When we had announced our intention to leave South Road Church to the elders there they had told us they were very concerned for us, in fact Wilf Lakeman and Charles Savage came to see us to warn us that we were moving into very dangerous territory spiritually. The basis for their warning was that Bee was a woman, and therefore shouldn't be leading a church fellowship. They didn't know her personally, but all of this came rushing into my mind, plus loads of other things! However, we were beyond the point of no return, and on a rainy Saturday we left Purbrook and started on our new adventure. Margot and Jim gladly moved into their new house, they had a really hard time selling their shop and had lost a lot of money. We sold number 8 to them for £36,000, and could probably have got more on the open market, but felt that was the price God had showed us, and it was a blessing to the Parkes. They were very happy there for a number of years, and eventually Jim died there peacefully after a short illness. From August 1981 to March

1985 the value of the house had increased by two thirds, so God had blessed us financially too.

The girls had already started at Denmead Primary School and were happy there. They made new friends, and especially enjoyed catching the school bus every morning. They caught it at the bottom of our lane, along with Amanda and William, who were the children of Bill and Vicky, our nearest neighbours. Bill was the manager of the famous Vineyard which was adjacent to Green Pastures. Vicky was a really nice lady, a Christian, who belonged to the local Anglican Church, and occasionally came to our Ploughwomen's Lunches. The school bus wound around all the little country lanes, picking up children from the farms and cottages on the way to Denmead, so it was an early start for our girls, but they didn't seem to mind. It was lambing time when we moved in, and Lizzie's sheep always seemed to have problems with delivering theirs (probably because she overfed them and they were too fat). This meant we were "on call" 24/7 in case of one of them needing a midwife. The combination of this and organising our new home, Robb working shifts, and also an increasing awareness that Bee had a long list of jobs awaiting our arrival, meant we were very tired. I caught a really bad cold, which developed into a chest infection, which was very unusual for me. Before we moved in we had talked to Lizzie about adding a room onto Bethel, and, with her approval, had plans drawn up for what we wanted to do. We hired some local builders, Atkins and Glasspool, and they said they could start the work in late spring. All this meant we were living a chaotic sort of existence, but it was wonderful to be there and actually doing what we felt God had brought us back to England for. Church was lovely, I loved the meetings, because there was always some fresh and inspiring input, either from visiting speakers or from the regular members – all of whom were "full on" for God and keen to share what He was telling them. That included the women, which also meant I could open my mouth at last! There were some great people there, and we were especially close to Lynne and her sister Terry, who had both suffered tragedies which had drawn them close to God. Terry was widowed in her 30s, and Lynne had lost her oldest daughter in a freak accident in their home. Lynne was my age, and was pregnant with Abigail, her second daughter, when we moved in. The girls were friendly with James, her oldest son, and David and Natasha, Terry's son and daughter. We met so many inspiring people there, the place was a magnet for whatever was "happening" on the Christian Charismatic scene, and living there meant we were totally involved with everything that went on. One of the most inspiring people was a little Indian man named Paul Pillai. He was one of the Trustees, and came to visit quite often. He had been converted from Hinduism after a Christian fellow student prayed for him when he was at university, and gravely ill. He had been dramatically healed. He now ran a Bible School and Orphanage in New Delhi, and sent out travelling preachers into dangerous areas of northern India, where Islam had a stronghold. He had some amazing stories of God's leading and protection, and had written many books. He also prayed non-stop, and told us to pray in tongues whenever we were in any kind of difficulty. We have done so ever since, and it has been a tremendous help to us.

15 – Room for The Prophet

After a few weeks of being there I began to feel really washed out. I still had a nasty cough and decided to go to the doctor to see if I needed some antibiotics. He gave me tetracycline, and it seemed to do the trick, but a couple of weeks after taking it I realised, with very mixed feelings, that there was a possibility that I was pregnant. This was a total surprise. Not only had we not really planned any more children, we had been so exhausted by our alternate nightly lambing watches and all the work we had been doing we couldn't think how it had happened. We had been falling into bed and into a deep sleep as soon as our heads hit the pillow! Amy was by now almost 10 years old, and I was 39, but gradually we started to feel a sense of wonder and excitement, and knew without a doubt that God was in it. He had already told us to "build on a room for the prophet", so the plans were drawn up and the builder about to start. Obviously He knew there was going to be an extra person around on a regular basis! I bought a testing kit, and as expected, it was positive, so I went back to the doctor to arrange antenatal care. He thought that I was there to get an abortion! I was very angry – he didn't seem to think that I could possibly consider continuing the pregnancy, because of my age and also because I had taken tetracycline, which was not recommended in the early weeks of pregnancy. I told him that there was no way I would consider an abortion, and neither was I interested in amniocentesis to determine whether the baby had Downs Syndrome, because not only did it put the baby in danger, I wouldn't do anything about it even if it was a positive result. To my relief he put me under the care of Dr. Tim Goulder, his partner in the practice, who was a great family man and whose wife was a Christian, and very opposed to abortion.

As the implications of being pregnant started to dawn on me, I began to feel such a sense of joy. I went for long walks in the mornings, praying and crying and singing to the Lord (good job there was no-one around). Across the other side of the valley there were beautiful Beech woods, and when I began my walks the bluebells had started to carpet the ground under the trees. To this day, when I see bluebells with the pale lime green of new Beech leaves above them it takes me back to that wonderful time. I felt the presence of God so powerfully, and was constantly worshipping and thanking him for this totally unexpected blessing. I started to read about John the Baptist every time I opened my Bible or a Christian book – even non-Christian books! I decided to look up all I could about him, and realised that he was a sort of "herald" of Jesus. A lot of the teaching we were getting at Green Pastures was about Jesus's imminent return, and about telling people to get ready – a similar message to the one given by John the Baptist, and we decided that God was telling us that this baby we were expecting was going to be some sort of latter day prophet, warning of the need to get ready to meet Jesus (one way or another!). All sorts of other seeming "confirmations" led us to announce to everyone that we were having a boy, and that he would be called John. Eventually, after all the building work and renovations were completed, we painted the baby's room blue and yellow, and put a sign on the door which read "John's Room". We decided that, after all this certainty about having a boy, if we had a girl we would call her Sarah Elizabeth. This was after the two famous elderly mothers in the Bible, and also because Sarah laughed when they told her she would have a baby, and we would laugh to think we had misheard God so thoroughly about John. We said this, never thinking that we could possibly have done that!

The girls found out I was pregnant when Jane, my friend from South Road, who had by now moved to Derbyshire, called one evening to congratulate us (I had called her and left a message with her husband). Robbie and I were next door, in Beulah, at a meeting, so the girls answered the phone. We had wanted to keep it secret from them a while longer, because we thought they would tell everyone, and they did – immediately! Nanny was over the moon. She had missed out on having Nicky and Amy around as babies, and couldn't wait for this new little one to arrive. My Mum was pleased for us, but her medical background meant she was also worried about complications. Lizzie was excited, but the biggest surprise was Bee's reaction. She seemed angry. Looking back on it can I see the reasons, but at the time I just took it as a criticism. I felt she was implying that our carelessness in my getting pregnant had resulted in us missing the whole point of being at Green Pastures, which was to be totally occupied with the place and its needs, not to be distracted by family needs. However, most of the people in the Fellowship were lovely. Lynne was a tower of strength. She had been in her late 30s when she had Philip, her second son, and had just given birth to Abigail. Both were born at home. I told her about my heart's desire to have a home birth for this baby, after being so regimented for Nicky and Amy's births, and she said "That's easy, just sign up with Dr. Goulder, he's all for it". I already had! Once again I could see God had prearranged things. I talked to Dr. Goulder and he told me that, provided all was well, and the baby and I were healthy, there was no reason why I couldn't give birth at Green Pastures, in spite of my age and of our home being a bit isolated geographically. The one "fear" I had, of getting the awful night-time panic attacks I had suffered whilst pregnant with Nicky and Amy, was only vaguely at the back of my mind. I wasn't born-again for those pregnancies, and had since learned enough about the tactics of the devil to know that overwhelming fear was often a symptom of a spiritual attack from him. I figured I would be immune this time. I was wrong! It was 100 times worse. I went to see the doctor, and he point blank refused to give me sleeping pills, and was horrified that this had been the previous treatment. He did give me some mild tranquillisers to take if I was desperate, but they had very little effect on what was one of the worst experiences of my life, a 2 hour long panic attack, when I was shaking and almost paralysed with fear of I didn't know what. Robbie prayed and held me and talked to me, but nothing seemed to work. It was pure hell, and I think I now have an inkling of what that place might be like. I was desperate for help, and told Bee about it. She was sure it was a demonic attack, and I was subjected to hours of so-called "deliverance", which didn't have the slightest effect. What did help was the whole fellowship praying for me, and I didn't have another full-blown attack, just the vague feeling that I might, which was bad enough. I didn't go anywhere without my tranquillisers, though, in spite of their ineffectiveness. I began to wonder why this happened only when I was pregnant. Obviously medication and "exorcism" weren't the answer, but prayer did help.

My due date was 8th December, and the intervening months were spent in a combination of domestic chaos (due to the building work and subsequent decorating), constant church meetings, and chores. I remember trying to milk the cow when I was about 8 months pregnant, and feeling like a failure, because I couldn't bend down to do it! We did take some time out to go on holiday to Cornwall, and stayed at a Christian guest house in Port Isaac. We enjoyed meeting other Christians, as well as being in Cornwall, and the girls spent hours on the beach at Polzeath, body boarding in the surf. They found the guest house a bit restrictive, but had some good laughs at the owner, Gavin, who would ask Robb to pray before meals, but kept calling him "Rod"! On our way home we stopped at Seaton in Devon, staying at "Peacehaven", another Christian guest house. It was a lovely big retreat centre on a hill overlooking the sea, with good accommodation, a chapel, a games room, extensive grounds, and lots of undeveloped potential. The owners had great plans for it, and we felt excited at the potential for something along those lines at Green Pastures. Nicky didn't enjoy our time here, however, because she was really ill with a tummy bug which we traced back to some cheesy garlicky spuds she ate in Cornwall. We spent an extra day here so that she could feel better before travelling, and got to know the owners, talking about GP and hearing about their plans, but then we returned to Green Pastures and fell back into our routine. As well as our regular meetings on Sundays, and Thursday evening prayer meetings, there were frequent elders meetings, plus extras like Saturday evening Praise and Worship meetings and Ploughwomen's Lunches. On top of that we had groups coming to stay for weekends and individuals coming for Retreats, all of these things needed either our attendance or help to arrange, organise and clear up after. We were expected to be at all the meetings, regardless of family or work demands, which meant that the girls were frequently left to their own devices (not that they minded too much!) Robb worked shifts, so often had to take time off to be there. He used his store of overtime for this, which he could have been paid for, but we felt at the time it was the right thing to do. We also became aware that we were expected to pay rent for Bethel to "The Trust", which we did. This meant that not only were we using our own money to improve Trust property, and paying our "tithes" (10% of our income, which we had consistently paid to our current "home" church since being born-again), we were paying rent and also using up a possible extra source of income in the form of Robb's overtime, all for the benefit of Green Pastures. Added to this huge financial commitment we were wearing ourselves out physically working there, and in spite of all this we constantly felt we weren't coming up to scratch. However, the friendship and true, heart to heart fellowship that we experienced with many people there was wonderful, and we loved meeting all the new ones that came along and seeing them touched by God.

We were all so excited about the baby coming, and loved seeing Bethel transformed, even though I felt it would never be in a fit state in time for me to have my home birth there! Quite a few visitors saw the need for more help around the place and some would come and give us a hand. Brenda was one of them. She helped Lizzie with the animals and did some wool spinning with her. Lizzie spun wool from Lily – one of her sheep – and knitted a blanket for the baby, I was so blessed by that. Mick and Rosa, from Cosham, came to some of the meetings, and Mick helped out a lot with painting and general maintenance. There were many others who mowed lawns and helped with the grounds. We had pigs, and I helped Lizzie with them, although as my pregnancy progressed I got a bit scared of being too close to them as they would knock anyone over to get to food! We bought a ram, Patrick, to save Lizzie having to take her sheep over to a ram in Droxford every year. Patrick was a Friesland, and seemed calm and friendly until he got with his little harem and became a bit overprotective! He actually charged Lizzie, butted her, and knocked her over, so in the end we got rid of him. We had bought a Friesland because they were good milk sheep and we'd had ideas of making sheep's milk cheese eventually, when we got a few Friesland babies from him. Another hare-brained scheme went wrong when we dug up a large area of meadow and planted potatoes, which caught blight and were absolutely useless. These had been intended to feed Russian Jews who were being deported from the USSR, and who someone had "prophesied" would be hiding in "The Ark" (the hay barn). Looking back, we were all incredibly gullible and easily manipulated by some frankly nutty people with totally stupid ideas. Some of them were also unscrupulous, but we believed good of everyone in those days! The milk cow, Vanessa, had a huge calf after a very difficult birth. She was a Jersey, which is a small breed, and some idiot had artificially inseminated her with Charolais sperm. Charolais cattle are very big, and Vanessa never really recovered fully, plus her beautiful creamy white heifer calf, which we called Vanilla, was infertile, so we never got any milk from her. Something else was happening during all of this. We began to feel that, in contrast to her overwhelming friendship and generosity towards us before we agreed to move into Bethel, Bee was becoming increasingly cold and critical. Lizzie was obviously being influenced by her, although when Bee wasn't around she was lovely, but there seemed to be a growing barrier between us and them.

My pregnancy went well. I was physically fit and healthy, and "John" was, too. As it got towards December I began to panic, because I didn't think Bethel would be ready for the home inspection by the midwife to give final clearance for the birth. Nanny and Pops were coming over every morning to help us get the place finished, and this was a mixed blessing. I don't know whether we would ever have been ready if it wasn't for their help, but they were there at the crack of dawn, and often I would wake up to the sound of their car arriving, which made my heart sink. I could just about cope with them if I had a few minutes to myself to pray before they arrived, but struggled all day if I didn't. Pops nearly drove us mad. He never listened to what we wanted, just did what he felt like doing, and went off in a strop if we had the nerve to tell him he'd done something wrong. Nanny fussed over and smothered me, and the strain of not telling her to "back off" was sometimes overwhelming! However, the place was coming together, and was looking lovely. We bought a second hand solid fuel Aga cooker, which I loved, but the daily cleaning and stoking up was a pain, and it made a lot of dust and dirt in the kitchen. It was lovely and warm though. We did eventually pass the midwife's inspection, and things had quietened down at Green Pastures as summer ended, so I settled down to do things like making curtains and a patchwork quilt for the baby. I bought some lovely fabric for curtains, which we hung in the new bay window in our living room. They were in shades of soft pink and grey, with a cloud pattern that often matched the sky over the hill at the opposite side of the valley. Our bedroom was lovely. It had windows on two sides, and was full of light. I hung curtains there which were covered with spring flowers, and we loved it. As had happened to us before, all the things we needed for the house seemed to be on sale for a reduced price, and we knew it was God providing for us, as most of our money had gone. Our resident potter made us a plaque to put up at the door. It had on it the name "Bethel" and a verse from Psalm 84; "I would rather be a doorkeeper in the house of the Lord than dwell in the tents of the wicked". Which could be also be translated "I would rather be a porter in Bethel..........." so it seemed very appropriate. That Psalm begins "How lovely are Thy dwelling places", and Bethel had certainly become a lovely home, full of light and warmth, transformed from the small, dingy, damp little cottage which we had looked at initially. We dedicated it to God and asked Him to be present there with us. Even now, when I hear that part of Brahms' German Requiem I feel overwhelmed with the goodness of God, now knowing that God's real dwelling place is in the hearts of His people, but also remembering the joy of seeing "Bethel" finished and living in it. The 8th December came and went, and I began to wonder what was going on, as Nicky and Amy had both arrived before their due dates, as had Anthony before them. I was more or less ready for Christmas, and the days dragged on and on, with the girls dashing home from school every day to see if John had arrived, although we had asked the school if they could come home when I went into labour, and they had agreed. My midwife, who was really nice, was going away on holiday just before Christmas, so I was beginning to worry that she wouldn't be around. The other worry was that if I was two weeks overdue they would make me go into hospital to be induced – or worse – I might need a caesarean, the nightmare opposite of my dream of a lovely natural home delivery! Dr. Goulder was reassuring though, and said that, as we were still fit and healthy, he was still happy to stay with the original plan. Robb had taken two weeks holiday to help look after us, and this was now ending, but on Sunday 22nd December, his last day before going back to work, we had a children's Christmas play in Beulah. This was brilliantly produced by a single Mum who came to Green Pastures regularly, Lynne Daley. Robb was moving staging around for her, when he dropped a very heavy wooden frame on his big toe, which immediately swelled up, with a huge blood blister under the nail. He could hardly walk, and we realised that he couldn't get his Police boots on to go to work the next day. In spite of the pain, we felt this was really a blessing, because he would still be around for the birth and to help afterwards!

That night I was so fed up. I was beginning to doubt that I would ever have this baby, and so was everyone else. I couldn't sleep, so decided to finish wrapping the last minute Christmas presents. (I should have recognised the signs, the night before Nicky was born I sat up playing

Solitaire until 3 a.m. and watched TV until really late before Amy arrived). Eventually I went to bed and slept until 5 a.m. when I woke up and realised I was in labour. I got up, had a shower, and made a cup of tea, then woke Robb just before 7.00 and phoned for the midwife. As I had feared, my own had gone on holiday the day before, so we prayed for a good replacement. At 9.00 a.m. an old battleaxe arrived, telling me that my blood pressure was sky high and that my doctor must be a lunatic to allow someone my age to have a home birth. Very encouraging and reassuring, I must say. She sat with me, timing my contractions, which had been about every 5 minutes, whilst I prayed. After about an hour my contractions had completely stopped, and she angrily told us she "didn't have time to waste, sitting around here when there was nothing happening" and left. We celebrated! She had only been gone about 30 minutes when my pains started again. As soon as we were sure that "this was it" we called for the midwife again. They couldn't find her! An emergency call went out, and to our great joy and delight we got a Christian called Mary, who was based at Havant. Dr Goulder arrived a little later. When I got to the stage of wanting to push we dragged out the "birthing stool" we had borrowed from the hospital, and I sat on it. This was supposedly an old method of giving birth, using a squatting position for the mother, plus gravity, to make the birth quicker and more natural, rather than the 20th century's favoured, un-natural, horizontal-in-bed position. I really didn't want to get out of bed, but thought I had better try the stool, as Mary and Dr. G. seemed to think the baby was a bit stuck! I sat there for about an hour and my pains wore off again, so I said I was fed up with it and got back into bed, whereupon everything started up again with a vengeance. So much for ancient and natural methods! Through all this fiasco Nicky and Amy were sitting outside the bedroom door, shouting from time to time "Can we come in yet?" We had discussed their being present in the room for the birth, but everyone – including them – had decided against it. Another thing that had been happening through all of this was that Robb and I were praying in tongues constantly. Dr. Goulder seemed to be watching us carefully, puzzled by what just poured out of our mouths without our even thinking about it. His wife was a charismatic Catholic, so he knew what we were doing, but he was obviously taking notice of all this, and we were so humbled when we heard that he had become a Christian not long after that. Mary, too, was watching us carefully, and visited us afterwards to tell us that she had been challenged by our obvious love of Jesus and had rededicated her life to Him and started going again to Paulsgrove Baptist Church in Portsmouth.

Robbie was encouraged to take an active part in the birth, and our precious little one was delivered into his hands at around 2 p.m, exactly 40 weeks from the day we moved in to Bethel. But then, as well as the wonderful sound of our baby's first cry, I heard Robbie shout out "It's a Sarah!!!" And there she was, all 8lb 13ozs of chubby girlhood. She was the sweetest thing in the world, with almond shaped blue eyes looking all around, a surprised expression, a fat little face and soft crumpled up ears. Her hair was dark, and came right down her forehead to a unibrow! We thought she was absolutely beautiful. I was a bit puzzled as to what all the so called "words from the Lord" about John the Baptist meant, but I had a beautiful healthy baby girl and immediately loved her more than my life. Nicky and Amy rushed in and cuddled and kissed her, then helped Mary to bath and dress her whilst Robb and I watched in a sort of daze, then someone made a cup of tea, and we all sat on the bed drinking tea, eating biscuits and taking turns to hold our little Sarah Elizabeth. Dr. Goulder had to go and buy a Christmas present for his wife, so Mary sorted out all the formalities. We called everyone to tell them the good news, Nan and Pops first of course, since they were sitting by the phone in Cosham waiting to come over and see their new grandchild – the first one they had seen newborn. Nicky had been 9 weeks old, and Amy 6 months old, before they got to see them. Nanny had asked to be at the birth, but I really couldn't face coping with her and her emotions as well as squeezing a baby out, as well as being very reluctant to have her gazing at my bits! Aaaaaagh! No thanks. Everyone was so happy that all had gone well. I think my Mum was wondering if the baby would have Downs Syndrome, because of my age, and we actually did look very carefully at Sarah, because she looked so different from our other two. They were skinny little ginger things, she was fat and dark haired. Her eyes were definitely almond shaped, her "unibrow" and funny little ears looked a bit suspicious, likewise her thumbs, which were really curly and set very low on her hands, plus she had a really long tongue which seemed to loll out of her mouth from time to time. However, we were reassured by Mary and Dr. G that she was perfectly fine! Nanny told us that she had known that both the baby and I were OK, because around the time Sarah was born, she had been looking out of her kitchen window towards Portsdown Hill, and there was a really bright double rainbow over in our direction. Everyone wanted to come and see her, but we kept it to family, apart from Bee and Lizzie, who only stayed a little while later in the afternoon. Lizzie was so sweet, she was delighted that a baby had been actually born at Green Pastures, and at Christmas, too!

The next day was Christmas Eve. I took advantage of my post-natal state and just lay in bed gazing at my lovely new daughter, falling more and more in love with her. The girls and Robbie were great, I didn't do a thing apart from sort out their presents and put them under the tree after they had gone to bed. There was a meeting in

Beulah in the evening, but for once we felt we had a good enough reason for staying away, and had a lovely family time together. Everyone who went told us that it was a very special meeting, full of the wonder and true meaning of Christmas, but I felt that I was experiencing personally some of that wonder when I held my baby, it was as if the miracle of creation and humanity was revealed to me alone – a truly spiritual thing. When I looked at the miracle of her, my heart broke for all the abandoned and starving babies in the world, and all the precious little lives snuffed out by the horror of abortion. A great deep sadness and poignancy became combined with the joy of having her in my life. Nicky and Amy had opened up worlds of wonder and joy to me (as well as anguish of one kind and another) but nothing like this first child God had given me as a Christian, with His eyes and heart for the world. Christmas Day was so lovely. Nanny and Pops came over with Big Nan, Popsy's mother, who was a bit "out of it" by this time, and living in a care home because she was on her own now that Auntie Vera had died. We sat Big Nan in a chair by the fire and told her to close her eyes because we had a present for her. I came out and put Sarah in her arms, and she opened her eyes and said "Ooh, it's a baby"! We all laughed, and I don't know if she ever really twigged that Sarah had just been born and was her latest Great-Grandchild. For once I didn't have anything to do with Christmas Dinner except in an advisory capacity, as Robb and Nanny struggled with the Aga! We eventually ate around 3pm but it was delicious, and we had a great day together, taking turns to cuddle Sarah. Nicky and Amy began to show what a blessing they were to be in the future, helping with everything from washing up to changing nappies. Lizzie's sister-in-law, Eileen, came up to see Sarah and brought a lovely posy of white Christmas Roses, another white flower for another new-born daughter! Nicky's was Bermuda Narcissus, Amy's

Magnolia, and now Sarah's was Christmas Rose. I felt so content and happy – but it was the calm before the storm.

The following Sunday, when Sarah was only six days old, we went over to Beulah for the regular Sunday meeting, but also to have her dedicated to the Lord. It was lovely, we really felt God's presence, and Sarah was admired and cuddled by everyone. As born-again Christians, we believed that "Christening" a baby to welcome them into God's family wasn't Biblical, so babies were simply presented to God and dedicated to Him, with parents and congregation promising to do all they could to love, care for, and instruct the child in God's ways until, as adults, they could decide for themselves to give their heart to the Lord and be Baptised.

Bee "prophesied" over Sarah, repeating a scripture she had given me when I was pregnant "This child is set for the rise and fall of many in the nation of Israel, and a sign that will be spoken against, that the thoughts of many hearts will be revealed, and a sword shall pierce your own soul also." I had puzzled over this scripture when she gave me it before. It was given originally to Mary by Simeon in the temple in Jerusalem when she and Joseph had taken the infant Jesus to be dedicated. At a low point during my pregnancy I had gone into the village church to pray, and looking up had seen a stained glass window depicting the Annunciation, and the words "Blessed art thou amongst women" written underneath. I knew that God was telling me that I was very blessed by Him, and that sometimes this meant suffering, and in Mary's case, deep anguish. "And a sword shall pierce your own soul also"? I had a feeling that this was going to be fulfilled in me as well as Mary.

16 – The Storm

I had started to go to the meetings in Beulah again, but only the day time ones, because Sarah had developed terrible colic, and screamed blue murder every evening. She also became extremely spotty, so bad that Nicky and Amy called her "Spot". The other nickname they gave her was "Squinima Fatbread" (after a popular athlete of that time called Fatima Whitbread, and because Sarah was always "squinnying"). She was not the perfect baby by any means! I was subjected to strong disapproval from Bee, not only because I obviously put my baby before compulsory attendance at the meetings, but because we had been so sure that God had told us this was going to be a boy, and had told everyone. We were on the leadership at Green Pastures, and this mistake exposed fallibility in us, which threatened her image. In one meeting, she asked me to stand up in front of everyone and tell them how I had got it so wrong! I did so, but very falteringly, as I was really hurt by her unfeeling attitude. Added to this, having a baby to care for meant I was not at their beck and call the way I had tried to be before the birth. I managed to go to a couple of the leaders meetings, where Robbie and I were "delivered" from so-called spirits of deception and the like. Ivy, a really lovely lady from the congregation who had become very close to Lizzie, helping her with housework and praying with her, had started to come to the meetings, along with us and David and Audrey (the other elders). Ivy regularly got "pictures" from the Lord when she was praying, and had started to announce regularly that she "saw" cracks in the foundation, and also a big black spider. Normally

Bee listened to her, as we had realised that God really did reveal things to her in that way, but as far as cracks and spiders were concerned, she didn't want to know, and either trashed Ivy's insights or interpreted them as signs of someone betraying her, usually with glances at Robb and I. Increasingly, a good part of these meetings were spent praying for Bee, asking God to heal her from her traumatic past, which included a disinterested husband and divorce (it didn't sound all that traumatic to me) and also for her son, who spent his life getting into debt and drifting from job to job and from one disastrous relationship to another. We had quite a few "prophecies" from Bee, delivered in a strident voice and declaring that her son was "the Prince on this land". All of this was so puzzling to us. Our hearts were so innocent and pure. We had come to Green Pastures because God had told us to go there and lay down our lives for His work there, and to the best of our ability we had in every way, financially, bodily, emotionally, spiritually, with our family and our future. We had committed to be there until Jesus came back if necessary, even if it meant taking care of Bee and Lizzie in their dotage, even if it meant wiping their bums and feeding them! Why were they turning against us?

We couldn't believe that what we were going through was because of anything other than our faults. We believed that all born-again Christians were as pure-hearted as we were, so if there was something wrong it was because we weren't living up to God's expectations of us. We didn't entertain the possibility that Bee had a hidden agenda and that she had realised we were going to get in the way of her achieving it. God was so good to us through all of this, and one deeply significant thing that happened was that we had a visit from the great Harry Greenwood from South Chard Fellowship in Somerset. Most Charismatics felt that he and his fellowship were the leaders of that movement in England in the 70s, and people flocked from miles around to hear him speak at one of our "Saturday Night Praise" meetings. I didn't want to miss this one, so bribed Nicky and Amy to put up with Sarah's screaming for a night. Right in the middle of Harry's talk, in front of Bee, Lizzie, and our fellowship, and a packed house of local Christians, including all the leading Christians in the area, he stopped and said "I feel God is telling me to stop and tell someone this – that my wife and I have five children, and that with four of them we believed God had told us their sex before they were born, and four times we got it wrong"! I just started crying, but when I looked up Bee was looking at me with such venom I would have dropped dead if looks could kill. Afterwards she collared me and accused me of "nobbling" the meeting, and telling Harry what had happened to us! I denied it, but could see she didn't believe me. Apart from anything else, when we had "famous" speakers staying at G.P. hardly anyone else got a look in, she monopolised their time totally. Even after that we still felt that our inadequacies were the cause of Bee's attitude towards us. A few more significant things happened around this time. One was that we had started the "Saturday Night Praise" meetings, asking a local Pastor to lead them. He played accordion and sang, and had a large and growing church near Romsey. He seemed a nice chap, but again, we couldn't get to know him well, as Bee "took him over" when he was with us. Elders meetings were becoming a joke. They were totally dominated by Bee, although supposedly being led by the Holy Spirit. Basically they were opportunities for Bee to set her agenda for Green Pastures and for us to rubber stamp whatever she wanted to do. This particularly applied to financial matters. If any of us voiced a concern or a differing opinion we were "ministered to". This usually meant being shown where we were wrong, us repenting, and then being prayed for. Often we supposedly had spirits of rebellion or contention, which we were duly "delivered" from. Another thing was that quite a few members of our fellowship had started to come to us, as leaders, with various concerns. We dutifully presented these concerns at the leaders' meetings, but didn't get anywhere. Everything became twisted around against the "complainant" or us, and eventually we were accused of having "an Absalom spirit" – in other words, of hearing complaints against Bee in order to win followers over to "our side". What was this "Our side"? We didn't have one! We were devoted to Green Pastures and to Bee and Lizzie! Robb tried talking to fellow elder Dave before he raised any concerns in the leaders' meetings, to get Dave's backing first, but sadly, he found that when he did speak out at the meetings Dave would stay silent and simply leave Robb to carry the can. We began to realise that Dave and Audrey were totally under Bee's thumb, and that we really couldn't expect any support from them in our efforts to sort out pastoral concerns in the fellowship. At one of these meetings Bee read out a letter from Jonathan McMahon, a business owner from a village near Emsworth who was one of the Trustees. He had moved away from the area and couldn't be involved with Green Pastures any more, so was resigning his trusteeship. I don't think he had been there for years, and I certainly had never met him in all the time we had been there, so we knew he wouldn't be missed!

Also around this time we had a visit from a "Prophet" named Roger Teale. He was a tall gangling man whose face looked a bit like an eagle (even though he had the name of a duck!), quite scary looking in fact, and quite intimidating! He spoke at one of our meetings, and also got together with us as leaders to give us "the Word of the Lord". What he did was to question us in order to find out our gifts and tell us our role and position in the leadership. He asked me to describe Robb, and I said that he was kind, caring, disciplined, and good with people. Roger immediately said to Robb, "You are the Pastor here". Again, I caught the look on Bee's face, and realised that this was another nail in our coffin – she was now sure that her position was threatened by Robb. This was augmented by Roger's "word" for her. He said that she had an itinerant prophetic ministry – something like his own, and that she should get out and get on with it. Of course this would mean her leaving G.P. in the hands of the rest of us when she was on her travels, so she never did fulfil this calling on her life (which we all felt was a true one) because of her fear of losing control of Green Pastures. Our understanding was that giving Robb the title "Pastor" meant that he was the one to care for the "flock" as a help to Bee, who wasn't good with people, and not to take over the leadership, as she obviously understood it to mean. He gave us another, personal "word" too, which we didn't understand at the time. It was "in the time of winter snow, shall we stay or shall we go?" This has been fulfilled in our lives many times over.

One day in the early Spring of 1986 we were driving into Waterlooville to shop. As we drove through Denmead we saw Ivy waiting at the bus stop and stopped to give her a lift. She sat quietly in the back of the car for a while and then just said "It's not right, the way they are treating you". Amazed that someone else had seen that things were going very wrong, and would actually sympathise with us, we started to talk. She told us that she was very concerned about a lot of things, but mainly about us and Lizzie. She was worried because Bee was behaving in a way that she felt would destroy us in one way or another. We couldn't help but notice that Bee's treatment of Lizzie was awful, in fact it reminded us of the way Robbie and I were towards each other on our worst days before Jesus stepped in. She also seemed to be isolating Lizzie from her family, and from her friends in the village. Ivy also implied that Bee was going around behind our backs trying to destroy our reputation, which is very easy to do to someone who trusts you completely and lays their life open before you, as we had done with Bee. After this we began to entertain the possibility that it wasn't our fault that things were not as they should be at G.P. Something else that helped this change of attitude was the fact that I wasn't going to all of the meetings. I would stay at home and read my Bible. This was mostly out of guilt at not being at the meetings, but nevertheless God used it to speak to me, and I also realised that I was actually free to hear from Him without going through the "filter" of Bee's opinions. I think I was breaking free from a kind of brain-washing. I began to see that things were really off balance at Green Pastures. I began to realise that if someone claimed to be filled with the Holy Spirit, they should act as Jesus did, and be full of love, joy, peace, patience, kindness, gentleness and self-control – the fruits of His Holy Spirit. Bee constantly claimed to be "in the Spirit until God showed her otherwise" (i.e. "I'm always right") but she certainly wasn't full of the fruits of the Holy Spirit! She also frequently quoted "touch not the Lord's anointed" (i.e. "don't you dare to suggest that I might be wrong"). I began to see that she had everyone completely stifled by this, thus making herself like some kind of pope – infallible! In my Bible I read things like "By their fruits you shall know them" and "a good tree doesn't bear bad fruit". I was sure God was speaking to me, and I actually went to Bee on one occasion to share what I felt He was saying. My goals were to be completely transparent, to pray with her, and to be a friend to her, because I could see that her behaviour stemmed from deep insecurity, as all controlling behaviour does. Looking back on this, her reaction was predictable. She was furious, and I realised that I had now sealed my fate, and I was out! I was so upset and confused, still believing, as Bee constantly emphasised, that God had put her in charge at Green Pastures, that she was God's anointed there, and that He called us to be servants there. She reminded me that I had been mistaken in the past (as I had with John/Sarah) and was now misinterpreting the scriptures because I was being influenced by demons that wanted to get rid of her.

Nicky and Amy had started going to Summer Camp at a lovely place in West Sussex called Southwater. It was just outside another typical English village called Lickfold, not far from Midhurst and Petworth. They loved going there, they had such fun and made some great friends. It was run by two older ladies who were Pentecostal Christians. They had gathered a team of people around them who loved kids and the Lord, and organised one of the best Christian kids' camps ever. Our girls both became aware of the Holy Spirit through these camps and looked forward to being there each summer. We had also booked to go to Spring Harvest in Prestatyn, North Wales, that Easter. We had been quite a few times with the girls before we moved to Hambledon, as well as to Royal Week in Cornwall. We all loved being with such large crowds of Christians, we heard some great speakers, and had been part of some sublime worship. The girls really enjoyed the kids and youth meetings there, and both of them had made a further commitment to the Lord and been Baptised in the Holy Spirit as a result of the ministry of Ian Smale, or "Ishmael" as he was called. He wrote some brilliant songs for kids, and we loved him, he was such fun. It took me so long to realise that what we were doing at Green Pastures was totally opposite to the girls' joyful experiences at Southwater and Spring Harvest. The only explanation is that it was some kind of spiritual blindness or brain-washing, as I mentioned before. The girls hated the meetings at GP. They were expected to just sit in the background and listen to hours of what they perceived as "boring grown-ups rambling on", and boring old songs with only occasionally a decent musician. Bee said that their spirits would soak in the "anointing", they didn't need special children's meetings! The Christmas play had been an exception, and they enjoyed doing that immensely – especially since it meant they would escape being in our meetings. As a result of all this, and because of what we were going through with Bee, we were really looking forward to being at Spring Harvest. I didn't get much out of it personally that year, as I felt Sarah was too young to be in the crèche constantly, so I didn't get to many meetings, but being away from the pressures of GP, and seeing Robbie and the girls learning more about Jesus, and being so free in their worship and enjoyment of Him, was wonderful and so refreshing. As the time to leave grew nearer I began to dread going back. It was a horrible feeling, it was our home, the fulfilment of our dreams of serving God and bringing up our family close to Him and to the land, the place where our precious Sarah was born, and unbelievably I didn't want to return to it. I remember, as we got close to home, a sort of cloud seeming to come down on us, a literal oppression. Our reception from Bee and Lizzie was extremely frosty, and I found out the reason later from Ivy. Apparently Bee had received "a word from the lord" that they should go into our home whilst we were away, and pray in it, because of all the "opposition" she was getting from us. I wonder whose lord spoke to her – it certainly wasn't my Lord Jesus Christ! They had a key to our back door – freely given to them by us, in case of emergencies, but we had put in a new front door when all the alterations were done to the building, and they only had a key to the old one. Apparently when they tried to unlock the back door they couldn't get the key in. Bee threw a tantrum and accused us of deceitfully changing the lock on the back door because we knew what they were going to do. They eventually gave up. When we got home we used the front door, so had no difficulty getting in. However, when I tried to open the back door I had the same problem as them, but when I knelt down and looked into the keyhole I could see a small piece of wood that appeared to have dropped down into it, stopping the key from going in properly. I got a pair of tweezers and removed it, and the door then unlocked easily. When I told Ivy she said "Praise the Lord, I knew it was wrong to go in whilst you were away, but they wouldn't listen to me." She had been invited to go with them, and in spite of great misgivings had gone with them to see what they would do. She had been praying against it all the time, and was so blessed that her prayers had been answered in such a practical way. So were we!

We knew now that we were definitely out of favour, but still didn't understand why. What had we done? And how could we put things right? We continued to try harder, thinking we could regain favour by working ourselves to a standstill! We were even sabotaged in this, because Bee started to give our responsibilities to others. She would ask us to do something, and then, before we had chance to start doing it, she would recruit someone else, implying that we were taking too long. She would pick out new people that came along to the meetings and "big them up" in front of everyone, whilst at the same time putting us down or ignoring us. It was a tactic I recognised, because it's what she had done to us in the beginning, at the expense of poor George and Win! The people she picked were usually lovely new Christians, or people of some standing in the local Christian community. They fell for it, as we had, wanting to be part of what God was doing there. My mind (and God) was telling me that this was all so wrong, but my over-active conscience was still giving me a hard time. However, over that summer, many things helped me to become confident that we were not disappointing God, nor were we out of favour with Him, and I came to the conclusion that it was Bee who wasn't hearing from Him, but from someone else entirely. Because I read a lot, and because "deliverance" seemed to be the main focus at G.P., I read quite a few things on that subject. One book in particular, recommended by Bee, was a bunch of lies and rubbish. It was written by two women who were emphasising the need to eat large amounts of meat when performing a deliverance ministry, because deliverance depleted one's serum protein! They gave figures and test results which supposedly proved this, and then more test results after eating meat. I knew from my pathology training that eating meat had absolutely nothing to do with raising one's serum protein, and also that Jesus recommended fasting to help in casting out demons – just the opposite of what this book said. I tried to tell Bee this, and once again, got an angry response. Another book I read was by Bill Subritsky, and this really helped me. He identified several spiritual "strong men" (as in the scripture where Jesus says that only if you bind the strong man can you take his goods) and described them as something like army generals. He described their various characteristics, and also the minor demons they controlled. I took particular note of one of these strong men – Jezebel – personified by a female in the Bible, but genderless in the spirit, and read that under "her" command came divorce, division, factions, perversion, seduction, religion, and witchcraft. Witchcraft, biblically, is far from being like our Shakespearean inspired image of an old hag dancing round a cauldron chanting spells, or riding around on a broomstick with a black cat behind her. In the New Testament witchcraft is listed as a "work of the flesh" which always opposes the work of the Holy Spirit, so anything man-inspired opposed to anything God-inspired. I was very interested to see my old bugbear "religion" listed (meaning the devil's substitute for a relationship with God, masquerading as spirituality, and driving other people away from God). In the book,

Bill defined the main ministry of Jezebel as replacing the power and leading of the Holy Spirit in the true church by substituting the power and the purposes of man, resulting in some or all of "her" minor demons being free to fulfil their purposes there. I could see that, if this was true, which I instinctively felt it was, it would explain a lot of the sad history of the church over the years, and also its unpopular modern reputation.

Robb had continued to be at all the meetings he could possibly be at, to show that we were totally committed to the place. I showed him all the things I felt God was showing me, and he agreed with most of it, but kept quiet and thought and prayed about it all. We were still being "lobbied" by members of the fellowship who had many concerns and some of whom had been deeply offended and hurt by Bee. Some of them left. We still tried to air some of these concerns in the interest of transparency, and also to show that we still acknowledged Bee as the leader. We didn't want to undermine her or get rid of her, we wanted to be reconciled and get on with God's business at G.P. Robb became totally convinced that Bee was way off beam after she accused him of having a spirit of rebellion in one of the leaders meetings. At that time he was the Vice-President of Portsmouth Full Gospel Businessmen's Fellowship International (FGBMFI) and Pete Sharpe was President. Robb and Pete had organised a special dinner with an ex-policeman and a boxer as after dinner speakers. Both these guys had fresh and dynamic testimonies of being born-again, and Robb had invited many of his Police Colleagues to the dinner (and paid for their tickets). Normally the dinners were held on Mondays and didn't clash with any of our elders meetings, but on this occasion it had to be on a Tuesday. Robb told Bee months in advance that this was being arranged, and explained that he must be there with his guests. He told her this even though no meetings were planned at GP on that evening. Exciting things were happening in the Police Force at that time. Robb had confronted a P.C. called Mark McDermott, and one of his Inspectors, Trevor Guilfoyle, because he had heard that they were Christians, and because neither of them were admitting it or showing it! They both made a fresh commitment to the Lord because of Robbie's challenge, and a small lunchtime Bible Study had begun at the Station at Havant. As a result of this, and Mark's overflowing enthusiasm when he realised what he had been missing, Police Officers were getting born-again, healed and baptised in the Holy Spirit left, right, and centre. It really was Revival, and most of them were coming to the planned FGBMFI dinner and bringing other cops with them. It was crucial for Robbie to be there, and anyone with a heart for God's Kingdom and for the lost would agree that it was. Bee didn't. She deliberately arranged for an extra leaders meeting that night.

Whilst all of this was going on I was struggling with a new, colicky baby and sleepless nights. Sarah would wake up 4 or 5 times a night, and even though she would go back to sleep quickly my sleep was disturbed for months, and I was very tired. Probably because of that I can't remember too much about that first year of Sarah's life, but it was also because we were so occupied with our role at GP and dealing with Bee's increasingly hostile attitude towards us. Sadly, we had to have our cat, Sam, put down around this time. He dashed out into the lane one day as Robbie was going to work, went under the car, and was badly injured. I don't think Nicky and Amy were too upset, however, and we didn't replace him. Because we were so busy the girls were left to their own devices much of the time, but I think they were happy, looking after the animals, helping with Sarah, and joining in with the various Youth Groups that came over for weekend retreats. One weekend a group of teenagers from Holy Rood Anglican Church in Stubbington were staying at GP. Their leader was a lovely man called Roy Spiller, who played guitar, could lead praise and worship really well, and knew some inspirational new songs. Not only Nicky and Amy, but Robb and I, joined in with some of their meetings. We had a great time with them, and many of the young people gave their hearts to the Lord or were touched by God in some way. They all wanted to stay for our fellowship meeting and tea on the Sunday afternoon, which was going to be special because a couple of our regular people were going to be baptised. One of those was Amy, who had pestered us and pestered us until we gave permission. We felt she was a bit young to appreciate the full implication of Baptism, but in the end we felt that it was OK, and that she knew what it meant. It would also be a wonderful climax to a great weekend. Our meeting started on time, although David and Audrey had not yet arrived, and Dave was supposed to be doing the actual baptising, along with Robb. Roy and his group came along, and of course Roy brought his guitar with him. In spite of all the newly saved young people being with us, and the planned baptisms, there was such a feeling of heaviness about the place. We didn't have a guitarist of our own that day, but instead of asking Roy to help out, Bee just stood up and started speaking, monopolising the platform, and even trying to lead the worship, singing old hackneyed choruses and ditties unaccompanied. Everyone dutifully listened to her and then joined in half-heartedly, not wanting to undermine her authority. I was getting more and more upset. I could see the kids' faces, and they were bored and incredulous, wondering what all this had to do with their fun, exciting, and inspiring experiences with Jesus over the previous two days. I decided that, for their sake, and because I wanted Amy's Baptism to be a wonderful and memorable occasion, as Robb's and mine had been, I had to do something. I waited until Bee paused to draw breath, and then stood up and said "God has provided us with a gifted and anointed worship leader in Roy today, and I believe He would be grieved if we didn't accept and use His gift. Please would you lead us in worship, Roy?" It felt as if something lifted from us. Everyone gratefully voiced their approval (except Bee, who was again looking at me as if she could kill me) and Roy started to lead us in a time of worship and praise the like of which we hadn't experienced in our regular meetings for ages. Dave and Audrey turned up during the worship, and afterwards we proceeded with the Baptisms. Amy's was lovely – she was crying when she came out of the water, really touched by God. Our friend Hannie was next, she too came up from the water crying. Robbie then said that if anyone else felt God was telling them to be Baptised that he and Dave would be glad to do it. The kids from Stubbington responded en masse, and by the end of the meeting over 20 people had publicly declared their commitment to Jesus and been baptised. Anglican doctrine forbade anyone who had been Christened as a child to be "rebaptised". Most of the Stubbington bunch had been Christened, but they knew that God was telling them to go ahead, and Roy decided that he wouldn't stop them and would just face the music from his church later! Whilst we were having tea afterwards Bee, Dave and Audrey joined Robbie and I. We chatted, and then, to my delight, Dave spoke to Bee and said "What was going on here earlier? As we drove into the car park from the lane we saw a huge black cloud lifting off Beulah." They had walked in just after I had spoken out and asked Roy to play for us. A victory for the Holy Spirit, but another nail in my coffin!

Other things happened over the summer to reinforce our conviction that Bee was not leading us according to God's plans and ways. More people left the fellowship, but new ones kept coming along. There were hardly ever any "exit interviews" with the people who left, and, if they did give any reason, everything was twisted around by Bee and they were blamed. She zealously courted the new ones, and as a result we felt ourselves being increasingly excluded from things. Some things saddened me, some made me very upset. A brilliant violinist had started coming to the praise meetings. He would pick up his violin and harmonise and improvise along with the songs – almost like singing in the Spirit. It was so beautiful. However, Bee didn't like it, and she asked him not to bring his violin any more. He didn't bring himself any more either! I was so sad. The meetings were open (in theory) for anyone to "bring a word from the Lord", and one day a visitor stood up and said he was having a very disturbing vision. It was of a high white wall with a small window and someone gazing out of it as if they were a prisoner. I can't remember how Bee "interpreted" it, but I knew it wasn't the real meaning. A couple of days later I happened to read Ezekiel chapter 13, about God destroying all the whitewashed walls the priests of Israel had built to hide their corruption. Bingo! Later I realised the person looking out was probably Lizzie. She was trapped in all of this. Bee had convinced her that she wouldn't have anyone if she didn't have her, and Lizzie saw very little of her family, and even less of her old friends. Around this time Stuart and Eileen, Lizzie's brother and sister-in-law, decided they wanted to be nearer the main part of the village, as they were getting less mobile. They bought a house opposite the bottom of our lane, next to the field where Stuart often showed his donkeys. Lizzie and Bee decided to sell their house – the original Green Pastures – and buy Stuart's house, which was next to the cow barn. We weren't too sure about this as Trustees. Was it actually legal to sell Trust Property without the full agreement of the Trust? More to the point, what about all these "prophecies" about God adding to the land? Along with the house "Green Pastures" they sold the small field behind the Pottery, which meant more land had gone than was gained. There seemed to be some Biblical significance in selling "The Potter's Field", but we couldn't quite work it out at the time! We didn't see much of Stuart and Eileen from then on, neither did Lizzie. No-one in the village wanted anything to do with Green Pastures, and Bee persuaded us all that this was because of "the offence of the Gospel". In other words they were all heathens and we didn't need them! What's more we were warned against being in certain places and with certain people in case we "caught" something from them spiritually. I compared this attitude unfavourably with the stories of Jesus mixing with tax-collecters and sinners, and being invited to their parties. Another thing was that the emphasis on "deliverance" started to disturb me, after someone came to us for help and finished up in a far worse state than when she came. She was having terrible nightmares and panic attacks, which actually did sound demonic. We prayed with her over and over again; Bee and others getting "words of knowledge from the Lord", supposedly telling us what demons we needed to cast out. Looking back on it I seriously doubt that the Lord was speaking these words to anyone. Any physical or emotional problems were totally ignored – the answer was always a spiritual one as far as our doctrines and methods were concerned. My personal experience of panic attacks and subsequent "ministry" for them had given me grave doubts about the effectiveness of it all, but because I could see that this lady was in such a bad state I stayed with the others, praying desperately for God to help her. In the end they gave up on her, blaming her for lack of faith, with such a lack of compassion for her suffering that I was disturbed and angry, and determined to continue trying to help her. She lived in Cosham, not far from Nan and Pops, so I would secretly visit her whenever I was in the area. The outcome of all this was that I discovered that she was addicted to Ativan, a toxic kind of medication that had been given her for menopausal symptoms, and that the nightmares and panic attacks were all withdrawal symptoms when she tried to stop taking it. Nobody bothered to find any of this out when she first came for help to GP, and she had meekly submitted to Bee's authority, thinking that anything medical was irrelevant. She eventually did get off the medication, and found relative peace, but she never went back to Green Pastures, or to any other church as far as I know.

We began to realise that we were in a real spiritual battle. One night I woke up with an overpowering sensation of being smothered, and fighting for breath. With all my strength I let out a strangled cry of "Jesus!" and at once I could breathe again. We started having vivid dreams, one in particular that Robb had was of a woman with two dogs walking onto the land and leaving a gate open, through which a fire came and spread all over Green Pastures. I had a dream which I can remember in detail 24 years later. I was at Buckingham Palace, standing at the bottom of a grand staircase in my school uniform. The Royal family were upstairs, getting ready for a state occasion. A door opened, and Princess Diana started to come down the stairs, dressed in a tight gold dress, a tall gold crown, and extremely high heeled golden shoes. She got about a third of the way down when she stumbled, fell and lost her crown. Another door opened, and Sarah Ferguson, dressed in silver, with lower heels and a smaller silver crown, rushed down to help Diana, who turned around with a furious look, and smashed Sarah's crown from her head with the back of her hand. I am convinced that this was a prophetic dream on many levels – literal fulfilment came in the eventual divorces of Diana and Sarah from Princes Charles and Andrew, but we also felt it had a relevance to our situation at GP, as had Robb's dream. Bee's chosen name had been Diana (which others had changed to Bee) and I found out that the name Diana symbolised religion, which in the Bible was embodied in the ancient goddess worship of Diana of the Ephesians. She was often depicted as a huntress with two dogs – as in Robb's dream. The name Sarah symbolised the true Church, as Sarah was the wife of Abraham and mother of Isaac, so symbolically also the mother of all who are children of God by Faith. In my dream I was dressed in school uniform – and I was certainly learning so much through our time at G.P.

The conclusion we came to through all this was that Bee was dangerously wrong, and that we shouldn't be supporting her in what she was doing, and that if she carried on, God's work at GP would be destroyed. We felt God was saying that the true church should not try to help the religious establishment when it came into disrepute (lost its crown through vanity and excess and hypocrisy), or else it would suffer the same loss of authority and honour. Diana (Bee) was "reigning" at GP, God had blessed us with a Sarah, born there by His plan and purpose (certainly not ours!) We should stop trying to uphold Bee in what she was doing, and let God show us what to do about protecting His work there.

Some good things happened that summer. Nan and Pops were such a help with Sarah. As she grew they started babysitting more, and they enjoyed her so much. Liz and Dave, with Richard and Rachel, came to stay with us, and we had a good time together. The kids all got on really well, and Liz and I did too! We were trying to keep things normal for the girls, and had another holiday in Cornwall, which was lovely apart from Nicky getting another tummy bug from eating creamy, cheesy, garlicky potatoes at the same restaurant as the year before. One would think she would have developed an aversion to spuds or Cornwall from this, but she still loves both! However, back at green Pastures, everyone in the Fellowship was starting to detect that things were not as they should be between us and Bee and Lizzie. We were being excluded from almost everything that was going on, and we could see people in the fellowship coming and going from Bee and Lizzie's house without ever making an effort to come and see us. The hay barn was being revamped to use as another building to provide accommodation for visitors, but in spite of our having been instrumental in starting the work, the responsibility of finishing it was given to a young couple whom Bee was cultivating, and who treated us with extreme coolness, bordering on rudeness. We couldn't give the project as much time or energy as them because of Robb's work and our responsibilities with a new baby and two adolescent girls. We still kept trying to find out from Bee what it was that we had done to upset her, and offered frequent apologies for "anything we had done to offend her". This was all to no avail. By the end of the summer Robbie and I, Dave and Audrey, and Bee and Lizzie, had all been approached by some of the "pillars" of the fellowship, asked what was going on, and told that we, the leaders, must sort it out and put it right.

A very significant thing happened around this time. We got a phone call late at night from Ivy, who was very excited. She had been to a "Prayer for Israel" meeting in Denmead, and met there, for the first time, our Doctor's wife. Mrs. Goulder had given her an audio tape by Derek Prince, a well known and excellent Bible teacher who was based in Jerusalem. She told Ivy that she felt strongly led by God to give this to her, not knowing anything of her circumstances, or her link to Green Pastures. Ivy had taken it home and listened to it, then phoned us to say that we must listen to it straight away. We actually picked it up the next day and listened to it in the car on the way home, but had to play it again and again because what we were hearing was so relevant to what was happening at Green Pastures, and so potentially earth-shattering! In it Derek described the behaviour of someone who was being influenced by "Jezebel" – my old "friend" from Bill Subritsky's book! It could have been a description of Bee. He stated that wherever there was divisive behaviour, manipulation, domination, and intimidation, the spirit of witchcraft was in operation. One of the major manifestations of this was refusing to accept blame, reversing it so that any problem was turned against the one who pointed it out, and also lack of accountability. He also stated that the strongest of men often felt overwhelmed by this spirit, and ran from it. In the Bible, the story of Elijah running from Jezebel in 1 Kings chapter 19 was the original of this. Even after he had single-handedly defeated all the priests of Baal on Mount Carmel her threats intimidated him. It took great spiritual strength to oppose this spirit. We found out that Derek Prince had first hand experience of Ruth Heflin's Mount Zion Fellowship, the ministry Bee had been part of in Jerusalem, and where she had learned a lot of her doctrine and practice. We gave the tape to Dave and Audrey, with great trepidation, because we still didn't know if we could trust them not to go straight to Bee behind our back, which would have resulted in our being kicked out with no opportunity to address the problem at GP, and to be reconciled to a repentant Bee, which was our goal in all of this. Fortunately Dave and Audrey had a lot of respect for Derek Prince, listened to the tape, and recognised that God was speaking to us all through him. As a result they were now willing to admit that Bee was causing a lot of problems, and that they too needed to do something about it. At our next Leaders meeting, after a lot of prayer, we suggested that we should call a fast for the whole fellowship. We were led to this after reading the book of Joel, chapter 2. The only person that didn't see the need for this was Bee, of course! For the first time we actually overrode her authority and announced to the fellowship that we should all fast in some way during the last week of September, then at that week's Thursday night meeting we would see what the Lord had to say to everyone.

That week we felt the presence of God so strongly. Our daily scripture readings were totally relevant to our situation, and the same thing was happening to others in the fellowship, even though we all had completely independent Bible reading plans. Robbie and I faced the possibility that we could be kicked out of Green Pastures, and lose almost all we possessed. Every bit of our savings, and the money from selling our house in Purbrook, had gone on the refurbishment of Bethel. However, we knew that we couldn't be part of what Bee was up to, so we had to ask God to lead us, and trust Him that He would look after us whatever happened. The night of the meeting arrived. I felt strongly that I should take a bath before I went over to Beulah. I did so, trusting that there was a good reason! When I got out we prayed, again asking God to lead and guide us and keep us from doing or saying anything not of Him. For some reason we felt we should read Hebrews Chapter 10, which talked about joyfully losing possessions and not casting away one's confidence in God, so we were reassured that God knew how we felt and what we feared might happen. It also mentioned "having our bodies washed with clean water"! We went over to the meeting. A large number of the fellowship was present, and the meeting started as usual, with Bee leading and all of us praying for various things that she brought to our attention. No-one else did anything to take the control of the meeting away from Bee, but at 9.30 p.m. which was our usual finishing time, she had still said nothing about the reason for the meeting, in spite of knowing that everyone had been fasting for it. Terry, Lynne's sister, then stood up and said "When are we going to do what we said we would? I have to get home to my children and we have wasted the whole evening as far as I can see". What a relief! We hadn't wanted to undermine Bee in front of the fellowship, but at last she had been confronted by someone else. Some of the others then joined in, and told Robbie and I, Dave and Audrey, and Bee and Lizzie to go somewhere and sort things out between us, whilst they stayed behind and prayed. We got up and walked out of the room, and Dave and Audrey followed us, but as Bee and Lizzie came up to the door, after the other four of us had gone through it, it was slammed shut behind us, and we heard Bee telling the rest of the fellowship, in a strident voice, that we were traitors who wanted to get rid of her, and begging them to help her! We stood there, totally shocked. After a couple of minutes I said to Robbie "You cannot stand here and let this happen, she is lying to them and leading them astray!" He hesitated for a second, and then opened the door, walked in, pointed to Bee, and said in a strong voice "Woman, in the name of Jesus, be quiet!" It was as if she was a pricked balloon, she seemed to physically shrink, and then she ran out of the back door of Beulah. Lizzie followed her. Helena, the young woman Bee had been cultivating, and who had been helping revamp the hay barn with her husband, started shrieking at the top of her voice. It was horrible. I really can't remember much of what happened after that, but people went home, and when Robbie and I got back to Bethel we were shaking and numb.

17 – Sent to Coventry

The next morning we tried to go over and talk to Bee, but she refused to see us. The following Sunday we held our usual meeting, but it was awful, because no-one wanted to talk about what had happened. I think that was probably the last meeting of the fellowship. We tried over and over to meet with Bee, to no avail, she was implacable. We phoned, called in at the house, sent gifts, wrote letters, begged her forgiveness for upsetting her, everything we could think of to move forward, but nothing worked. We tried to visit members of the fellowship to explain to them what had been going on, but the ones we did see became angry with us, and stopped speaking to us too! We gradually realised that our character and motives had been so blackened, behind our backs, that if God didn't tell them what was going on we were wasting our time trying to, and might as well keep quiet, whatever they thought of us. The worst, for me, was that Lynne and her husband, whom we had felt really close to, turned against us. However, God knew our hearts and we had to trust Him alone. Through all of this we were still trying desperately to be reconciled to Bee and Lizzie, so that we could bring the Trust and the fellowship back into order by getting Bee to be accountable, but it was to no avail. We were praying and fasting constantly, and tried everything we could think of. We asked the Pastor who had been leading our Praise and Worship evenings, whose church was becoming quite prominent in the area, if he would mediate. We knew he was a friend of Bee's and would not be seen as being biased towards us, but he refused to get involved. We later found out that he was, at that time, in the midst of a seven year affair with someone from his church. I guess he thought that people in glass houses shouldn't throw stones! Every so-called Christian leader in the area that we asked said the same. All we wanted was to follow Biblical steps to reconciliation, and take someone with us because she would not speak to us on our own. The one person who reluctantly agreed to come with us was Paul Pillai, who was briefly in England at the time. We went over to Bee and Lizzie's house with him, and Bee simply stood in the kitchen with her back turned to us and refused to speak. Paul just giggled nervously and tried to placate her, apologetic for his audacity in confronting her. He was under her thumb, too! We couldn't believe it! Here was a man who had a huge ministry, a Bible School which was training and sending out hundreds of missionaries into the most hostile areas of northern India to plant churches, and an orphanage rescuing abandoned, starving children in New Delhi. He had been beaten and slandered, and physically battled against militant Moslems and Hindus, who were trying to stop him spreading the Gospel, and had even seen hordes of angels come to his rescue, but he was totally intimidated by Bee. We were absolutely gutted and so disillusioned.

Bee's next step was to "close the fellowship" – she just dumped everyone! Robb and Dave got together and decided reluctantly that they should consult a lawyer to find out what the implications were as far as the Trust was concerned. They went to a solicitor based in Petersfield, who had become a Christian through an FGBMFI rally in Portsmouth Guildhall. He didn't want to take the case, because he knew so many of the involved parties, but advised them that they were right to seek legal help, because they had a responsibility as Trustees to see that everything was dealt with properly. He referred them to another Christian solicitor, who told them vehemently that they must do something to combat what he said was "spiritual tyranny". He said they should call an extraordinary meeting of the Trust, which they did, sending out formal letters, worded by him, to all the Trustees. This, in fact, would be the first proper Trustees Meeting there had been since Robb had become a Trustee, which in itself meant the Trust had not been run on legal lines. We realised that things would not be straightforward when Jonathan McMahon indicated that he would be at the meeting. He had not been sent a letter because he had resigned some months previously. Robb phoned him, and asked what was going on, and was told that he "couldn't recall whether he had resigned or not". All of us had heard his letter of resignation read out! Had Bee made it up, or was he an out and out liar? What were they up to?

After the fellowship was closed, we started to attend the Anglican church in the village, and got to know the vicar and some of the congregation. There were some lovely people there, and some of them were obviously Christians. So much for Bee's explanation that they didn't want to know us at GP because of "the offence of the Gospel"! We realised that the offence had nothing to do with the Gospel, but everything to do with Bee and her isolation of Lizzie. I took Sarah to the local Mother and Toddler Group, and in chatting to the women there, found out that we were the last in a series of people who had moved into GP and been squeezed out because of falling foul of Bee. We worked out that this was the 7th time it had happened if we included Win and George. One lady, who ran the village Antique Shop, brought her grandchildren to the group, and told me that she used to get regular visits from a young pregnant woman who lived at GP with her husband. This woman would just come into the shop and cry brokenheartedly. Percy, the vicar, was such a blessing to me. When Robb was at work and the girls were at school I would often feel very lonely and vulnerable, because of seeing many people that we knew going to Bee and Lizzie's house, and never attempting to come over and see how we were. It was very painful. Percy would take his dog for a walk along the footpath to the vineyard that ran behind Bethel and would pop in to make sure I was OK. He also wrote us a lovely letter assuring us of his prayers during this difficult time. Vicky, our neighbour, invited me for coffee regularly, and she was a great listener, so a great help to me, because I found myself talking a great deal! We met Win and George when shopping one day, and went to their flat for a coffee afterwards. They were so sweet, telling us that they had gone through a similar thing, although without the financial commitment. As soon as they had dared to call Bee's methods into question they had been gradually excluded and eventually forced to leave. They had realised that there was no point telling us about it because we wouldn't have listened, Bee had blackened their characters before us!

One thing they did tell us reinforced our conviction that it was a spiritual battle we were in. Apparently they had found out that Bee would eavesdrop their private conversations, standing under the high, opened window next to their dining table, where they would sit for their meals and devotions. We realised that this was the exact place that we had put our telephone after the renovations, and I always felt as if someone was listening in when I was on the phone. Added to this I remembered a dream I had before we moved in to Bethel, where an evil looking clown had been standing in the garden and looking up at this very same window with absolute malevolence. One evening, when a group of us were in Bethel, walking up and down and praying in tongues for the situation at GP, Dave, without any knowledge of this, stopped at the telephone and felt he had to pray for God's protection in this very area. When we were talking afterwards he said he had walked past the phone and been overcome with a feeling of panic and claustrophobia, likening it to a time when he was a mile underground in a mine under the sea and suddenly realised where he was! Things like this seemed to happen all the time. A situation would arise, and then someone would call us with a scripture that was perfectly relevant, or we would read a passage in the morning and it would be totally fulfilled during the day. One day I looked out of the window and saw Bee's son's car outside our house, for some reason I looked at the number plate and the letters LYA jumped out at me – phonetically it spelt "liar". There were certainly a few of those around! Someone called us and said they had a dream that two black and white sheepdogs had come onto the land to try to bring the flock into order. Later that day two men in black suits with white shirts, one of whom was Roger Teale, came to visit Bee. We saw them get out of the car and knew they were the "sheepdogs". We found out later that Bee had completely rejected their help. I began to find obscure words running through my mind which I had to look up in a dictionary, finding that they described what was going on at that time. Two particularly stand out – Sycophants, and Nepotism, and I found out that they were two things that typified a "dictatorship" situation. This was confirmed, around that time, when I was watching a documentary about Mussolini, and these two words were used constantly! The dictator surrounds himself with sycophants, or "yes-men", giving them all the positions of power, which is nepotism (classically these are family members, whose unquestioning loyalty and "controllability", whatever the situation, can be depended upon). As soon as one of these people begins to show signs of thinking independently, they start being edged out by the others, and eventually are totally excluded, and in some cases killed! I knew this must be God because I hadn't a clue what these words meant before I looked them up. It was a perfect example of the Holy Spirit giving wisdom as it was needed in a special situation, and very faith inspiring.

Behind the footpath, which ran from the village to the vineyard, behind Bethel and all of Green Pastures, there was a huge wheat field. The wheat had all been harvested in August, and during the week that we fasted and then confronted Bee the farmer was burning off the stubble, which was spectacular. The weather was warm and dry, so fierce fires ran quickly around the field, giving off huge plumes of smoke that drifted across to us. During the weeks after that he ploughed the field, then tilled it, and eventually sowed winter wheat. Every time something was happening in the field there seemed to be something significant going on at Green Pastures, and we realised that this could be prophetic symbolism. God was producing spiritual bread at GP, just as the farmer was producing wheat to make actual bread. This involved hard work, and in the spiritual sense, pain, because "we are God's field". The burning of stubble, ploughing up the ground, removing obstacles, and sowing seed to produce a harvest are all pictures of God's work in us. God was speaking to us in everything. We felt so safe, in spite of all that might happen, because He let us know constantly that He knew exactly what we were going through. One funny thing that happened to me was that I was driving behind a van with the logo "Folly Fires" written on it. I felt it was significant, and looked up the word "Folly" in the dictionary, finding that one of the definitions was "a costly and foolish undertaking; unwise investment or expenditure". I felt God was saying that He was going to destroy the "follies" that people had built in His name. What Bee had "built" at GP wasn't his idea, it was hers. Lizzie had dedicated her land to Him, and He needed it for His work to be done there. He also was probably telling us that we had invested in a "folly", but He also reminded us that whatever we lost in all of this, we had given it as if it was directly to Him with pure hearts and motives, and He would always more than repay us.

A very significant thing happened that October. FGBMFI had organised a conference at the local Holiday Inn (which later became the Marriott Hotel, North Harbour). A group known as the School of Ministry were invited, and there was a week of teaching, prophecy, and praise and worship. It was almost like a travelling road show, gathering people as it went along. Most of them were based in America, but there were also people from South Africa, Zimbabwe, Scotland, England, and elsewhere. The leaders of the group were a couple from South Africa, James and Abigail Von Welk, an American pastor called Steve Chase, and an English guy called Gerald Vane, who was based in upstate New York. Robb went along to the first session, which was in the evening. I was in bed when he came home, but was woken up, as he came into our bedroom, by a sensation of beams of light "bouncing" around the room, almost as if he was swinging a filigree lantern around. I sat up and asked him what on earth was going on. He was bubbling over, and told that me I must come with him the next day, which was a full day of teaching. The next morning we arranged for Sarah to go to Nan and Pops so that I could be at the meetings. Nicky and Amy were at school, so that wasn't a problem. It was such an amazing day. It started off with Gerald Vane's baby daughter being dedicated to the Lord. She had been born recently in England, and was called Sarah Elizabeth! I was immediately so excited. We found out later that Gerald and his wife, Wanda, had four children, all born on different continents, and that God had shown them that their lives would be prophetic for the places they were born. This was exactly what God had shown us for our Sarah!

The teaching was so refreshing and exciting, and we could see that all of them were deferring to one another in a way that we had never seen before, giving each other preference and respect. James and Abigail led the worship, singing songs that they had written, which were mostly scripture set to music and were really inspiring. They welcomed any other musicians present to join them, and it was a wonderful time. During one meeting Gerald called Robbie up to the platform and told him that he felt he had a prophecy to give, and to "go for it"! Robb started to speak, waffled on about something vaguely scriptural, and then stopped. Gerald just said to him "Now really prophesy", and suddenly Robb's voice literally rang out with a powerful message about God "blasting away the veneer that was hiding His beautiful timber", meaning in one sense the religious pseudo-spirituality that people had used to cover the true Gospel, but also in a personal sense, getting His people back to their true selves by removing all the masks they hid behind. I hardly recognised Robb! After the meeting he spoke to Gerald, and they realised that Robbie had been the inspiration for James and Abigail to write one of their best songs "Stand to Attention all you in Heaven". Robb's conversion testimony had been put into the international FGBMFI magazine, "Voice", along with a formal picture of him, saluting, dressed in his white Bermuda Police Dress Uniform. Gerald had seen this, and thinking that he bore a resemblance to James, had sent it to him in South Africa from America, with the words "Heaven stands to attention" written next to it. When Robbie was telling him about us, he mentioned Bermuda and Gerald exclaimed "You're the guy I saw in the "Voice" magazine!" We talked for ages, sharing a bit more about what was happening to us, and about our Sarah Elizabeth's birth at Green Pastures, and its significance, and we learnt a bit about him. It was a real and immediate "heart connection". Robbie knew he was "one in the Spirit" with Gerald. The School Of Ministry team were heading for Israel soon after leaving Portsmouth, and Gerald invited Robb to go with them, telling him that he felt strongly that it was right for him to go. We were really excited. We realised that Robb had been gradually crushed, spiritually and emotionally, by Bee's treatment over the past couple of years, and that something wonderful had happened when Gerald called him up to prophesy. As he spoke out he broke free from whatever had tried to stop him from being all God had called him to be. It was an almost tangible deliverance – and a true one this time!

One not so good thing happened during that conference. Pete Sharp had been Robb's friend since he joined FGBMFI on our return from Bermuda six years before, and was President to Robb's vice-president of the organisation. They had worked together, played together, travelled together and spoken at dinners together, and knew each other well – or so we thought. Bee and Lizzie came to some of the meetings, and had been at the one where Robb had prophesied, and I knew that Bee knew that she had lost control of Robb. We had seen her going from one person to another, speaking to them in a way we somehow knew was defaming us, and one of the people she influenced was Pete Sharp. He came up to Robb, and in an angry voice said "Robbie, how could you do this to two poor old ladies!?" Robb replied "Oh, come on Pete, you know me!" to which he replied "I thought I did", and turned away from him. It was like a knife in our hearts. We realised that we couldn't rely on anyone to stand with us in our situation. As well as this, other Christians that we had known for ages started to "blank" us, or said things like "We're not going to take sides" and then refused to listen to anyone but Bee! We felt so lonely, but thanked God for the encouragement of the School Of Ministry team.

Although the thought of going to Israel was so exciting, and, I felt, a lifeline for Robb, there were some major hindrances to deal with. Firstly, we had no spare money! We had given it all to Green Pastures in one way or another. Secondly, he couldn't take time off work because he had no holidays or overtime left, for the same reason. He had used it all up on being at GP meetings, or so we thought! The other major problem was that the extraordinary Trustees meeting was set for a date when he would be in Israel. We prayed hard about it, and came to the conclusion that he had to go, almost for his own survival. He dug around and discovered that he had a couple of days overtime owed for working bank holidays, and that if he changed around some days off and combined them with the overtime days it would give him exactly the six days he needed. We eventually scraped together enough for his fare, trusting God to supply spending money, and then, out of the blue, we started to get letters and cards with cheques and money in them! Eventually our expense was covered, right down to the last penny of spending money, and we knew God wanted him to go, in spite of the Trustee's meeting. Our confirmation was that Dave agreed that Robb should go, in spite of the fact that it would leave him to face the meeting alone. On my 40th birthday, the 2nd November, I drove him to Heathrow to join the team flying to Tel Aviv. He came home a different man.

The scheduled Trustees meeting never happened (as a result of Bee sabotaging it, I'm sure). All of the Trustees (including the somehow reinstated McMahon) said they wouldn't or couldn't consider meeting. As I mentioned before, there hadn't ever been a proper Trust meeting that I could remember, so the Trust was never run legally, but this was ridiculous. They wouldn't even meet to sort out a major problem. Bee's next step was to put padlocks on Beulah, so that we couldn't get in! In spite of finding all this on his return, Robbie was absolutely overflowing with joy and excitement. He had met some wonderful people, some of them whose friendship we still value greatly, and some who inspired and influenced us in a life-changing way. As well as Gerald and Wanda Vane and James and Abigail Van Welk, there was Francois Du Toit, whose teaching on righteousness has been a great blessing to us. Steve Chase and his future wife Marietje were on that trip. Steve and his friend Mike Engler became close and encouraging friends to us, as well as inspirational teachers. Susan and Jack Pryor became close friends, as did Angelo and Yvette Parisi, who were married on the Mount of Olives during that trip. Gerald was such an encouragement to Robb, drawing out of him gifts of prophecy and teaching that had been lying dormant under the "veneer" of the Brethren and the domination of Green Pastures. Also whilst Robb was away he felt God speaking to him, telling him that America would figure in his future in a major way. There was an immediate fulfilment of this by a phone call I received whilst he was away. It was from an American cop called Dennis Smith, who was the President of the "Alaska Peace Officers for Christ" organisation. He was calling from his home in Anchorage, Alaska, and wondered if Robb would come and speak at their conference the following June. We were so excited by this. The scripture "You will be my witnesses in Jerusalem, Judaea and Samaria and in the uttermost parts of the earth" seemed to be literally coming to pass in Robb's life! We delightedly accepted the invitation, learning that the Peace Officers would pay both our fares to Anchorage.

Gerald and Wanda came to stay with us at Bethel, with their four children, soon after the return from Israel. Fitting all of us into our 3-bedroomed cottage was a bit of a challenge, but it was a very significant visit, establishing a friendship that would change our lives. We thought that Gerald might mediate with Bee, as we found out that they knew each other from the time they were both at Ruth Heflin's Mount Zion fellowship in Jerusalem, but he, too, didn't want to get involved. We didn't think too badly of him in this, because he didn't really know us well, or the situation. I quite liked Gerald, although he could be very bombastic, and this, combined with his height and size, could be quite intimidating. However, I loved what he had done for Robbie, and found his teaching absolutely gripping. I wasn't too happy when he lapsed into "pentecostalese", preaching in a peculiar style and voice typical of some of the wild preachers we had seen on American TV "God Channels". They explained it as "the anointing coming upon them". Spare me! I wondered if Jesus or Paul sounded like that when they preached in the power of the Holy Spirit. I don't think so somehow. I also had a few misgivings about Wanda, as she wasn't very open or friendly, a bit aloof in fact, and the kids weren't very well behaved, but we definitely wanted to get to know them all better, and felt that we had some kind of special connection with them.

Christmas that year was very strange. We sent cards and presents to Bee and Lizzie, but didn't even get an acknowledgement from them, and Lizzie actually came over to Bethel on Sarah's 1st Birthday to return our gifts. She almost weakened when she saw Sarah toddling to the door in her lovely little red birthday frock, and I asked her to come in, but she wouldn't. I was so saddened by this, we loved Lizzie, and increasingly felt that she was being used by Bee, who had finally persuaded her into thinking that she would have no-one if she didn't have her. I think we had Christmas Dinner at "The Haven" that year, because the atmosphere at GP was so awful. It should have been a joyful time of celebrating the birth of two very special babies, but it was very subdued. Life went on, with visits from various people with "messages from the Lord" for us. One man, Mike Harrison, was around a lot. We had taken an instant dislike to him when he first appeared on the scene some months earlier. Bee had invited him to speak at a meeting (after consulting the other elders about it and then ignoring their prayerful counsel not to). He had toadied up to Bee immediately, and had been very dismissive of Robb and Dave. He came over to us and said that the Lord had told him we must get out of Bethel, because "Christians didn't have any rights". We knew he was a dishonest man, because our friend Diane knew of him. He had ripped off a minister friend of hers in Somerset with the result that the minister's family were on the bread-line. We knew and trusted Diane, and we instinctively didn't trust Mike Harrison, and we felt he was definitely up to something with Bee. Others came and went. Pete Sharpe actually relented and came to see us with his wife, Mary, and after we explained to them what had really happened he reluctantly agreed to talk to Bee and try for a reconciliation. The result was that he conveyed to us that if we got out of Bethel we would be given £10,000 to compensate for what we had put into GP. We had actually given well over twice this amount, and were never motivated by money anyway, so this offer made no difference to us whatsoever, we only wanted to do what God wanted, whether by staying or going. We continued to have Thursday night prayer meetings, with just a few people coming along to pray with us for the situation in general, and for us in particular. I had misgivings about the wisdom of holding these meetings in Bethel, because I felt it would be seen as an effort to start up an alternative fellowship. Some of the ones who came definitely had that in mind, but we weren't having any of that! We would just pray in tongues until we felt that God gave us specifics to pray for or against, and sometimes it was inspirational. We really knew the power and leading of the Holy Spirit in doing this, being given insights and scripture references that were so accurate. This was very reassuring, because it showed us that God knew exactly what was going on and was directing us. Other things happened during this time of "waiting on God". Nicky's bike was stolen from our garage, and it felt like a confirmation of our vulnerability. We tried going to Pete Sharpe's "Living Waters" Fellowship in Waterlooville, but I was reduced to sobbing by an angry Jim Latham shouting at me and accusing us of destroying Green Pastures. We didn't go there again.

18 – In the Time of Winter Snow...

In February 1987 we had one of the worst spells of snow in living memory. The girls loved it, and had a great time falling into deep drifts along the lane behind the school house, building snowmen, trekking through knee deep snow down to the school bus, and having epic snowball fights at school and at home. The village looked absolutely beautiful, and some of the villagers were even skiing down the hill opposite our house! On February 28th Robbie was shovelling snow with our neighbour, Bill. As they shovelled, he looked up and saw the postman picking his way on foot through the deep snow in the lane. Robb knew in his heart that there would be a letter for us, and that it would be bad news. He was right, it was our eviction notice. Through a series of totally illegal moves they had come to the position of supposedly being able to tell us to get out of Bethel. It was addressed to Robb, and the wording was, more or less, "Since there is no longer a fellowship at Green Pastures, you can no longer be considered an elder. Since you are no longer an elder, you can no longer be a Trustee, and since you are no longer a Trustee, you can no longer be a tenant of Bethel." Here it was - "In the day of winter snow, shall we stay or shall we go?" None of this had been done legally or through acceptable channels, so we decided to ignore it. This was with deep sadness and trepidation, I might add, and was only to try again to force some kind of communication and reconciliation, not to grasp onto what wasn't ours to grasp. From then on, though, the gloves were off as far as Bee was concerned. She phoned the Chief Constable and complained about

Robbie "squatting on their property". Robbie explained to him what was happening and he understood our position, but advised that we should just get out and cut our losses, saying that we might be eligible for a Police house if we did. This was slightly reassuring, knowing that we wouldn't be homeless, but still a heart breaking prospect to all of us. Bee and Lizzie returned our rent each time we tried to pay it. I suppose they didn't want us to look as if we were doing the right thing. A good friend, Hannie Smithson, called us and said that she had a "word" for us. It was from 2 Samuel 5:24 "When you hear a rustling in the mulberry leaves, the move is on", meaning that we shouldn't move until God showed us to go, and that we would have a sign. There certainly weren't many of any kind of leaves around at that point, so we knew it probably wasn't yet, and it confirmed that we were doing the right thing in ignoring the eviction notice. Although we knew that all this had been done against us illegally, we felt strongly that we ourselves shouldn't make any legal moves against Green Pastures. Having been assured by our solicitor that we were on safe and strong legal ground, we felt that was all we needed to do. This too was confirmed when we read 1 Corinthians 6, where Paul was berating the Christians in Corinth for taking each other to a heathen court and not settling their differences in a Godly way amongst themselves. We just had to sit tight and wait for God to tell us if and when to make a move.

Our invitation to go to Alaska in early June of that year was formalised, and we received our tickets. We decided to scrape the money together to buy another ticket, and take Sarah with us. Nanny and Grandma were going to look after Nicky and Amy, moving into Bethel and splitting the 3 weeks we would be away between them, but Sarah would only be 18 months old, and it didn't seem fair to leave her, especially with my Mum, as she hardly knew her. By the time we flew to Anchorage we were despairing of the situation at GP. We hadn't made any progress whatsoever, Bee and Lizzie were still not speaking to us, and the atmosphere was so tense and antagonistic that I was reluctant to even step out of the house. We made tentative enquiries about a Police House, and were told that we might be able to get one in Cowplain. Percy, the vicar, was still calling in to make sure I was OK, and our few "prayer partners" continued to come up to Bethel on Thursday evenings, but it didn't seem that we were getting anywhere. The one thing we did do outside was to replant a fig tree that we had put into the garden at Bethel. It wasn't thriving, and we decided to put it against the south facing wall of "The Ark". We had planted it as a prophetic thing, since the fig tree symbolises God's people and we wanted to see it growing and bearing fruit at Green Pastures, not shrivelling up and dying. We did wait until we saw Bee and Lizzie going out before we moved it, however! The trip to Alaska was such a welcome escape for us. We flew British Airways, which was the only airline going there direct from England. It was a long nine hour flight, going over the North Pole, landing at Anchorage and then flying on to Tokyo. Robb was invited up to the flight deck as we flew over the Pole – what an experience. I could have gone up, but Sarah was sleeping at the time, and I didn't want to disturb her – one of the few regrets of my life! The plane was full of lovely little old Japanese tourists, who made such a fuss of Sarah that she was entertained for the whole trip. They made her origami animals out of sweet wrappers and gave her little presents, they took her to see their friends in other parts of the plane, and played "peepo" with her over the back of the seats, it was great. We just relaxed, enjoyed the Japanese food and a few glasses of wine, and looked out of the window at the snowy wastes below us! Landing at Anchorage was awesome. The airport was surrounded on all sides by beautiful snow-capped mountains. Dennis Smith, the cop I had spoken to when Robb was in Israel, came to meet us in his gorgeous old Cadillac. We were staying with him and his wife Esther on the outskirts of the city. Their house was lovely, it was new, made of russet coloured timber, glass fronted and with big skylights. Dennis was a dog handler and had a huge German Shepherd that he was training, which took me aback, but he was such a well trained and placid dog that I lost any misgivings I had about Sarah being around him. I was a bit concerned by the guns lying around in Dennis's office upstairs, but decided to just keep Sarah downstairs and out of there rather than worry whether Dennis had remembered to put them away. Esther was really sweet. She was Mexican, and told us that Alaska is full of Mexicans, mostly illegal immigrants escaping to the last frontier. She cooked us some amazing meals and taught me a lot, too, for instance what to do with a tomatillo (I'd never even heard of them!) and she gave me an Alaskan cookbook which I still use to this day. The recipe for our most favourite family meal – Chicken Enchiladas – comes from that cookbook. Dennis and Esther had two children, Yolanda and Sean, both friendly and fun. They all made us so welcome, as did the other Christian cops and their wives, inviting us for BBQs, lending us a Winnebago, taking us up in their planes, you name it! The conference Robbie was speaking at was on the middle Saturday we were there, but he also spoke at a few Full Gospel dinner meetings. At one of those, where Robbie was the main speaker, we heard the testimony of a young guy who had nursed his wife through terminal cancer in a cabin in the Alaskan wilderness. What he and his wife, had gone through, before she died in his arms, and the way God had been so real to them, made me realise that our trials at GP were truly trivial in the great scheme of things, and I was totally humbled. Robb wondered how he could ever follow a testimony like that, but of course, what he shared was a great blessing to others that had heard the other guy's story before.

We had some memorable trips whilst we were there. We took the borrowed Winnebago on a trip to Valdez, on Prince William Sound, taking in the famous Alaska oil pipeline, which runs to Valdez from Prudhoe Bay on the North Coast. The scenery was incredible. We went over snowy mountain passes, through wilderness and deep forest, past amazing waterfalls and rivers, and saw moose, eagles and bears. The pipeline was spectacular, stretching for hundreds and hundreds of miles across the wilderness. At one point we stopped for a good look at it, and met two bikers who were riding their gorgeous Harley-Davidson Electraglides cross-country all the way from Ontario, heading for the West Coast. Valdez looked like one of the sea-ports where prospectors landed during the Gold Rush. There was a high, tree covered mountain behind the town, with waterfalls cascading down, and a honeycomb of docks, piers and moorings for the mass of little fishing boats which sailed from there to catch the abundant local seafood, which they sold from the boats. They had everything you could wish for, including huge lobsters and crabs, all as fresh as they could be. We bought King Crab and shrimp, which tasted out of this world. The end of the pipeline couldn't be seen from the town, and everything looked absolutely pristine, so we were very sad when the Exxon Valdez tanker leaked millions of gallons of oil into Prince William Sound two years later, in 1989, and damaged so much of that beautiful environment.

Another trip we took was to "Beautiful Downtown Talkeetna". One of Dennis's friends had a light aircraft, and offered to take us to see Mount McKinley (now Denali), the highest mountain in America. Unfortunately, on the afternoon we went, the weather was too bad to actually get close to the mountain, and the nearest we could get was to a little town called Talkeetna. It took us over 2 hours to get there, and we flew over wilderness for 99.9% of the way. One of the most spectacular things we flew over was a glacier. I couldn't believe how massive it was, and the amazing deep turquoise colour of the crevasses which covered it. Somewhere, frozen in time, in that glacier is a paper sack with my lunch in it. Esther had treated us to a delicious Mexican lunch before we took off, and sadly the bumpy ride made me throw it all up! Talkeetna itself was a real frontier town, the last outpost of "civilisation" where mountaineers stocked up with supplies before beginning their climb of Mount McKinley. It was also the home of the world famous "Mountain Mother Competition", and the annual "Alaska Moose Dropping Contest". We bought some great souvenirs there, Mosquito Traps that looked like mouse traps, and Jewellery made from lacquered moose poop (yes, you can polish a turd!) I bought some for my friend Thelma, so that she could offend some of the middle class religious types at her Anglican church by telling them her earrings were made out of shit!

We took day trips to lots of places not too far from Anchorage, and saw so much. We went to look for Beluga Whales passing through a sea channel nearby, but unfortunately there weren't any that day. We went to an Information Centre near the Portage Glacier, which was really interesting, as it gave the history and geography of the area, plus all the local wildlife. In the Matanuska Valley we saw vegetables bigger than we had ever seen before. Apparently they grow to a huge size because of the rich ground, fertilised by the retreating glaciers, and because of 24 hour daylight in the summer, which makes them grow at an incredible rate. The midnight sun was something we found really hard to get used to. Further north it was daylight all night long, and of course in winter it was dark all day long, but in Anchorage it wasn't quite so extreme. At about 2 am there was a sort of twilight period before it started to get light again, but as the school holidays had started kids were still playing out in the street at 11 pm. We even saw an Ice-Cream Truck opposite Dennis and Esther's house, selling popsicles at 10.30 pm, and Esther went to the supermarket at 2 am one night, to buy a mouse trap! This was before Sunday trading was legal in the U.K., and many years before 24 hour shopping, so we found it very strange. We loved the supermarkets, as they stocked loads of American food that we hadn't seen since we left Bermuda, plus they had wonderful buffet bars selling various Salads and Soups, and this was of course long before we got them in England. The weather was pleasantly warm when we were there, but the mosquito season came with the warm weather, and it really was a plague! Robbie went out on patrol with Dennis one night, and almost got eaten alive by the pesky critters when he and Dennis staked out in a wood, waiting to catch some criminal. The violent crime and murder rate in Alaska was the highest of any U.S. state, as was the number of cops killed on duty. Dennis put it down to the "last frontier" status of the place, meaning that there were many fugitives from justice there, as well as people who had tried everything and had nothing left to lose. It was certainly an amazing place and we met some amazing people. I'll never forget the guy who told us he had met an angel. He looked almost like a hobo, but apparently was an ex Gold-Prospector and was very wealthy. He had visited London some time in the past, and before he left Alaska he had booked into what sounded like a grand hotel, only to find when he arrived that it was a sleazy old place where prostitutes took their clients. He went to his room, thinking he would look for somewhere else the next day after a good night's sleep, but had felt so uncomfortable and disturbed by the "dirty" feeling in the room, that he knew he couldn't sleep there and decided to go out and get a drink before rethinking his plan. As he left the Hotel, he saw an old lady sitting begging on the steps, so gave her a generous tip, telling her to go and get something to eat, then walked off. He didn't go back for hours, not finding anywhere else to stay, and being very reluctant to return. When he was desperate for sleep, he went back, and to his surprise the old lady was still sitting on the steps. He smiled at her, but then, as he went past her, she said "Your room is clean now, you will be able to sleep", then she stood up and he saw she was 9 feet tall! He said that he was so shocked he couldn't remember what happened next, but when he looked again, she had gone – he couldn't see where or how. He went back to his room, which felt totally different, and he slept like a baby.

The conference went well, and Robbie was very well received, although the feeling still lingered that people we were meeting had probably experienced the stark realities of life in ways we hadn't even dreamed of. The whole trip was a blessing. We felt loved and respected, we were spoilt and feted, and we knew God was in all of it. Dennis and Esther were going through a church situation very similar to our Green Pastures experience. They had been part of a group of Christians who had all given sacrificially to build a beautiful new Church to house their growing congregation. They had all helped practically, as well as financially, to build it, and it was their spiritual home. Shortly before we were invited to go to Alaska a few of the congregation had been recruited by a cultish group from the Southern U.S., led by a guy called Earl Paulk. To cut a long story short, this cult gradually took over the church and congregation, and when we arrived Dennis and Esther were on the point of leaving, with heavy hearts. We actually went to the church with them and were pounced on by some of the Paulk groupies, who told us that God had sent us there so that we could take "the message" back to the UK. Not on your life, mate. I actually read one of his books and got such a creepy feeling about it that I was never remotely tempted to follow it up. We also went to the mega-church that looked as if it was going to be Dennis and Esther's new "home" and it was good. They met in a huge warehouse, which had a coffee bar where the congregation could get great coffee at any time before, during or after the service! It was so relaxed and informal, I loved it. We were able to encourage our new friends that what they were going through was going on all over the world, and had always been a tactic of the enemy. I had been reading about similar "take-overs" ever since things started to go wrong at GP, and realised that our experience was typical of the church's experience through the ages. There would always be pioneers and settlers, one group moving into the future and into inevitable change under the guidance of the Holy Spirit, and the others grabbing onto the status quo by refusing to change and making rules and regulations to try and control everything and everyone else. By their very nature, the pioneers would be moving on, and the settlers staying put, physically, mentally and spiritually. It was Jezebel again, trying to kill Elijah, the true voice of God.

We had one last blessing as we arrived at the airport to fly home. One of the Full Gospel guys met us with a present – a huge King Salmon! He had caught it a couple of days previously, gutted it, cleaned it, wrapped it, and frozen it so that we could take it home with us. We were so touched by the love, hospitality, and generosity of everyone we had met, and were really sad to be leaving them. We said goodbye to Dennis and Esther, but with the prospect of seeing them again, as they were planning a trip to Europe, and would love to be able to stay with us when they were in England. The flight home was long and dreary. Fortunately for us Sarah slept a lot. We were both tired and so full of conflicting emotions. We couldn't wait to see Nicky and Amy, but were dreading going back to the situation at Green Pastures. As we had feared, nothing had changed apart from Bee's increasingly nasty efforts to force us to go. No-one had spoken to my Mum all the time she was there, and she had been very lonely. One day, as she was walking down to the village whilst the girls were at school, she saw Lizzie coming towards her. Her heart had sunk, because she didn't know whether to greet her or cross over the road to avoid her. Suddenly, into her mind came the opening words of an old hymn, and she felt peace, knowing that God was with her. When she looked again she realised it wasn't Lizzie after all! When we looked up the words in my old Methodist Hymn Book we couldn't believe how appropriate and comforting they were to all of us.

> In Heavenly Love abiding, no change my heart shall fear,
> And safe is this confiding, for nothing changes here,
> The storm may roar without me,
> my heart might low be laid,
> But God is round about me, and can I be dismayed?
> Wherever He may guide me, no want shall turn me back,
> My shepherd is beside me, and nothing shall I lack.
> His wisdom ever waketh, His eye is never dim,
> He knows the way He taketh, and I will walk with Him.
> Green pastures are before me,
> which yet I have not seen.
> Bright skies will soon be o'er me where the dark
> clouds have been.
> My hope I cannot measure, my path to Life is free,
> My saviour has my treasure, and He will walk with me.

When I read these words, I somehow felt that the "Green Pastures that were before us" were going to be in America, and knew, with a quiet sense of excitement, that the adventure would carry on, whatever happened to us in England.

19 – The Rustling of the Mulberry Leaves

On the Thursday after our return we had our usual prayer meeting, but the atmosphere was very subdued, and when we discussed what to do next we realised that everyone was giving up hope of the situation ever changing. Someone read out another scripture they felt was for us "He who goes out weeping bearing precious seed, will return with joy, bearing sheaves" Psalm 126 v 6. A couple of days after that, I was walking Sarah down to the village in her pram when I saw one of our neighbours trying to cut up and move a tree that had fallen over in her garden. I called to her to ask what had happened, and she said "Oh it just fell over, I guess it was weakened by old age, Mulberry trees tend to do that, you know". No, we didn't know, but we did know that it could be our sign to move out of Bethel. This could be the fulfilment of the scripture given to us about the "rustling in the mulberry leaves", these leaves had certainly rustled! Only days later we were offered a house in Cowplain; number 23 Wheatsheaf Drive. It was perfect. It had 4 bedrooms, an enclosed garden, and was a short distance from both of the schools Nicky and Amy were attending. Even the carpets were the same colour as the new ones we had put in Bethel, and all our furnishings matched the décor. It seemed that scriptures we had been given all came together. Not only had the mulberry leaves rustled – we had been provided with a home, fulfilling the promise in Psalm 23 that God would always provide us with a dwelling place – this was number 23! We had just been given Psalm 126 v 6 – telling us we would be bearing sheaves (a harvest) and the house was on Wheatsheaf Drive! It was hard to leave the lovely (and expensive) things we had put into Bethel, such as the Aga, the Wood Stove, and the beautiful bay window overlooking the valley, but my first and biggest struggle was leaving the curtains from that window! They often seemed to blend with the evening skies they framed, and I knew God had found them for me. I was praying and feeling sorry for myself, telling God that I knew He had picked them out especially for that room, and it was as if I heard an audible voice saying "Well then, perhaps you had better leave them". Once I had come to terms with that, the battle was as good as over, and I got on with packing our stuff, focusing on the future and knowing that God had good things planned for us, according to Jeremiah 29 v 11. We hired a self-drive van to move ourselves. It cost us about £50, and it was the last penny we had. There was no goodbye or thank you from anyone at GP, and the last straw came when they accused us of stealing the wheelie bin! We had taken it to the end of the footpath a day too early for the collection because it was so full we wanted to spare Lizzie from having to put it out. Someone must have stolen it before she realised we had left it there (wheelie bins were very rare and desirable objects back then). We did receive lots of good wishes and farewells from people in the village, and my friend Percy, the Vicar, wrote us a lovely letter, telling us he was full of admiration for the way we had dealt with all of our problems, and assuring us of his prayers. By the time we moved I think we were over the worst of the disappointment of seeing our dream crashing around us, but we will always feel the sadness and loss of seeing so many Christians deceived, of friendships that ended, and of Green Pastures never becoming the place of restoration and renewal God wanted it to be, and which we had a vision for. However, it was such a relief to be able to look forward to a "normal" life again. We never did receive the £10,000 Pete Sharpe had been offered for us, but thanks to loving and generous friends such as Mark and Viv McDermott we had everything we needed. We moved out on July 23rd 1987, and into a house which was to be our family home for one of the happiest periods of our life.

I think this is the time to make some sense of what happened to us at Green Pastures. God clearly led us there, and also to invest all we had in what we felt was His plan for the rest of our lives. The fact that we lost it all was part of that plan too! We learnt so much about Him, about the true church, about prayer, provision, faith, persecution, and also joy in the face of it. We learned what Christian leadership was and was not, and what fellowship was and was not. We learned to give until it hurt and saw God give us back a hundredfold and more. We met some wonderful people and some very un-wonderful ones! We learned to worship with total freedom and we saw God's power clearly demonstrated. We saw the life-giving relevance and importance of the Word of God, and clung to it more and more until it became as essential to us as food and drink. Our trust in Jesus, our gratitude towards Him, and our love for Him, grew in ways that could never have been if we hadn't "jumped out of the boat and started to sink". We also had our precious little Sarah, our great and unexpected blessing, who was made, formed and delivered there! However, just to confirm to us that God knew exactly what had gone on both spiritually and practically, and that He was both in it and in control of it, at the beginning of 1988 something amazing happened. He led us both to start reading right through the Bible. We used a version of The Living Bible which sectioned it off into 365 readings, one for each day, comprising a chapter from the Old Testament, a Psalm, a verse or two from Proverbs, and a chapter from the New Testament. When we got to the book of Esther we almost fell over! In that translation the Jewish dates had been translated into our western calendar, and we read that the day Haman had set to annihilate the Jews and steal their property was February 28th (we got our eviction notice on February 28th!) The day that the edict was revoked, and the Jews could fight back, destroy their enemies and keep their homes, was July 23rd (we moved into our new home on July 23rd!) Some years later, as part of a study of the Book of Esther, I looked up the Jewish months in my Bible Dictionary. 28th February falls during the month of Adar which was the season of "The blossoming of the Almond Trees". Almond Blossom was a sign given to Moses and Aaron that God was with them, and symbolises a promise of abundance to come. 23rd July falls during the month of Sivan, which was the season of "The beginning of the wheat harvest"! All this – wonderful as it is – isn't the end of the story. Almost 20 years later, the Christian Counselling Organisation I worked for rented office space at Green Pastures. It was hard for me to go back in some ways, but the Lord blessed and there was a welcome reconciliation with some of the people who had "persecuted" us. In fact, the people who had gathered around Bee to "protect" her from nasty old us had become the new Trustees. Bee was no longer there, and Lizzie had died a few years before. After years of coping with her troublemaking, and realising that she was not the Godly leader they had thought her to be, the Trustees had asked Bee to leave. Added to this she was growing old and was no longer capable of leading anything! After I had worked there for a couple of years, renewing friendship and fellowship, I was asked to sign, as a witness, a legal document removing Bee from the board of trustees; the person who had instigated all of the illegal moves against us 21 years before! God is so amazing – He can ALWAYS be trusted in every tiny detail!!

I want to tie up some other loose ends before I leave Green Pastures for good. We went back to visit Bee and Lizzie a few years after we left, to show that there was no animosity and unforgiveness on our part. I think we took Nicky's wedding photos to show them. Sadly, they still didn't acknowledge any wrongdoing on their part, but delighted in pointing out all the ways we had hurt, and supposedly judged, them! We apologised for hurting them once again, but we could see that there was not the slightest change of heart in them. We were eventually proved right about Bee's motives for getting rid of us. She wanted the land for her son. He was still drifting from job to job and relationship to relationship, and must have been on the wrong side of 35 by then. Before we left we wrote to Lizzie's family in Scotland, telling them briefly what had happened, and that we were leaving, but that we were very concerned for Lizzie's welfare, as we truly were. We wanted them to watch out for her, because we had seen how ruthless Bee could be, and were also convinced that there was a serious and evil spiritual element to our conflict there. This, we were sure of, would transfer to anyone else getting in the way of Bee's goal, as it had in the past. After we left we heard that Bee persuaded Lizzie to make her co-owner of the house they lived in (to protect her from people like us trying to get rid of her!) The rest of the property should have legally belonged to the trust, but a few years later, when Lizzie died, we heard that she had left "Bethel" to Bee's son in her will. He immediately put it on the market, sold it, pocketed the money and went to Indonesia, buying a house there and marrying a local girl. The legal wrangles over boundaries and what was trust property and what was not were still going on, and still costing thousands of pounds, 20 years later, when I was working there. Another bad, ongoing situation developed from a decision made by Bee just after we left. A local builder was persuaded to do some work on the cow barn, converting it to a chapel and accommodation for visiting speakers. It was a listed building and planning permission had been turned down, but the builder agreed to do it illegally in exchange for a piece of land. He was given (trust property again!) the copse at the end of the fields, next to the village school and the little lane going past the church. He tried to build a house there, again without planning permission. He told the council that the shell of his house and an indoor swimming pool was a fish farm! They didn't fall for it and made him pull it down, and whilst I was working at GP 20 years later he decided to give up trying to build there and sold it to a local woman. The woman in question was the scourge of the village, who had connections with a bunch of "travellers", who we suspected were behind a break in and theft of a computer from my office. She had planned to turn the copse into a permanent travellers' camp-site, but fortunately she was legally stopped by planners. However, the trouble caused by all the original illegalities still goes on and on. The Trustees of Green Pastures eventually "bribed" Bee into leaving there by buying her a First-Class ticket to Indonesia, where she planned to live with her son and his new wife. She only lasted a few months before becoming ill, and, as her son hadn't arranged any health cover for her, she had to return to England. The last I heard, she was living in an old peoples' council bungalow in a nearby village. I'll finish on one last thing, which is merely a hunch of mine. As I mentioned earlier, we really were fearful for Lizzie when we left. It almost seems crazy now, but we even feared for her life. When she died of heart failure we were really surprised, because she was an extremely healthy person, having spent most of her younger life farming and riding horses. She still kept herself very fit, walking everywhere she possibly could. When I was working at GP I met up for a coffee with someone from the village who was part of the fellowship in the 80s when we were there. She had renewed her contact with Bee and Lizzie after the Fellowship was abandoned and we had gone, and she too had become concerned for Lizzie, who had lost a great deal of weight. She had discovered this when, one winter, she'd had to help her to put on her boots (as she was too weak to do it herself) and saw that her legs were extremely skinny under her long thick tweed skirt. When she commented on this, Lizzie had said "I am so exhausted with all this fasting we have to do". Bee always had "plenty of padding", and to my knowledge never lost any of it. She certainly still looked very portly when we saw her at Lizzie's funeral, so "all this fasting" obviously hadn't involved her, except to order it! Could Lizzie's heart have been physically affected by her obedient fasting? She certainly wasn't the type of person to say one thing and do another, and would naively expect that she wasn't the only one fasting if "God" had instructed them both to do so.

One of the first things we did after moving to Cowplain was to start attending the local Evangelical Church on Durley Avenue. We knew a few people from there, and, after our recent experience of our Church Fellowship isolating itself from the community, we wanted to be involved in every aspect of life in the area we lived. I had read somewhere that, ideally, one should be able to walk to church, not commute to some place on Sunday mornings without having any other involvement in the area, and this seemed sensible to me. Durley Avenue was a bit conservative compared to some of our wilder Charismatic experiences, but they were nice people who loved the Lord, and we liked the Pastor, Maurice Redmill. Some of the people who had been part of our prayer support before leaving GP wanted to carry on meeting in David and Audrey's home, but I found it even more oppressive than GP! They got quite upset when we refused, telling us that we had been brought together by God etc, but I'd had enough of holy huddles. Incidentally, they were still doing it 23 years later, and became hyper-critical of almost every other Christian group. Keith and Diana Baker were members of the Durley

Avenue Church, and we became good friends with them. Keith was a Police Officer too, and also the treasurer for Full Gospel Businessmen, so Robb knew him well. They had 6 children, and Becky, their youngest, was Sarah's age. We had some great times with them over our years at Wheatsheaf Drive. One of the best things about being there was that the girls had friends and school within walking distance. They joined the Youth Group at the church and made some good friends there, too. We still had to drive Amy the short distance to Denmead School at first, but Nicky started becoming more independent, and was doing well at Cowplain Secondary School. Amy eventually went to Oaklands Catholic Secondary School in Waterlooville, but was able to catch a bus there.

One of the great things about our new home was that we had lots of space. Having four good sized bedrooms meant that we could easily accommodate visitors by getting the girls to double up, and we certainly had plenty of them! Our house was constantly full of people, and I spent good chunks of my time driving back and forth to Heathrow, making up beds, and cooking meals for crowds. I loved it! I have so many great memories of sitting around our table, laughing and eating and talking about Jesus. We met Yves and Annick Baron through FGB, they stayed with us a few times, and we visited them in Paris. We stayed in close touch with Gerald and Wanda Vane, and they not only stayed with us frequently themselves, but sent many of their friends and contacts to us as they passed through England from America and on to the 3rd world on Mission trips. Robb had met some of them in Israel, but there were many more. Some of them were a wonderful blessing, and we got to know and love them; people like Angelo and Yvette Parisi, Steve and Marietje Chase, Mike and Elise Engler, Leslie and Marianna Leman, John Muench, Danny McMullen, Nick Small, and Dave Hart. Jimmy Rice from Taunton in Somerset was another visitor. Some were a "mixed blessing"; people such as James and Abigail Von Welk, and Chris Scarinzi. We had some very strange ones, too, Todd Carter and Elijah Mukabi spring to mind. Todd, or Darren, as he was sometimes known, would spend all night pacing around and praying loudly in tongues! He also went down in family history because of blowing his nose loudly on one of my best linen table napkins as we sat at dinner one evening. Elijah, with his "slave", Gladstone, came to us from Zimbabwe, and he cost us a lot of money. We took him shopping one day because he wanted some duvets and bedding, but when we got to the checkout we realised he expected us to foot the bill! Poor Gladstone had constant orders barked at him in the Shona language and wore himself out running up and down the stairs fetching and carrying for Elijah. They brought me a present of a carved wooden bird when they came. In an effort to make conversation, and to look as if I knew something about Africa I thanked them and said "Ooh, lovely, is it a Hornbill?" to which Elijah replied abruptly "It is a bird". Nicky and Amy were standing giggling in the background. They spent half of Elijah and Gladstone's stay chasing each other with the little curly black hairs they found everywhere. Another gruesome object they found and tortured each other with was one of Mike Petzer's toenails. Amy made Nicky laugh, and when she had her mouth open and eyes closed the toenail was carefully dropped onto her tongue. The vengeance attacks came thick and fast after that one! It started with Amy covering Nicky's toothbrush with soap, then gradually escalated, but we called a halt when Amy ran into Nicky's bedroom and chucked a bucket of water over her as she sat up in bed. Most of our visitors were connected with Gerald through a ministry called "Elyon" in Nelspruit, South Africa which was led by the same Francois Du Toit who shared a room with Robb in Israel, and whose teaching would eventually be the start of a radical change in our lives.

Just after we moved in to Wheatsheaf Drive James and Abigail Von Welk came to stay with us. The School Of Ministry conference at the Holiday Inn in 1986 had been so successful that they decided to put on another one. The only trouble was that most of the people involved in the previous conference had gone home to concentrate on their own ministries. James and Abigail went ahead with it anyway, and we booked the rooms and advertised it all. Actually - this was our ministry for most of the time we lived at 23, we arranged many itineraries and speaking engagements for lots of different people. The conference was very poorly attended, and I became a bit wary of both James and Abigail. They were trying to get their son out of South Africa and over to America at this time, and spent hours on our phone making calls to people all over the world. They also spent hours calling various airlines to arrange tickets for him on what sounded to me like dodgy credit! James "did my head in", he was so intense, and I actually thought he preached a load of twaddle. I loved some of his songs and had been blessed by his music ministry at the first conference, but had never heard him preach before. We had a couple of meetings at our house but I made excuses not to take part, making a big deal of things like putting Sarah to bed or cooking a meal. He took me aside at one point and told me that I was like Martha, and should make time to sit at his feet, like Mary. What a nerve! Did he think he was Jesus? He also took Robb aside and told him that God had told him (James) that Robb should leave the Police Force and travel with him and Abigail to be discipled by them! I don't know what he had planned for me and the girls! Robb just told him that God hadn't said anything like that to him, so he wouldn't be taking up the offer, thanks very much! One night he told Robb that he needed to go on a "prayer walk" and spend time on his own with Jesus. He went off in a big woolly balaclava, even though it wasn't winter, as he really felt the cold, being used to a warmer climate. He looked positively manic, with his face peeping out of the woolly hat, eyes staring and gold teeth flashing. At midnight he still wasn't back. He didn't have a key, and we started to get worried. We got a call from the police in the early hours. He'd got lost and knocked on some old lady's door for help. She panicked when she saw this strange apparition and called the police, thinking he was about to mug her or something! Robb had to go and pick him up from the Police Station. The last straw in all this fiasco came after James and Abigail left. They blessed us with a lovely Sunday lunch at Holiday Inn to thank us for all we had done, and we enjoyed it tremendously. Sadly, a few days later we got the bill from Holiday Inn, not just for our lunch, but also for the whole conference! They hadn't paid for a single thing. We just shoved all the bills in an envelope and sent it to the UK representative of School Of Ministry (who was also a latter day Trustee of Green Pastures). We wrote a "polite" letter along with it, reminding him that we hadn't as yet been paid any compensation by GP and were penniless as a result of being kicked out of there with nothing, plus pointing out that James and Abigail were also well aware of this. It was quite a satisfying thing to do, and we didn't hear from him, or from Holiday Inn again. The mammoth phone bill they ran up came a while later, but we managed to gradually pay that off. Some time later we got to know a lovely couple, Rick and Jane Franckeiss, who actually moved to Israel to be "discipled" by James and Abigail, but came home sad and penniless as a result. We heard that James was eventually accused of fraud, tried, and found guilty, after ripping off someone else during a guided tour of Israel. I think he was given a very large fine – so justice was done. One good thing came out of their stay with us; Nicky and Amy perfected a "take-off" of them harmonising some of their songs, and we got loads of laughs from that.

Most of our neighbours seemed really nice, but the girls didn't like the ones next door, who spied on them and told us what they got up to. I think this was mostly because they obviously disapproved of normal behaviour for kids. Their son was kept on a very tight leash, and wasn't even allowed to play in the street. The wife was often caricatured by the girls, and we caught Amy one day galloping around the garden on a broomstick imitating her voice and facial expression. They called the husband "the French farter", after a character in a TV comedy show. At the other side were a very quiet couple and their grown-up son. I got to know the wife a little bit, and she told me about the previous tenants of our house. A Police Inspector, who was to figure quite significantly in our future, had lived there with his wife and family. He had been serially and blatantly unfaithful to his wife, even bringing girlfriends home and sleeping with them there. He was, in fact, a nasty piece of work, and had an extremely bad reputation among the guys in the Hampshire force. His poor wife had killed herself in our garage by attaching a hosepipe to the car exhaust. This made us even more sure that God had brought us there, we definitely had some damage control to do! Opposite us, across the road, was a strange couple who didn't speak much, and who fostered loads of children. I once reported him to Social Services for his horrible verbal abuse of some of their foster-children. He thought it was his next door neighbours, Ellie and Dave, who had reported him, as he didn't get on well with them (actually he didn't get on with anyone!) so he retaliated by reporting Ellie for leaving her children at home alone. They were aged 13 and 11, and came home from school only half an hour before Ellie got home from work, so his complaint was totally disregarded. He and his wife carried on fostering, too, so my complaint was probably disregarded too, but hopefully he modified his behaviour as a result, although I doubt it. He used to hang out of his bedroom window taking photos of us doing things like washing our car or clearing out the garage – very strange! Ellie and Dave were friendly, and the girls got to know their kids, Gemma and Jonathan. Dave worked for the Portsmouth Evening News, as did Dave Kill, another neighbour, who lived further up the road with Rita, his Irish wife, and their kids, Michael, Vicky, and Joanne. Nicky became good friends with Michael. Amy had such fun times with Vicky and Joanne. They hung out with a bunch of other kids from the neighbourhood. I remember some of their names; Chris Budgcon or "Budge", "Matt the Prat" and "Terry the Mong"! We used to crack up laughing even at the names, and goodness knows what they all used to get up to. I also remember Amy and Gemma scaring a neighbour's son. He was an amateur "Goth", and, as his parents had gone away on holiday, he had decided to have a big party with his little Heavy Metal friends. Amy and Gemma called him "the Heavy Metal Ralph" ("Ralph" was a derogatory name at that time). They waited until the party was in full swing, then hung over Gemma's fence and shouted "Hey, Ralph, your Mother's home"! Panic ensued, Goths scattered over the neighbourhood, and Amy and Gemma ran off and hid. Amy supplied us with regular near disasters as she got older. I'll never forget waking up to an almighty crash one night when she had been out clubbing with Joanne and Vicky (using Nicky's birth certificate to "prove" she was 18). She came home a bit the worse for booze, and decided to swing down the stairs on Sarah's "twizzler" – a sort of circular rope contraption that we had hung in the stairwell over winter. She grabbed the rope and flew down the stairs, crashing feet first through the front of Sarah's dolls' house, demolishing it completely. She had her adenoids out when she was about 11, and the surgeon had warned her that she must never smoke, as her respiratory system wouldn't take it. She still had the odd asthma attack if she had a heavy cold, so we never imagined that she would start smoking, and when friends from church told us they had seen her walking down the road with a cigarette in her hand we airily dismissed it, telling them they must have the wrong person. Later we found out that in fact it was her and the little pest had been smoking like a chimney! I think she still sneaks the odd one. I remember her going off to the hairdressers in secret and paying all her pocket money to get a huge matted lump of hair cut from the back of her head, caused by her not bothering to brush her tight curly hair properly for weeks. She fought regularly with Nicky, usually because she wound Nicky up, and one afternoon it almost caused a disaster. She had taken something from Nicky's room as they were getting ready to go off to a Youth Camp. They chased each other out of the house and up the road, and eventually Amy ran back, slamming the door in Nicky's face. Nicky put out her hand to stop it and it went right through the glass panel. The glass shattered and cut Nicky's forearm badly. We had to take her to A&E to get it stitched, and then drive her to camp because she missed going on the minibus with all the others. She still has a big scar. Nicky always had nice clothes and money. She had good taste and worked hard after school and on weekends at the Coop, but we found out in later years that for a while she supplemented this with a bit of shop-lifting! Amy was younger of course, but even when she was old enough to work she never seemed to be able to keep a job. I wonder just how hard she tried, or maybe it was because of her attitude! She was always borrowing Nicky's stuff. Usually she asked, but occasionally got into big trouble for wearing Nicky's things without permission. The main problem was that Amy was a walking disaster area, and clothes seemed to self destruct on her. One morning, when she was doing her B. Tech Nat. in Health Studies at Southdowns College, she asked me if she could borrow Nicky's best sweater, because she didn't have anything to wear. Nicky had already left for college, so I told Amy that she could, because there didn't seem to be anything else suitable. I made her swear to take care of it. I will never forget answering the door to a stricken looking Amy that afternoon. Her eyebrows, eyelashes and fringe were singed, and she was still wearing Nicky's best sweater, which looked as if it had been put into a toaster. One of her friends had thought it would be funny to spray her with lighter fuel, and when she lit a cigarette afterwards a sheet of flame had shot up the front of the sweater and her face. Fortunately someone had the presence of mind to throw a coat over her and put out the flames, so she wasn't hurt, but the sweater was never the same again and Nicky was understandably furious. I totally lost it when I saw Amy standing on the doorstep. I couldn't help it, and laughed until I cried. Of all the days! It couldn't have happened to anyone but her – she is totally unique! Once she sneaked Joanne's Hamster into her room. I had refused to let her take care of the little thing whilst the Kills were away because I knew how often the blasted creatures died when their environment changed. We once looked after a neighbour's Guinea Pigs whilst they were away, and half of them pegged it. Anyway I didn't want a smelly rodent in my house – especially in a bedroom! A few nights after her request, in the early hours, Robbie woke up suddenly and said in a loud voice "There's something creeping up my leg!" We shot up and threw the covers back, to find the hamster in our bed. She had smuggled it in, and it had escaped from its cage and gone walkabout into our room and up under the duvet. Probably Amy hadn't fastened the door properly, but thank God it didn't choose my leg to creep up or it would have been history (or I would).

Other neighbours we got to know were Liz and Steve Wilkinson and their children Matthew and Cally. Steve left Liz for another woman after we had been there a year or so, and I'll never forget hearing Matthew crying out "No!

No!" when his Dad told him he was leaving them. It was a terrible sound. Liz's friend, Jenny, lived across the road, a few doors away from the Kills. She was a young widow with two little boys, and became both a friend to me and a fellow-Christian. Her husband had been a Portsmouth Harbour Pilot, who had a heart attack on board ship and died on the way, by helicopter, to Haslar Hospital. When I got to know Jenny I found out that her parents had been strong Christians. She was struggling to cope emotionally, and desperate to give her life to the Lord, but felt that if she did it would be like consigning her husband to hell. He had refused to become a Christian many times, in spite of hearing the Gospel over and over again from her Dad, who had also died a few years before. I told her that she couldn't possibly know what had happened to her husband in the time between his heart attack and getting to Haslar, and she should trust God that He knew everything and wanted the best for both of them. She did give her heart to the Lord, and a few nights later, after being woken up from a deep sleep, she saw what seemed like a vision of her Dad and husband, standing next to her bed with arms around each other and smiling joyfully. God is so amazing. She had complete peace after that, and came to church with us for a while, before she moved to Widley.

We got to know a bit about the history of the road, and apparently the house opposite had once been occupied by an ex-Navy man who was subsequently convicted of spying, and imprisoned after selling secrets to the Russians! Not long before we left a Chinese guy moved in there. He used to disappear for weeks on end, and whilst he was away big black cars with darkened windows, occupied by scary looking Chinese "heavies", would park outside his house and wait for hours. In what looked like a quiet suburban street there was an awful lot going on! The guy who lived on the corner opposite Dave and Rita was convicted of murdering his girlfriend's husband and disposing of the body by setting fire to it in their garage. I used to say hello to his wife each day as she walked their little dog past our house. Amy was one of the last people to see this guy before he went on the run, so the Police had to come and interview her. Rita had to give evidence too, as he had made several passes at her over the years! I like to think that we were put in the street to bring a bit of light into a dark place, and I think we did, but I expect most streets have stories to tell – because all the people living in them have their stories too.

We had quite an assortment of cars whilst we lived there. The first one we bought was the most awful old brown Cortina. We still had hardly any money and this was cheap and it moved! It was disgustingly dirty inside and stank of cigarettes and wet dog. I hated it. The seats were shredded by what must have been hordes of animals jumping all over them. We did our best with it, but it never looked or smelled good! I remember picking up Nick Small from Heathrow and bringing him back to Portsmouth in it. He was uncharacteristically quiet for most of the journey, then said "I'm going to pray for you to get a better car". Amen brother. I'm sure that this car was a great source of distress to our neighbours, too, especially Ellie, who had to look out of her suburban palace windows straight at the horrible thing festering in our drive! The best car we ever had (to this day) was "The Green Machine". It was an old, bright green Citroen Dyane, and we all loved it. We bought it for £180, although it cost us hundreds more than that to keep it going during the time we had it. It had a hole in the floor by the foot pedals and we used to joke about its being like the Flintstones car, needing us to put our feet through the floor and run to make it move. It had a soft top, and in summer it was lovely to drive along with the roof down. This was before back seat safety belt regulations came in, and we used to pack it with kids and drive to the beach with them all hanging out of the top and sides. On one occasion I bought a hanging basket and drove along with the top down and a basket of flowers hanging from the roof frame! We had a great bumper sticker, which read "Only Visiting This Planet" referring to the Bible verse which says that we are strangers and pilgrims on this earth. I don't think Ellie took much delight in that car either. She had a bright, shiny red 2CV with her name on it – a much more civilised version of our old green banger. We did get better cars eventually, but I remember the times when we had rubbish ones with great fondness. We eventually sold the green machine to a guy round the corner. It was costing us more and more money, and the roof had started leaking, so we reluctantly got rid of it. We used to see him bombing round in it for ages after that, and really regretted losing it. Gerald said that we should have had it crushed flat and hung it on the wall as a work of art and a family heirloom – I wish we had!

Sarah was growing up, and was such a delight. She still didn't sleep very well, and would creep into our bed at night, but I would lazily snuggle her in and go back to sleep. I was so much more "laid back" with her than I was with Nicky and Amy when they were small. The girls were happy to babysit most of the time, so Robb and I had a bit more freedom than we did during the early years with them. All the neighbours loved her, too. Dave Middleton was advertising manager for "The News" and ran a publicity campaign with a picture of Sarah on the front cover. She was so cute. Her hair was white blonde and she had the sweetest little chubby face, turned up nose, and rosebud lips. She was a stubborn little thing, though, and even then couldn't let anyone else have the last word, and wouldn't look you in the eye either. If I was telling her off for doing something naughty she would roll her eyes up to the ceiling, or to one side, and refuse to make eye contact! I bought a bike with a baby seat on the back of it and a basket on the front, so I could ride into Cowplain to do the shopping, get some exercise and give Sarah some fresh air all at the same time. We had a branch of Waitrose in Cowplain and I became an expert at finding their bargains. They would reduce the prices by half if stuff was nearing its sell-by date, and we ate pretty well sometimes thanks to that. I must have looked quite a sight pedalling around with shopping bags hanging off the handlebars, the basket full, and a podgy toddler on the back! I remember one day walking through Cowplain to get my bike, which was locked up outside Waitrose. I had Sarah on my back, as she refused to walk. I also had heavy shopping bags in each hand, so when I tripped on a loose paving slab I couldn't save myself from falling forward because of being so weighed down. I staggered along in a Quasimodo type run, trying to straighten up and save myself, then I lurched forward onto my knees, slamming my ribs into the end of the wooden bench next to the bus stop. Sarah flew over my head and landed on the lap of an old lady who was sitting on the bench. I was kneeling on the pavement, desperately gasping for breath, as I had totally winded myself, and trying to apologise to her, as she looked on aghast at this groaning bag lady who was about to die at her feet and leave her with an orphaned Sarah. We did have some lovely bike rides, though. Not far away from Wheatsheaf Drive was the open countryside around Denmead, which ran right through to Purbrook Heath, my old jogging area. There were fields, woods full of bluebells, and trickling streams, and favourite of all was the ford at Sheepwash, where we played "Pooh Sticks" from the little bridge. In May we picked beautiful bouquets of bluebells, starry white stitchwort and lime green beech leaves. We also discovered that wild garlic, which grew in abundance by the ford, was absolutely delicious cooked like spinach. Blackberries, sloes and rose hips were the bounty in Autumn, plus the occasional wild mushrooms and giant puffballs. Favourites were Shaggy Inkcaps, which are amazing if they are picked whilst very young. We found oodles of frogspawn and took it home to watch the tadpoles hatching out and turning into frogs in a bowl full of water outside the back door. Later we put the little frogs into a plastic tub and took them over to one of the streams to be released "into the wild"! There was a big free-range pig farm at Closewood, too, and we loved going there to watch the little pink piglets running around and playing in the fields.

20 – Joy in the Morning

It was around this time that I started thinking about finding Anthony again. The years were rushing by, and he still hadn't come looking for me. Mum was still living at 3 Appleton Road. Auntie Eileen had moved in with her by now, so Mum had an obvious need for a 3 bedroom house, but one of the reasons she gave for staying there was that Anthony might find it easier to trace me if she was still living there. I had heard about a Government post-adoption contact register where I could put down my name, stating that I was willing to be found by him, so I sent off for the appropriate forms. When I got them there was a letter included, asking me to examine my motives and whether I was prepared to face any possible consequences of finding him. All sorts of things went through my mind. What if he was a drug addict, or extremely needy? What if he was a homosexual dying of AIDS? Could I cope with it? What about my little family? What would that sort of situation mean to them? I had heard adoption horror stories, about the emotional damage that could be caused by the ultimate rejection of a baby by its mother. If I couldn't cope with what I found, what would it do to him if I rejected him again? I shoved the forms in a drawer, and put off making a decision until I felt peace about it.

We really enjoyed having Sarah, and decided, on the basis of this and because everyone said that having three children of the same sex was a mistake, that maybe we should have one more try for a boy! I became pregnant quickly, but I think I instinctively knew from the start that it was another girl! We were still registered with Doctor Goulder, so again we planned a home birth. This time, knowing we had no major alterations to make to our home, it was all a bit more relaxed and I sailed through the pregnancy with no physical complications (apart from feeling tired) in spite of being 42 years old. We announced our good news to the family at Christmas dinner of 1988. I taped some Christmas wrapping paper to my tummy, then put an apron over it whilst I cooked and served the meal. After we had eaten, Robb and I said that we had another present for the whole family, and I stood up and lifted my apron. They all realised what it was right away, with varying reactions! Nicky rushed, screaming and horrified, out of the house and ran along the road shouting "My Mother is pregnant, my mother is pregnant!!" Nanny looked terminally worried, and said something like "Please God, all will go well". I can't remember much else, I was a bit concerned about Nicky. She was just 15 by then, and turning into a really beautiful young woman. She had boyfriends locally, at school and at church, and I guess it must have been quite embarrassing for her to have a pregnant mother, especially one my age!

I must mention our pet rabbit at this point. He was actually a birthday present to Amy, but, typically, I was the one who did most of the day to day caring for it. Our garden was enclosed, and, as I hated the idea of animals being imprisoned in a cage, we used to let him out when the weather was good to have the run of the garden. He ate everything in sight, including my wisteria! I was desperate to have a wisteria vine in my garden, and had planted one at 'Bethel', but of course I'd had to leave it behind, just as it was getting established. I think we tried twice to grow one at 23, but the rabbit got to it each time. He also gradually ate a pair of wellies, and chewed holes in numerous paddling pools, when people carelessly left the shed door open for him to get in. I got vengeance for this later. Another of his nasty habits was encircling anyone who went into the garden, running around them in ever decreasing circles then flicking his rear end and peeing on them. He did it to me one summer day in 1989, but because I couldn't see him for my huge pregnant tummy, I caught him with my foot as I walked forward, sent him flying, and he landed in the middle of Sarah's paddling pool, which was full of water. I hesitated at first, but in the end I did actually save him from drowning! It was quite difficult catching him to put him back into his cage at the end of each day. We often heard urban foxes at night, so we had to do this to protect him. One day we saw him "dribbling" a black and white football around the lawn. We thought we'd got a new animal sensation to send to Esther Rantzen's "That's Life" programme – a footballing rabbit! But as we watched, he cornered the ball and jumped on top of it, obviously mistaking it for a lady rabbit. Even though we couldn't film him for TV we realised we could use his fondness for the ball to distract him, grab him, and put him into his cage. From then on, before it got dark, we would kick the ball out into the garden (nobody would touch it apart from with covered feet!), wait for him to jump on it, then grab him and throw him into his hutch. He must have been the most frustrated rabbit in the world, and we were the only family in the world to discover how to trap a rabbit by coitus interruptus. I wonder if the pope would have been proud of our creative use of one his chosen methods of population control, or is it one of the ones he forbids? I can't remember. Poor old Smudgy was despatched to bunny heaven in later years by Mike Petzer. Smudge had become really ill, I think because of some problem with his teeth, and we couldn't afford to take him to the vets. It was going to cost us £7 to have him put down, and at that point we really didn't have a penny to spare (I heard someone later ask if they charged that much because they were going to shoot him with a golden bullet!) Mike was staying with us, and, after serving in the South African army for years, he had no problem bumping off a rabbit, but enough said about that. We took the girls out one day, and whilst we were out, Mike got a garden spade and quickly put him out of his misery, then buried him in an unmarked grave. I don't think anyone missed him for days!

Although we had many visitors, and not all of them were a total blessing, mostly I loved having a house full of people, getting to know new Christians, and learning more about the Lord from them. We loved our tremendous "feasts", full of fun and laughter and oodles of food! Somehow we managed to provide for hundreds of people on only a modest income (I think the Man who fed 5,000 people with 5 loaves and 2 fishes had something to do with it). The only time I ever felt that it was too much for me was when I looked after the Vane kids for 2 weeks. Wanda had just given birth to their 5th child in South Africa, and Gerald had been invited to speak in Scandinavia. It had been an extremely difficult birth, and Wanda had needed a blood transfusion as a result. She was exhausted from that, and from schlepping 4 kids around South Africa for months before the birth. They left the 4 oldest with us and took the baby with them, after taking over my washing machine for days on end with suitcases full of dirty washing accumulated over their travels. I don't think I have ever wished time away as I did when looking after those children. The oldest was sneaky and greedy, conning pocket money out of both our kids and the Baker's. The next one was about the best behaved, but was very boisterous. The third one was rude, disobedient, stubborn and very naughty. The youngest was sullen and unresponsive (at less than 2 years old!) They all closed ranks and became very challenging and aggressive if we tried to discipline any of them. I have never seen Robbie lose his cool the way he did once during that time. He actually smacked one of them, and was not gentle! Diana

Baker refused to have them in her house, in spite of being used to the chaos of having 6 children of her own. She also formed an opinion of Gerald and Wanda based on the behaviour of their children, and wanted nothing to do with them from then on. On Gerald and Wanda's return they came to pick up the kids, but they also brought Gerald's mother, Iris, with them, so we had a houseful of Vanes for a couple of days. I managed to keep going because the end was in sight. Iris was an interesting woman, but very over-assertive, and hadn't hesitated to invite herself to our home along with them. I was so relieved when they all left, and probably for the first time realised that I was not superwoman, and what's more, I didn't want to be!

Another visitor we had, in fact more of a lodger, was a Chinese Malaysian girl, Pauline Chan, who was with us for a couple of months whilst her guardian, Dennis, went back to Malaysia in an effort to bring her mother, his wife, over to England. Dennis was the newly appointed head of bakery at what was then the Coop owned Havant Hypermarket. We had introduced ourselves to him in the supermarket after reading about him in Popsy's Coop newspaper. He had mentioned being a Christian in the article, as well as the fact that he was looking after his wife's three daughters, so we thought he might need some local Christian friends after working abroad for years. It turned out that his wife, Julie, was in prison in Malaysia. At that time she was on remand, accused of murdering her sister. It was a very strange story, of which, I am now convinced, we only heard a part. Apparently the two sisters had been sharing a house and had fallen out, not speaking to each other for years. One of them met a violent death and the other was imprisoned for causing it. Apparently Julie had become a Christian in prison, and had started praying for an English husband. Somehow Dennis got involved, and had become the answer to her prayers. He left her in prison in Malaysia, brought her daughters to England with him, settled not far from us in Cowplain, and enrolled the girls at Amy's school, Oaklands. Pauline was a lovely girl, who was in the middle of her A Levels when Dennis went back to Malaysia, so she couldn't go with him, and we put her up in Amy's room. Amy moved in temporarily with Sarah. All three Chan sisters were incredibly hard working, motivated and diligent, almost driven, and they put most of the English kids in the shade. When I eventually met Julie after she was acquitted and came to England, I understood why. She was one of the most ambitious, mercenary people I have ever met. The marriage eventually broke up – probably confirming the suspicions of the Immigration people here in England, who thought it was a marriage of convenience. The sad thing is that I think Dennis was a victim who believed that he really was Julie's answered prayer. I think he was, but it wasn't prayer for a loving husband, but for a way to get her kids a good free education far away from, and without involving, her ex-husband, their father. Through them we met a young Chinese pastor and his family, Richard and Jaqui Chung and their two year old daughter, Faith. They later stayed with us for a week or so, and that was another hair-raising experience. Faith suffered from "night terrors" and would wake up in the middle of the night screaming in the most blood-curdling way. Her parents, unable to do anything (as she wasn't properly awake and couldn't be woken) would add to the noise and chaos by running around, yelling at each other and at Faith in Chinese. I wonder how we kept our sanity sometimes!

Robbie studied for promotion during our early years at Wheatsheaf, and eventually became a Police Sergeant. He actually didn't particularly want to be a P.S. because it meant a lot more responsibility, plus some grotty jobs, with not much of an increase in salary. However, we felt it was the right thing to do for our future, and that God would want him to strive to be the best he could be (Gerald had actually "seen" 3 stripes on Robb's arm). After he got promotion he was offered a chance to go up to the Police College at Harrogate to study to become a Police Trainer. I was so torn by this. My typical pregnancy feelings of terror and panic were hovering constantly in the background, although I don't think I had more than one full-blown attack during this pregnancy. The thought of being on my own at night for 2 months at this time was so frightening, but I knew that this was a wonderful chance for Robb, and for all of us. Eventually, with great trepidation, I encouraged him to go, praying desperately for God to help and protect me from night-time panic attacks. He did, although I lived in fear of it happening all the time Robb was away. It was quite a traumatic time for Robb, too. There was a lot of psychological content in the training, and for the first time he had to face some painful facts about himself! If it wasn't for the Lord I think it might have broken him, I know that quite a few people dropped out of the course early for that reason. When he finished he was offered a post in training, at the lovely new Police Training School at Netley, on Southampton Water. He accepted, loved it there, and enjoyed the most fulfilling time of his career in the Police.

Around this time he went over to Paris to run in the annual "Le Figaro" Bois de Boulogne 10K race with John Mohammed, a friend from Cowplain Church. The pastor of an Evangelical Church in the suburbs of Paris, who had contacts at Cowplain, was running in the race himself, and had invited runners from England to join him. Robbie didn't run in the end, as he had a bad sinus infection, but he and John went to the French church on the Sunday and met Yves and Annick Baron, who belonged to the local Full Gospel Businessmen's Fellowship. They invited Robbie to come over to Paris again and speak at an FGB dinner, which he did soon after this, taking Keith Baker with him on the first of many enjoyable trips over the channel for all of us. Yves and Annick became good friends to us and the Bakers. Yves was a brilliant musician – composing his own worship music as well as being a very good keyboard player and writing books on the importance of praise and worship in our experience of God. Annick taught English at a secondary school, and could speak perfect English, so she was a real blessing. We were typical Brits, and hardly spoke a word of French – although to my surprise I found myself able to follow conversations thanks to what I had learned at St. Mary's Grammar School without even knowing it. Responding to the conversations was a different matter! The Barons came over to England and stayed with us a few times too.

When I was about eight months pregnant, Francois Du Toit came over from South Africa to fulfil some speaking engagements. We had started to realise that his teaching was completely different from most of the stuff we were hearing elsewhere, and we were desperate to hear more of it! Gerald, Angelo, Dave Hart, Steve Chase, the Mikes (Engler and Petzer) and others, had been radically changed by his teaching. He emphasised God's Grace, as opposed to the usual "working hard to be a good Christian" message preached in most churches. I struggled with what he was saying at first, thinking that it was an encouragement to go out and sin. The message was that nothing we could or couldn't do would affect our standing with God, or His love for us. I reasoned that, if that was the case, we could just go out and do what we liked. In fact, we could, and that was IT, the key! As someone once said - "Love God, and do as you like". I had unknowingly discovered the essence and uniqueness of the Gospel, and Christianity, after being a Christian for years. In a conversation with Gerald, I had asked him "So we can go out and sin as much as we want, then?" He replied "Well, yes, but what does it make you want to do? Does knowing that you are His precious child, and that you could go out and sin as much as you want, knowing that God's love will never change towards you in spite of it, make you want to rush out and "sin" as much as you can?" My reply was a heartfelt "No, it makes me so grateful, and makes me want to love and serve Him even more". His reply was the beginning of such a joyful discovery and realisation of God's love for me that it really was life-changing, and I will be eternally grateful to Gerald for this. At last, the full implications of Grace dawned on my heart and soul. "He who knew no sin, became sin for us, so that in Him we might become the righteousness of God". The Gospel – The GOOD News! The end of self-condemnation. The end of trying to score brownie points with God. The end of taking on board the condemnation of the "coulda, woulda, shoulda" message preached in most Evangelical circles, or the pressurised emphasis on super-spirituality amongst the Charismatic bunch. Instead it meant a heart full of gratitude and wonder and love for Jesus, overflowing to everyone it met. It was the beginning of discovering my uniqueness and value to God, and of gradually becoming free of anyone else's opinion but His, and free from beating myself up with guilt and condemnation every time I failed to live up to my own or someone else's churchy standards! "You shall know the Truth, and the Truth will set you free". God wasn't interested in us just turning our back on all the "bad" things we did, but on all the "good" things too. Our "Good Works" can't earn us points with Him, nor can our failures score black marks against us. He just wants our obedience to what He's telling us to do so that He can "Work all things together for our good and the good of all those who love Him". "Those who are led by the Spirit of God are the sons of God". Adam and Eve were warned not to eat of the Tree of the Knowledge of Good and Evil, because only God can know what is ultimately good and bad! I guess we would say that giving to a charitable cause was good – but what if, at that specific time, God wanted us to use that money to buy a significant gift for a child or a parent who really needed to know they were loved? Most people would say that cancer was bad – but what if having that disease caused us to rethink our reason for existence and put our trust in God, thus gaining eternal Life? The error of the teaching we got at Green Pastures also dawned on me. Every problem had been blamed on demons, and the solution had been "deliverance" from them by some expert, but most of the people there were already Christians, with Jesus living in them, and they in Him, so how could a demon live in such a place? It was religion again - another mind game to make people feel helpless and dependent on some spiritual leader, and therefore easier to dominate and control. The Bible said "Greater is he who is in you than He who is in the world" (in other words "Greater is He who is in you than he who is not in you"!)

Francois was speaking in Bromley in late May. Robbie and I went up for a one day conference at the home of a couple who were involved with his ministry. Their son had gone over to Nelspruit to train there with Francois. They had a lovely big comfortable home, and about 20 of us were gathered there for the conference. This couple were also brilliant professional caterers, and they had organised a fantastic lunch for us all, which we made the most of! For the first session after lunch Robbie and I sat on a squishy overstuffed sofa, which was a big mistake. Late pregnancy, a big lunch, and a comfy sofa at siesta time all combined to put me to sleep! After a little while I woke up with a jump. Francois was speaking about the difference between being clinically alive and having real life. He shouted out the word "Zoe" (which means "the Life that flows from God"), and at the same time my baby did a sort of "flip". Robbie and I just looked at each other and knew. This baby was another little girl, and we would call her Zoe!

Zoe was due on the 7th July. In June the weather was hot, and I was getting really tired and fed up with being pregnant. I was 42 years old, for goodness sake, what the heck was I doing going through all this again? I definitely knew that this would be my last baby! I was really conscious that my little Sarah wouldn't be my baby any more, and I remember snuggling up to her on the sofa one day (with difficulty because of "the bump"), cherishing the last few days of her being the littlest one, and sad because I knew how my feelings would change when I had care of another little life even more vulnerable than hers. Wimbledon started on Monday 3rd July, and I think I watched more of it that year than I have ever done. I was so uncomfortable that I couldn't sleep properly, and every night would see me walking up and down watching the highlights of the day's play, because I couldn't sit for long either! The night of 4th July was so hot. I was more uncomfortable than ever and knew there was no point trying to sleep, so about 11.00 p.m. I turned on the day's highlights. Everyone else had gone to bed, but by about 12.30 a.m. I realised that my discomfort was getting worse, I was in labour. I woke Robbie about 1.00 a.m. and we called the midwife. She was there by 2.00 a.m. and Dr. Goulder came shortly afterwards. I didn't mess about with birthing stools or any other such contraptions this time, just walked around, and eventually got into bed. My labour progressed steadily, with no interference whatever. Amy's bedroom was at the front of the house next to ours, so she was woken up by all the cars arriving and doors opening and closing. She was a great help, making cups of tea and praying. Nicky and Sarah were both at the back of the house and slept through the whole thing! At about 3.30am I was pushing hard, concentrating fiercely on getting this over with, shutting my eyes tight in concentration, and at about 4.00am our precious little Zoe Hannah was born. I opened my eyes to find a beautiful summer's day dawning. The room was full of soft dawn light, and there, on my tummy, was another sweet little red-headed baby girl. Straight into my mind came the scripture "Weeping may endure for the night, but joy cometh in the morning". We almost changed her name to Joy on the strength of that, but decided finally to stick with the name God had given her before she arrived. Nicky and Sarah were finally woken up by Zoe's first cries, and they all came in to cuddle their baby sister after everything was cleared up. My very favourite photo of all time was taken then, in that lovely sunlit room, by Robbie. In it were Nicky, Amy and Sarah, all in their night clothes (just a little vest for Sarah as the weather was so hot!), with no makeup, and their hair all over the place. Nicky was holding Zoe in her arms, Amy was looking over Nicky's shoulder, with one arm around her and the other around Sarah, and they were all looking down at their new baby sister with love and delight. Oh, what a morning, gloriously bright! We were so grateful to God. We had another beautiful, healthy daughter. She was weighed (7lbs 7 ozs) and measured and examined, and declared absolutely perfect.

One of the first things we did, after phoning Nan and Pops, and Mum and Liz up in Hull, was to phone our friends in America. Gerald pointed out that being born at 4.00 a.m. on 5th July in England meant that Zoe was born on the 4th July in America. This was to have great significance for Zoe when we moved to America later, as we always celebrated her birthday on the 4th so that she would feel that all the fireworks and celebrations were in her honour! Nan and Pops rushed over to see her, and our neighbours all visited with gifts and flowers. I waited to see if there would be any white flowers – as all our other girls had white flowers given when they were born, Nicky had white narcissus, Amy had Magnolia, and Sarah had Christmas roses. Sure enough, a friend from church came to visit with a lovely bouquet of summer flowers mixed with white Baby's Breath.

I will always associate those flowers with each of my girls. Right from the start Zoe was a far more placid baby than Sarah. The heatwave continued for weeks, and I would put her to sleep in her pram in the garden, wearing nothing but a nappy and the tiny embroidered cotton lawn tops Amy had worn as a baby in the summer heat of Bermuda. I covered the pram with a cat-net, made sure she was in the shade, and she would sleep for 6 hours or more at a stretch. My Mum came down on the coach to visit and see her new little Grand-daughter. She often came to see us when we lived there. The coach fare for pensioners was very cheap, and she could be dropped off at Cowplain Police Station, opposite the old-fashioned sweet shop near Durley Avenue, where we would pick her up in the Green Machine and take her back to to 23 for a few days stay. We often took her with us for days out in Dorset or the New Forest if she came in the Summer. Nicky and Amy would say that the only time they ever heard Robb swear was when we had days out with Grandma! She always was a very difficult person to be around, very impatient and irritable – especially with Robb, and he would become even more slow and stubborn the more impatient she got – pondering every little move or response for ages before acting, and seemingly deliberately keeping everyone else waiting as long as he could. It was unbearable sometimes, and the girls thought it was hilarious. We did have some lovely days out though.

Not long after Zoe was born we had a visit from Steve and Marietje Chase and their growing family, and Mike and Elise Engler. By then the Chases had a little daughter, and a son – Joshua – born the day after Zoe. They were all on their way back to the States from South Africa and were holding some meetings in Portsmouth. In spite of having a new baby to cope with we were desperate to hear more of the liberating teaching we had heard from Francois and Gerald, so Robbie and Keith Baker set up a series of meetings so that Mike and Steve to do some teaching too. I didn't make it to many of the meetings, but after each of them we had a "de-brief" at Keith and Diana's house, and these were like heaven on earth! There would be Keith and Diana and all their 6 children, Robbie and I, Sarah and Zoe, Steve and Marietje and their 2 little ones, Mike and Elise, and occasionally other people who had helped with the meetings. We all sat round the big dining table and had a meal together – sometimes lasting for hours, as we often did the cooking as we went along – filling the gaps between courses or dishes with conversation and questions and prayer, and, for Marietje and I, feeding our new babies. In spite of the large amounts of food we had to provide, it was never a chore, and the children all seemed so happy and occupied. We drank some great wine, and Mike and Steve discovered that English cider packed quite a punch, unlike American apple cider, which is just Apple Juice (albeit delicious). They actually took some back to the States with them, as it was a great way of avoiding the condemnation that would be heaped on them by the Christians over there if they caught them drinking alcohol! I realised that these extended meals together, absolutely focussed on Jesus and his grace and righteousness, learning about Him and from Him, talking to Him and each other alternately, revelling in His presence and each other's company, eating together, feeding both physically and spiritually, were actually what the early church must have experienced when they met in each other's houses and had everything in common. This was real "communion", and as far removed as it could possibly be from the uncomfortable, silent, self-recrimination and subsequent bit of dry bread and sip of juice that was the communion experience in most churches! Mike played guitar, and had written some wonderful songs that he and Elise sang together. After we had eaten, Keith joined in on his guitar and all of us sang our hearts out in praise and thanks to God for all that He was doing. It was such a special time in our lives, a foretaste of Heaven. During this visit Steve conducted Zoe's dedication service one Sunday evening at Cowplain church, and it was lovely. The church was packed, but not many of the "regulars" were there, only our friends and a few of the old guard who wanted to keep an eye on things.

Steve's preaching was really inspired, but he made the mistake of saying that he hadn't prepared a message, just prepared himself to speak as God led. This was later thrown at us as a criticism of him and of all the visiting speakers we had introduced to the church. Actually, some of them had been a bit flaky, especially a bunch of South Africans who put on a musical based on the Song of Solomon at the church. During the wild unhinged performance they had operated a smoke machine, which set off an asthma attack in the wife of one of the most miserable elders. Most visiting speakers who had made it as far as our church, however, had been inspirational people and given Spirit-led messages. Sadly, we were beginning to feel more and more at odds with the set up at Cowplain. Maurice Redmill was moving on – I think because he was constantly opposed by the elders, who were all dyed-in-the-wool Evangelicals, scared stiff of the Holy Spirit. We were feeling increasingly starved of good teaching, blocked from doing what we felt God wanted us to do, and "put down" when we spoke out about anything. We decided reluctantly to move on, and started to attend the Elim Church in Arundel Street, Portsmouth. Keith and Diana came too. Elim was a large and growing Pentecostal Church, and we knew quite a few people there because of FGB and Green Pastures. They were very open to visiting speakers, and we were encouraged to arrange meetings and teaching sessions for the people that were "passing through" from

Higher Ground Farm and its associated ministries. The church was pastored by Len Cowdery, whom we found a bit distant, but the junior pastor was Steve Potter. We liked him, and he was completely sold out for whatever God wanted to do through the church. Len, with his wife Bridget, had once spoken at a Ploughwomen's Lunch at Green Pastures. I had been a bit suspicious of him since then, because his message was, word for word, exactly the same as a memorable one I had heard from David Pawson in Guildford some months before. If he had acknowledged David it wouldn't have been a problem to me, but he didn't, and the fact that it was, as far as I could remember, a word for word recital made me wonder where Len was coming from, as he claimed to be led by the Holy Spirit. He later developed Alzheimers Disease, so that may have been something to do with it. Len's son by a previous marriage, Andre, was the worship leader at Elim. He was very "camp", and a bit of a prima donna, but the music was very good, and we enjoyed feeling a lot more free to express ourselves than we felt at Cowplain.

One of the hilarious highlights of our hospitality ministry happened around this time when we had friends over for a barbecue, and afterwards decided to sit in the garden and get the guitars out. Danny McMullen was staying with us on his way back to Florida after a stay with Yves and Annick in France. He had a lovely voice and could play guitar really well. Several of the neighbours had mentioned to us previously that they loved it when our guests sat in the garden playing and singing, so we knew it wouldn't upset them. Some of them were out enjoying the warm late afternoon sun, or gardening and mowing lawns. We were really getting into it and singing our hearts out, when we noticed some of the neighbours waving and shouting. We thought they were encouraging us so we smiled and waved back at them and carried on. After a while someone said "Maybe they have a request" so we reluctantly stopped and asked them if they wanted to hear anything special, only to hear Liz, next door but two, pointing in our direction and shrieking "Your fence, your fence!!" It took us a little while to realise that it wasn't the name of a song, but eventually we turned around and saw a large plume of smoke rising from the wooden fence at the back of the garden, with flames just starting to burst out and spread to Jan and Dave's shed next door. Robb dropped everything, dashed into the kitchen, filled the washing up bowl with water and galloped down the garden, yelling to everyone to grab whatever containers they could and chuck water on the fence and the smouldering compost heap before it demolished our next door neighbours' property. I was no help whatsoever, because I lost it completely and just sat in the garden cackling with laughter at the spectacle and the thought of Jan and Dave's shed going up in flames. It was brilliant! Apparently we had thrown our barbecue coals on top of the compost heap before they had cooled off properly, and they had rolled down and rested on the fence. We did manage to put the fire out in time, though, and saved the shed, but our fence looked a bit the worse for wear, and the whole neighbourhood laughed about it for ages.

21 – Grandparents

Zoe grew and thrived, she was a happy little thing, but as skinny as could be, apart from a really fat tummy and an umbilical hernia which sat like an egg on top of it! Life was pretty hectic. Amy was getting on pretty well at Oaklands School, keeping us regaled with funny stories about the teachers and her large group of friends. All her teachers told us she was a born leader, but that at the moment she was leading people into mischief! They teased some of the teachers mercilessly. One of them had terrible bad breath, and they called him F.B. (short for fart breath). He asked them one day why they called him that and they said it was short for "favourite boy". The poor guy believed them. They used to put grotty food on his desk – mashed sandwiches and trampled pork pies – and hide behind the desks, taking bets on whether he would eat it or not. One of my favourite stories about her schooldays was when it was her turn to pray in class at the beginning of the school day. By prayer, the Catholic teachers and Nuns meant some pre-set liturgical recital, but Amy knew it wasn't that. Her friend, Shakira, had just been kicked off the tennis team for some misdemeanour, so Amy mentioned this in her morning prayer. The teacher reprimanded Amy, telling her that she wasn't praying properly, but Amy replied "Don't tell me how to pray, I'm born-again, I know how to talk to God!" I didn't know whether to tell her off for being rude to a teacher, or be proud of her for speaking the truth. She had her first date around this time, arranging to meet Brian, a guy from school, outside MacDonalds one Saturday morning. After several phone calls from both of them we realised that Amy was at the Commercial Road branch, and Brian was at the North End branch. They got together eventually, but after that bad start it never really became anything more than a friendship. Nicky carried on working after school at the local Coop, and studying for GCSEs. She had become very friendly with a boy from school, Ben, who seemed to be at our house a lot. They had been friends ever since Nicky started at Cowplain School. His family were Jehovah's Witnesses, which we were not too happy about, but since we thought they were just friends we didn't worry too much, and thought Nicky might have a good influence on him. Amy's friends were constantly knocking on the door, but they all usually finished up at Joanne and Vicky's house in the evenings, as I would be trying to get the little ones to sleep and wanted peace and quiet. In May Nicky had finished school, apart from going in for her exams, and she seemed to be spending more and more time with Ben. The relationship had been going on for so long that we hadn't been paying it much attention, until they began spending so much time together that we suspected that it had become far more than friendship. We didn't really know what to do, as any action to discourage them from seeing so much of each other would seem to be too little too late, and Nicky was in a frame of mind which would prompt her to do just the opposite of what we wanted her to do. I was worried, as she seemed to be getting more and more detached from us. Her GCSE results were good, she only failed one subject – Spanish – and gained a place at Havant College to do A Levels and retake her Spanish GCSE. Ben, although he was a very bright kid and did well in his GCSEs too, was going to leave school and work for a local double glazing firm. I was horrified, but apparently Jehovah's Witnesses don't encourage further or higher education, and they seem to push their children into trades and manual labour whether they show academic abilities or not. Early summer

1990 was one of mental turmoil for me, I was so worried about their relationship, and soon I realised that Nicky's period was late. I had charge of the Tampax stockpile, so I knew it hadn't gone down as far as it should have done! I remember cycling into Cowplain one day, forcing myself to make it to the top of the steep hill on Sylvester Road without getting off to walk – hoping the pain and concentration involved would take my mind off the unthinkable possibility that Nicky could be pregnant. This turmoil went on for a couple of weeks, until I could stand it no longer, and confronted her as she sat in the kitchen picking at her breakfast one morning. I simply asked her "Nicky, could you be pregnant?" and she burst into tears, so of course I knew that she was. I can't begin to tell the relief I felt when I actually knew rather than suspected. I just threw my arms around her and she sobbed her heart out on my shoulder. Robb was away for a couple of days, but when he came back I poured him a beer, sat him down in the garden and said that I had something to tell him. He said "She is, isn't she?" and then told me that he had a dream in which God told him that Nicky was pregnant. It was all so easy, and so far from the terrible disaster I had been imagining for weeks. Our joint and immediate response to the situation was an overwhelming love and compassion and desire to protect Nicky, and the new and precious little life she was carrying, our first Grandchild. I think Ben was incredulous when he found out that we knew, and weren't going to chuck him out. They weren't in any position to marry, and we would never force them into it, one reason being that we had begun to see how moody and sulky he could be. There was also the problem of his religion. He thought of himself as a Christian, but his experience of God was a dry and sterile adherence to a strict set of rules and beliefs. At its heart, this so called Christian religion denies that Jesus is God incarnate, and in fact states that He was merely an angel, which the Bible refutes completely. Ben had turned his back on his religion to a certain extent, but the "family thing" is very strong in the Witnesses, and his mother was a very controlling woman. We tried to get to know his family, and invited them over for dinner. We got on fairly well, but they were very wary of us. Ben was "dis-fellowshipped" by his local Kingdom Hall because of Nicky's pregnancy, and apparently this was a major shame to his parents. The Witnesses have some weird doctrine about children born out of wedlock, and say that God never intended them to exist. What a contrast to what Robbie and I knew from reading the Bible; that every single life, however long it lasts and how it starts, is precious and ordained by God before the foundation of the earth, and has a unique purpose. The world can never be the same again when a life is created, because it changes everyone involved with it, and "no man is an island".

Once the news had sunk in, we started thinking about the logistics of it all. Nicky didn't want to miss out on her 6th form education, so we contacted Havant College and they were very helpful. She could carry on there and take her A Levels, with more flexible hours than students would normally be allowed. In the meantime we were all booked to fly out to New York for a visit to Gerald and Wanda. We had been so excited, but now were distracted by Nicky's situation. We did go, however, and had a great time. We were met at JFK by Gerald, in his big Dodge Ram 12 seater van. He was also picking up two guys from South Africa the next morning – Mike Petzer and Philip Smethurst, who were to figure in our future in a big way, and who were also going up to Higher Ground Farm, where Gerald and Wanda lived, in upstate NY. Because of this we stayed that night in Queens, at the home of Gayle and Andy Giardino and their children. We were blessed straight away, as they had a little girl called Joy, who was a couple of months younger than Zoe (another "coincidence", as we had considered giving Zoe the name Joy). She had been a big surprise to them, as their son Danny was about 10 years old. We loved the family right away, they were so sweet and generous, and we had such a lot in common with them. They put on a delicious barbecue for us that evening, out on their deck, and we tasted "squirters" for the first time (smoked sausages stuffed with cheese) whilst watching the planes taking off from and landing at La Guardia Airport. It was August, and New York City was hot! However, we all slept well, and I remember waking up early the next morning and feeling somehow as if I was "at home". It had rained in the night, and the breeze coming through the half open windows was fresh and cool. I could hear the garbage truck further down the street, and the clanking of the trash cans as they were emptied. I fell in love with New York all over again!

We left after breakfast, and drove back to JFK to pick up the guys from South Africa. Philip was friendly and outgoing, but Mike was slightly aloof and withdrawn. Gerald drove us around the city to see some of the landmark sights, Battery Park and the Statue of Liberty, the Empire State Building, the twin towers, Central Park, Trump Towers, and Macy's. We stopped at a deli and bought some amazing sandwiches and fruit for lunch, then set off for Lexington. It was a 2 hour drive, but once we got out of the city the scenery was wonderful. We drove across the wide Tappan Zee Bridge, which crosses the Hudson between Tarrytown and Nyack, and the view was amazing. We could see down the river as far as Manhattan, and upwards almost to West Point. The Thruway snaked upstate past Newburgh, Bear Mountain and Poughkeepsie, until, just before Kingston, in the distance we saw mountains jutting upwards suddenly from the flat plain. It was our first view of The Catskills. We left the thruway at Exit 20 – Saugerties – the same exit that had been the goal of thousands of people backed up on the Thruway twenty-one summers before. It was the exit for Woodstock! The place names seemed so magical and emotive. After stopping at a roadside "vegetable stall" which had the most abundant and varied jams, preserves and pickles section that I have ever seen, before or since, we started to climb up into the mountains. The scenery became even more beautiful. In particular we saw the amazing Kaaterskill falls, just before we got to Tannersville, where the water fell from a high crag into a narrow gorge beneath. Eventually we arrived at Higher Ground Farm, a lovely old 5 bedroomed farmhouse, set in a hollow, 2,000 feet up a mountain, at the end of a country road, which had been named after the previous owner of the farm. We got out of the van and looked around at one of the most beautiful places I have ever seen. Down from the house was an old red barn, and behind that the land sloped down to a little creek, rushing down the mountain to join the bigger river in the valley where the "town" lay, (it was smaller that most English villages!) In the distance, were hills and peaks, covered by pines and maples, and in the far distance we could see two high mountains with a v-shaped valley between them, which reminded me of Narnia, when the White Witch told Edmund that her house lay "Between those two hills"! The farmhouse was painted white with "American Blue" shutters on the windows (a kind of slate blue) and had a big deck in front of the kitchen window, which joined up with a covered verandah stretching across the front of the house. There was a lovely cool breeze, but the sun was warm, and children were playing in the fields surrounding the house. There was a little spring bubbling up in front of the house, and Wanda was standing out on the newly built deck, waiting to welcome us. I fell in love with the place immediately.

We were given a room at the back of the farmhouse with bunk beds, a cot, and a double bed. To be honest, it was a bit tatty. There was hole in the wall, which on investigation proved to let in daylight! The bathroom we were assigned was tatty too – more holes in the wall, and a floor that looked as if it would collapse any minute. It was also shared by anyone and everyone that came into the house. However, we unpacked and made ourselves as comfortable as possible, before going out into a big all purpose room with a kitchen at one end. There seemed to be people appearing from everywhere, and Wanda conjured up meals for hundreds in what seemed like no time at all. Gerald told us that Mike Engler was now based at Binghamton with Chris Scarinzi, and that he was lending us his new "people carrier" to tour around in whilst we were in NY. What a blessing! A young couple from Chris's church brought it over to Higher Ground Farm and we set off on some exploring. In spite of the fact that we were always aware of Nicky's pregnancy, because she was feeling very nauseous by now, we had a great time. We went to Loon Lake, near Rochester, to stay with Jack and Susan Pryor, a lovely couple Robb had met in Israel. They had the most beautiful 3-storey house right on the lake, and made us so welcome. We sailed and tubed and water-skied and swam – it was wonderful. We drove for hours to visit Niagara Falls, which was more than worth the effort, in spite of long queues of traffic. We went to Binghamton to meet up with the people we knew there. We ate at all the iconic fast food joints we could think of. We shopped at K-mart and Walmart, and Sears, and thought we were in food paradise when we visited supermarkets where you could seemingly buy any food from any national or ethnic background. They even sold dandelion leaves in the salad section! A lot of our time, however, was spent around the farm and we loved it. Gerald was pastoring a church which met in the local town, in the old Baptist church opposite the Country Store. We went there to the Sunday meetings when we were in the area, and met Ricky and Joan Duplessis and their 4 daughters, Shiyra, Ruth, Siobhan, and baby Cara, and the Radelich family, who all felt like our family! We renewed our friendship with Angelo and Yvette Parisi, who now had a 6 month old daughter, Sharlene, and we met lots of others. We have a lovely photo of the congregation all standing together at the front of that little church. It was a very special time. After the meetings we would all go over to the store for coffee. Jim and Candy Boyle ran the store, but they didn't seem very happy to see us all. It was the first time in our visit that we met with anything but a welcoming friendliness.

The Radelich family became close friends. They invited us over to dinner at their home in Windham, and when we got there we thought we had died and gone to heaven. They ran a Bed and Breakfast – "Albergo Allegria" on Route 296, a road which ran through awesome mountain scenery between the two ski resorts of Windham and Hunter. The building was absolutely beautiful, with Victorian stained glass, fan shaped and keyhole windows, balconies and verandahs with French doors into the rooms, shutters and gingerbread trims on the eaves. The atmosphere of the place reflected its name – Inn of Happiness. It had lovely mellow wood floors and was filled with beautiful antiques and sunshine. What a place! Vito and Lenore, their son Stefan, daughter Marianna, and Stefan's wife Alta with their new baby daughter, Miriam, welcomed us. There was also their big white fluffy dog, Shalom, who was the nicest dog I have ever met, and loved by all of our girls. We had an amazing meal cooked by Vito (who we later found out was one of the most respected chefs in America) and heard the history of the Inn and the family. We loved them and were fascinated to hear their story. Vito came from one of the islands off Croatia, and had escaped from Yugoslavia by rowing across the Adriatic when President Tito took over the country. He finally made it, after a life-threatening journey, only to be put in a prison camp near Trieste, where he saw people killed for a piece of bread. He came to America eventually, living in Brooklyn and working in construction, whilst always enjoying cookery on a non-professional level. Interestingly – he had been offered a construction job in Bermuda, but by that time he had met Lenore, who came from a close Sicilian family also living in Brooklyn (she was from the first generation to be born in the USA). She didn't want to be so far away from her family so he didn't take up the Bermuda offer. Lenore had been to college, earning a diploma in business studies, so they decided to use that, and Vito's cookery skills, and they opened a Seafood Restaurant on Long Island. This became famous and very popular, but as they got older they decided to opt for an easier way of life, so they sold up and moved to the Catskills, taking half of Lenore's family with them! They bought land and property in Windham, took 2 old houses, joined them together, refurbished them, and opened them as a B & B – Albergo Allegria. They also refurbished a building across the road, and rented it out to Vito's student chef Eddie, who ran it as a successful restaurant - "La Griglia". The Albergo stood next to the Batavia-Kill Creek, and they built a lovely deck behind the Inn, under the trees, which looked out over a little waterfall. When they joined the two houses together they did so literally. They moved one of them down the road, complete with furniture and furnishings – even the china and crystal in the cupboards – and put it behind the other one so that they could join them up. Apparently nothing was broken during the move except one glass! Vito ran cookery schools in Windham, with people like Paul Prudhomme coming to learn from him.

Our time in New York went all too quickly. The weather was so lovely. It was hot and sunny, but the cool mountain breezes made it perfect. Our loaned transport had air conditioning, so even the travelling was comfortable, although we often turned it off and opened the windows to experience things like hearing the rushing mountain streams or the scent of woods filled with the pink and white flowers of Sweet Rocket – even to get our first whiff of skunk! The latter was quite a revelation, and nothing like what I had expected. It was like a combination of every strong smell I had ever smelt, including coffee, burnt rubber, garlic, onions, hydrogen sulphide, bleach, hoppy beer, all in varying proportions. From a distance it didn't seem too bad, but I could imagine it would be devastating if it was experienced at close quarters. We explored the local area, and loved it. Down at the bottom of the mountain, on the road between Lexington and Jewett, was a beautiful Ukrainian Orthodox church, built entirely of wood, and held together with wooden pegs - not a nail in sight. We saw deer, raccoons, skunks, possums, chipmunks and wild turkeys, and we also saw snakes and heard bears rumbling around in the darkness. The bridges over the Schoharie Creek were iconic. We all went swimming one day near the bridge at Mosquito Point where the creek was deep and slower running. We could see trout swimming around in the deep pools, and apparently it was a favourite fishing hole when there were no kids splashing around in it. We also swam at Red Falls in Ashland, which was a lovely series of rapids, pools, and high rocks on the Batavia-Kill Creek as it ran down from Windham to meet the Schoharie in Prattsville. It was so called because of the colour of the water when it was in full flood in winter. The earth around ZPM was rich and red, and it reminded me of Devon and the cliffs of Teignmouth and Dawlish that I used to see on our epic train journeys down to Plymouth when I was a little girl. I jogged a little bit whilst we were there, and Wanda joined me a few times. We ran up to the end of the Road, and then back to the farm. It was only about a mile, but it was exercise, and meant I could try to get to know

Wanda a bit better. I didn't really succeed. She was very closed and distant. I even gave her my favourite dress when she admired it, in an effort to melt her standoffishness. I regretted it later, because the next time I saw her oldest daughter she was wearing my lovely dress chopped up and made into a skirt! I found Wanda really difficult. One thing that really surprised and upset me was that she refused to let me use her washing machine! Not only did I have mountains of dirty washing from travelling with the whole family, I remembered that I had willingly allowed her to take over my machine completely for days on end when they came back from South Africa and stayed with us after their youngest child was born. Shades of things to come?

Robbie and I were very taken with the place, and with what Gerald dreamed of doing there. His vision was to build a Discipleship School, mainly to train up gap year students who wanted to go on short term Third World missions. One evening Robbie and I stood on the deck in the dark watching the fireflies dancing. The air felt like warm velvet, we could hear frogs and insects chirping in the distance, and in the clear moonless sky the stars seemed close enough to touch. I felt I knew what Keats meant when he wrote "tender is the night". We talked about leaving England again and coming to help at the farm and found we both wanted to do it with all our hearts, but it seemed like an impossible dream. Robbie's police pension was at least 15 years in the future, and I had no income. What would we live on? What about the girls' education? Would the US give work permits to an unskilled man with a large family? However, having stepped out in faith often – especially in leaving Bermuda and later moving to Green Pastures – we were convinced of the truth of the scripture "delight yourself in the Lord, and he will give you the desires of your heart" (Psalm 37). We prayed, and asked God to give us a sign that it was Him and not just our infatuation with the place. We opened our eyes and immediately a bright shooting star streaked across the sky. Was it a coincidence? Just to make sure, we asked God that, if it was our sign from Him, He would send another one. Again, immediately, another one streaked across the sky, but this time in the opposite direction! We felt so excited, but because of the enormity of the idea, didn't really speak to anyone else about it. I did ask Wanda if she saw us being at the farm in the future, but she just gave me a strange little smile and said "We see everyone here". One of the things I remember best about the trip was sitting on the covered porch watching an amazing thunderstorm. The rain was torrential, and the thunder and lightning were deafening, dazzling and constant. We had never seen anything like it – it was apocalyptic! Apparently it was a regular occurrence up there, only the newcomers took any notice of it. I think the electricity went off for a while, but that was a fairly regular thing, too, and could be caused by anything from a thunderstorm to beavers felling trees onto electricity wires!

Sadly, our holiday came to an end, and we flew back to England, to face adjusting our lives to Nicky's advancing pregnancy and our future grandchild's arrival. Nick started at Havant College, and Ben started his double glazing job. He would occasionally surprise her by meeting her from college, and sometimes phoned her in the morning before she left, asking what she was wearing. She just presumed he was being loving and protective. We had a few visitors that summer too, and in particular enjoyed having Marianna Radelich and Jane Ricci, who were on their way to Africa on a mission trip. We took them to lots of very English places, and they loved it. Yves and Annick were over at the same time – I think they stayed with Keith and Diana. Nicky's pregnancy was uneventful. Both she and the baby were healthy, and she seemed happy. Christmas was good that year, with little ones around to enjoy it, and big ones to help with all the extra work! Nicky was quite large by this time, I remember watching her, with her big tummy (and big hair), decorating the tree. Sarah's 4th birthday party was an event, she was growing up and enjoying things like that more. She wore a beautiful little dark green velvet and taffeta dress which looked lovely with her blonde hair.

By the time March 1991 came along we were well established at the Elim church, and were planning to put on a Passover meal there, for all those who were interested in the Jewish roots of Christianity and, specifically, of Easter. Loads of people signed up for it, and we realised that it was going to be a lot of work! We arranged it for 28th March. I marinated about 10 legs of lamb, which then had to be roasted, and soaked kilos of chickpeas to make houmus. The menu was supposed to be more or less what a traditional Passover meal would be – roast lamb, bitter herbs (chicory salad) and unleavened bread. In the end I didn't get to go to the meal, because Nicky went into labour on that very day. Nanny stepped in, even though it was her birthday, and spent the day boiling mountains of chickpeas and mashing them into Houmus! What a blessing she was, and the meal went really well, in spite of not having me there to help. Ben and I took Nicky to St. Mary's Hospital, and began the long wait with her. I remember that Ben and I ate all the sandwiches she was given, whilst poor Nicky gulped down gas and air non-stop! It was quite hard for me not to interfere when I thought that there was far too much medical interference in what was a perfectly natural process, especially when the contractions seemed to stop and they decided to put up a pitocin drip to hurry things up. I mentioned that this was a pattern of all my labours, and that maybe Nicky was the same and would get going again on her own in a while, after a little rest, but they ignored me and put up the drip anyway. It did "get things moving" very quickly, but poor

Nicky was in agony, and really overdosed on gas and air. Our lovely Lauren Abigail was born by late afternoon, but had become distressed during the birth (could it have been because of the drip?) and had to be monitored for a while, but then attention turned dramatically to Nicky. She was haemorrhaging, and her uterus wouldn't contract down to stop it. I just stood and prayed in tongues, feeling very helpless. Ben looked terrified. Eventually they managed to stop the bleeding, but Nicky was very weak by then, plus sick and dizzy from all the gas and air, so not feeling well at all. I remember holding Lauren, looking down at her beautiful little face. She had lovely strawberry blonde hair, bright red cupid bow lips (she had been given oxygen!) and the bluest eyes. She was the image of Nicky when she was born – and didn't seem to bear any resemblance to Ben, who was dark haired and brown-eyed, although his Mum and two sisters had red hair. I called Robb, and told him Lauren had arrived, our first grandchild, and Nanny's first great-grandchild – on her birthday! What a present from the Lord! Nicky was feeling really ill, and in fact she fainted when trying to go to the loo when she was back on the post-natal ward. The hospital wanted to give her a blood transfusion, but I strongly advised her against it – I knew better than anyone the risks involved and the possible future consequences. I told them that Nicky would be at home with me, and that she didn't have to do anything apart from feed Lauren, plus I would wait on her hand and foot until she had built up her store of iron again. To my relief Nicky decided she wouldn't have the transfusion. Ben's family were rejoicing at that. I think it was because they thought we had "seen the light" and were all about to become Jehovah's Witnesses like them!

Nicky and Lauren came home, and we had another little member of our household to love and care for. Zoe was only 20 months old, Sarah was 5, Amy was 15, and Nicky was

17. Ben was on the doorstep all the time, understandably wanting to be with his baby daughter, so life was pretty hectic!

Although we didn't tell our friends in America about Nicky's pregnancy when we were over there, we told them eventually. Everyone had responded so lovingly and with such understanding and compassion. I think they must have seen our hearts through it all, as Nicky could easily have had an abortion, and none of them would have been any the wiser. We got a lovely "Congratulations to the new Grandparents" card from Gerald and Wanda with money for a present for Lauren. He wrote in it "When are you coming over to Higher Ground Farm to buy some of those cows you were talking about?" We had been talking to him about our self-sufficiency ambitions, and about our fancy for a herd of Charolais! It seemed a bit jokey, but it was another nudge towards fulfilling our dreams. Robbie went out to the farm that summer for a couple of weeks, during the annual Bible Camp. I didn't want to go – I was too busy – there were so many little lives to look after. I felt as if it would have caused me too much stress to take a holiday! He had a great time and met loads of lovely people. It looked as if everything was coming together for the proposed Discipleship School. Gerald was getting a team of good men together, including Stefan Radelich, Mike Petzer, Ricky Duplessis, and others, all good teachers and strong, Godly and gifted leaders. The local church had moved to a lovely new building in Windham, and Ricky Duplessis was pastoring there, whilst Gerald had started a small church down in Queens. He was also making contacts in lots of places all over the world, resulting in many young people wanting to train up to be missionaries – both at home and abroad. When Robbie came home he brought a young Australian guy, Leslie Leman, with him, who stayed with us for a week or two. During his stay

Robbie took him to the 17+ Young People's Group at
the Elim Church, where they asked him to speak. Two of
the young leaders there, Wayne Keeping and Andy Elmes,
were to become very important to our family. Andy Elmes
was quite touched by what Leslie had to say. As he talked to
them at the end of the meeting Leslie and Robb challenged
him, telling him that they thought that God had far bigger
plans for him than running a youth group in his home
town, so why not consider going out to New York for
a Discipleship Camp? Andy was engaged to a girl in the
Youth Group at the time, but they were not sure they
would ever get married, and it looked increasingly likely
that they would break up. He also said that not only did he
have no money, but his Dad needed him to help run his
Fruit and Vegetable Shop in Cosham High Street. However
- Robb and Leslie were persistent! In the end Andy said that
if God provided him with £300 for the air fare he would go.
Less than 2 weeks later he called Robb. He'd had a phone
call from a Building Society telling him that he had £400
in an account that seemed to have been forgotten. It had
been forgotten! It was left from an old mortgage account
he'd had some years before, when he shared a house with
a friend. The house had been sold and the account emptied
– or so he thought. After making extensive enquiries to
verify that the money was actually his, he had to admit that
perhaps God was saying something to him! At the same
time the teenager who helped out in his Dad's shop on
Saturdays asked if there was any chance of a full time job!
The last thing was that he and his fiancée finally agreed
that they had to break off their engagement. All of his
reasons for not going out to New York were completely
eliminated, and he flew out there as soon as he could the
following spring. Robbie and I felt that if we supported him
financially we would be making an important investment
in the Kingdom of God. Money was pretty tight, so it was
only a small amount per month, but it paid big dividends,

both for our family and eventually many others, both in Portsmouth and further afield!

Our years at Wheatsheaf were so full; it was such a special time for our family. Schools, pre-schools, colleges, church, family, friends, boyfriends, visitors, teachers, babies, pets, came and went. We never had any decent furniture, and were glad of it because it would have been wrecked by the constant traffic, but we were comfortable and very happy most of the time. Most of our family traditions, silly expressions, and jokes originated in our time at 23. These were shaped by things like our love of the Narnia and Anne of Green Gables stories, and movies like "The Three Amigos". We became big fans of the stars of that film, and we all knew the songs from "Annie" off by heart! Robbie and I loved Gene Wilder and Richard Pryor's movies, especially "Hear no Evil See no Evil" and "Silver Streak". One of my favourite expressions; "or something similar" came from a line in "Silver Streak" when Gene Wilder is asked to milk a cow. He replies that he doesn't know how, and is told by the old farmer's wife "Oh, come on Steve, you're a grown man, you must have done something similar"! I cried from laughing at the look on his face. Our very favourite movie was Richard Pryor's "Moving", but it was a bit too explicit to show when the little kids were around. Sarah started at a little school called "Woodlands" just around the corner on the Wecock Farm Estate. We found out about the school from a friend at Cowplain Church, Rhoda Mercer, who taught there. She was a lovely Christian, and told us that Woodlands had a few Christian teachers, and that the classes were very small. People avoided sending their kids there because of Wecock Estate's bad reputation, hence the low numbers of pupils, but a lot of kids from the church went there, and it seemed ideal for Sarah. She loved it, and the teachers loved her for her sense of humour and happy attitude. She turned out to be very artistic, and won quite a few prizes, including a national one for designing a stamp. The Head teacher was a bit of a dragon. Her name was Mrs. Morgan, and the girls called her Mrs. Mawgrim – after the wolf in Narnia. The BBC series of "The Lion, the Witch, and the Wardrobe" had just been shown on TV, and we all loved it. I had a run in with Mrs. M quite early on, because she wanted the kids to celebrate Halloween by dressing as witches and making up spells, so I took Sarah out of school after failing to change Mrs. M's mind about it. I knew I was within my legal rights, because Sarah wasn't yet 5, but "the dragon" tried to scare me with threats of legal action. It was quite satisfying to know I was on solid ground, and she didn't try pushing me round again after that! Zoe eventually went to preschool there, and started there full time later on. It was a lovely school and we grew really close to some of the teachers over the years that the girls were there. I also loved chatting to the Mums at the school gate. Some of them were a bit challenging, but others were like us, wanting their children to be well taught in small classes, so had ignored the prejudice against the Wecock area and seen all the good things about the school. I used to ride my bike to pick up Sarah, with Zoe in the baby seat at the back, if no-one was home to babysit. One day I rode up to the school, and one of the waiting mothers asked me "Why are you so f...... happy all the time?!" She was a biker chick, covered in tattoos and piercings, and her little girl, Tatanya, was in Sarah's class. Her husband was always there with her, he didn't ever seem to be working. He had a bleached blonde Mohican, and had chains tattooed on his scalp at each side of it. They both dressed in black leather, even in sweltering heat. Her name was "Riz", his was "Camel". They were quite a sight. Riz's real name was Maxine. I don't know if she was named after the character in "Grease", or because of their excessive use of Rizla cigarette papers (enclosing various plant substances). Camel's name was David Camilleri. I replied to Riz "Do you

want the long story or the short one?" and she told me
the short one would do, so I just said "Jesus". She said
"You're not one of those born-again Christians are you? My
mother-in-law is one!" It turned out that Camel's Mum was
Edna Camilleri – a member of Elim Church, and we knew
her! Camel had been born-again in his early teens, but as
he got older he had become interested in Biking, and was
told that he couldn't be a Christian and a Biker as well.
He left the church and became a Biker. Sadly there was a
large and famous Christian Biker group over at Leigh Park
in Havant at that time, led by a guy called Brian Greenaway,
but no-one knew about it at Elim. I invited Camel and Riz
over for a barbecue, and we spent hours talking about
Jesus. Camel was a lovely guy, who had been really hurt
by the church and then fallen in with a "heathen" crowd.
He had A Levels, but had never followed it up with
college or a career, and after a few bad bike accidents
was now on benefits because of the resulting damage to
his back. Riz had been a Mormon, but had given up on
that (fortunately for her). Camel couldn't hear enough
from us, he was hooked - we could tell. He kept saying
things like "It's all starting to make sense again". Soon he
prayed, and recommitted his life to Jesus, and Riz made
her first-time commitment. They came to church with us
a few times, but they didn't really fit in with the mostly
middle class commuter congregation who drove in from
the leafy suburbs for a weekly spiritual knees-up and then
returned home again until the next Sunday. Eventually
they got angry with us because we suggested that there
might be a better use for their small income than going
out and getting another tattoo! Riz did get "Property of
Jesus" tattooed on her shoulder, so probably we should
have kept quiet. It was actually quite a relief when they
stopped coming round every 5 minutes, because Robbie
was getting a bit twitchy about them sitting in our garden
smoking dope, as he was still in the Police Force! One of

the craziest things that happened was when their second daughter was born. They named her Natarka, after a native American sea monster. I was really into cross-stitch at the time, and made a little birth commemoration plaque for her, with her 2 given names, date of birth, weight etc. I was so careful to ask for the right spelling and to stitch it correctly, so when Riz told me I'd spelt her name wrong I couldn't believe it! They had called her Natarka Amba, and I hadn't bothered to ask how to spell the second name, just spelt it in the normal way - Amber. I nearly lost the will to live at that point.

22 – Sweet Land of Liberty

Nicky had slowly regained her strength after Lauren's traumatic birth, and eventually I started to babysit for her whilst she went back to Havant College to finish her course. I remember lying in bed one night around this time, wide awake in the small hours. Everyone but me was fast asleep, Robbie was lying next to me, Amy was in her room, Nicky and baby Lauren in their room, Sarah and Zoe in the room opposite ours. The thought came to me that this was probably a moment to treasure for me as a Mother, because it might not be too long before my little family started to go their separate ways. I think it must have been God warning me! We had begun to notice that Ben was getting more and more possessive. He was absolutely neurotic about Zoe playing with Lauren's baby toys, and vice versa. We often heard the sound of them arguing in Nicky's room, and he would frequently slam out of the house in a rage. He now phoned Nicky nearly every morning to see what she was wearing to college, and more often than not she found him waiting for her at the college gate in the afternoons when he should have been at work. Nicky was miserable, and we didn't really know what to do to help. They talked about getting married some time in the future, but that prospect didn't thrill us at all, we didn't want our Nicky married to this moody control freak! He had a motor bike for a while, but wrecked it not long after getting it. He passed his driving test and then had a car, but had an accident in that. He didn't seem to ever be happy, he was at our house most evenings, and always looked like a thunder-cloud. He was not fun to be with! When Lauren was about 6 months old, Jane Ricci came to stay with us again for a couple of weeks after her African mission trip. The trip had been with Mike Petzer and Philip Smethurst, and it marked the beginning of Philip's "Overland Missions" organisation. Marianna had gone back to the States earlier, but Jane stayed in Africa longer because she and Mike had fallen in love and become engaged. She was on her way home to get their wedding organised. We had fun looking at wedding dresses, and in fact she bought one here in Portsmouth and had it shipped over to Connecticut. Nicky and Jane became quite close, and they would sometimes talk late into the night after Ben had gone home. One of our favourite relaxing pastimes in the evenings after the little ones had gone to bed was to watch a movie, and one night, whilst Jane was still with us, we watched "Sleeping With the Enemy". It was quite a gripping story about a woman who was being physically abused by her husband. Everyone was watching it, including Nicky and Ben. Halfway through the movie Ben did one of his spectacular enraged exits. We didn't know what it was all about, but had become used to it. The next day, when Nicky was at college, Jane said she wanted to talk to us. We sat down together, and Jane told us that whilst we were watching the movie the previous night God had shown her that Ben was physically abusing Nicky. Ben's exit had been caused by a guilty conscience! She had confronted Nicky with it after Ben had gone, and Nicky broke down in tears and admitted it was true. We were so angry and upset, and so sad and worried for Nicky! After we calmed down we began to see that it fitted in with his usual behaviour – it was the ultimate control tactic. What were we to do? When Nicky came home we told her that we knew, and she told us more. She had been wearing jeans and long sleeved tops to conceal the bruises, and told us that Ben's bike and car accidents had been deliberate. Every time she had tried to end their relationship he had threatened to kill himself, then gone out and wrecked whatever vehicle he was driving. Not only was he beating her up, but was blackmailing her emotionally, and she was feeling more and more depressed and trapped. Later we found out that he had once pushed 3 year old Sarah over, and that he often angrily shouted at her when she wanted to be with Nicky and Lauren. We all started to pray, and Jane came up with the suggestion that Nicky should go back with her to the States to help her with the wedding preparations; not telling Ben, just disappearing. We instinctively knew that this was the right thing to do, in spite of college and any other commitment Nicky had. She had to escape from this deadly relationship. Jane was leaving in less than a week, so we somehow found the money and bought tickets for Nicky and Lauren to leave on the same flight as Jane. We then dashed around, getting them ready for an indefinite stay over there. We had to buy return tickets, as they had no visa, but we figured we could change the return date some time when things became clearer. So, only a few days from finding out that our beloved daughter and grand-daughter had been trapped in an abusive, dangerous relationship, we waved goodbye to them as they set out into the unknown. When we explained to Havant College what had happened they were very understanding. Ben came round as normal that day, and we told him that Nicky and Lauren had gone and why. I think we did it in the right spirit. I was so relieved and happy that they had managed to escape without his finding out that it was easy to be kind to him, in spite of all he'd done. I actually felt very sorry for him. He wanted their address, but I refused to give it to him, just told him that I would tell Nicky he'd come, and leave it to her to contact him. He came round once more to try again to get their address, and brought a little locket to give to Lauren from him. I don't know what Nicky did with it, but she never contacted him again, nor he her.

Life carried on almost as normal, but our lovely Nicky and Lauren were gone and I missed them terribly. I couldn't bear to go into Nicky's room for days and days, I got such a desolate feeling when I did. I guess it was the first taste of the "empty nest syndrome". I remembered my sleepless night of only weeks before, and cried. Nicky stayed in Connecticut with Jane's Mum for a while, then moved to NY, staying in Maplecrest, near Windham, with Stefan and Alta Radelich. She got a little pocket money job cleaning at the Albergo whilst she was there. Alta and Nicky became good friends, babysitting for each other and watching silly soaps together when they weren't busy with the children. The Radelich's have been a blessing to our family in so many ways, and they really took care of Nicky and Lauren. When Jane, Nicky, and Lauren first got to NY they had gone to Higher Ground Farm, where Jane would be staying, but, surprisingly to her and to all of us, she had met with an angry reaction from Gerald and Wanda. Perhaps suddenly having another 2 unexpected mouths to feed was a bit of a shock, but they had certainly given everyone the impression that was what they were used to. Being flexible, generous, and open to whatever God sends, was what Gerald preached. He phoned Robbie and berated him for not confronting Ben and dealing with the situation at home. The implication was that we had dumped our problems on them instead! Robbie tried to explain, but didn't meet with any understanding from Gerald, so Nicky and Lauren moved in with Stefan, Alta, Miriam and their new baby, Sebastian. Thank God for Christ-like Christians.

Nicky spent the winter in Windham, sending back lovely photos of herself and Lauren in the snow, and telling us about all the people she was meeting. A lot of young people were moving to the Windham area to hear the great teaching that was being offered by Gerald and his team, and to be involved in the discipleship school. Nicky mentioned John Muench quite a lot, and he took her and Lauren to meet his Mother in Poughkeepsie, so we thought that maybe something was going on there, but it turned out they were just good friends. Everyone loved Lauren – she was really spoiled – especially by Lenore's Mum and her sister, Aunt Rose, who often invited Nicky for Sunday lunch after church. She seemed to be coping financially. We were sending her what small amount of money we could, as she had no work permit. This meant that, although she could help friends at the Albergo and get pocket money, she couldn't be officially employed. She had travelled to the US on the Visa Waiver scheme, and when we tried to extend her stay we were told it was impossible, they had to use their return tickets, come back to the UK, and apply for US visitors' visas. Nicky was sure that she wanted to stay in America, convinced by everyone that she should enrol for the Discipleship School at the farm the following summer, and we were sure she should too. It was so lovely to have them back with us, even though it was only for a little while. Sarah and Zoe didn't know they were coming back, and we managed to secretly pick them up from Heathrow and smuggle them into the house, then they jumped out from behind a chair and surprised the little ones. They were so excited to have their big sister and little niece to play with again! Lauren was nearly a year old and had grown a lot, Nicky had changed a lot too. Of course, if she had stayed "on the tracks" with God, her relationship with Ben would never have happened, but she hadn't really been interested in God (or anything to do with Him) since well before getting together with Ben. Now she seemed so different, and was excited by the thought of the coming summer at the farm, although a bit apprehensive about the logistics of staying in a hut on a mountain, with no electricity or running water and a 1 year old baby to take care of! She got 6 month visas pretty quickly, and once again we waved goodbye to them at Heathrow, relieved that Ben hadn't found out they were home, or at least that he hadn't tried to see them. Looking back, I don't know where the money came from, as we were always strapped for cash! Nanny helped us out a lot over the years, so it could be that she paid the fares. Amy decided that she wanted to go out for the Discipleship camp too, and because we were so thankful for the inspiring teaching that was coming to us all from Gerald and the team, we wanted her to go too, and pulled out all the stops to get her there. She was only 16 when we put her on a plane to Newark NJ after calling the farm to point out that she needed picking up from there, not JFK, as we hadn't been able to get her on a flight to the nearer airport. Ricky Duplessis took the message, Leslie Leman was picking her up. She was a pretty strong character by then, but we still had reservations about her making such a long trip on her own at such a young age. We were on tenterhooks until she called us from the farm the next day, and we were even less reassured of her safety when she told us what had happened. Ricky had forgotten to pass on the message, and Leslie had gone to JFK, leaving Amy sitting on her own at Newark for 4 hours wondering if she had been forgotten. Eventually everyone realised where she was, and she did get picked up, but she was a bit shaken – so were we!

That summer was a special time for us as a family. Nicky rededicated her life to the Lord and was baptised in the Schoharie Creek at Mosquito Point. Amy decided she wanted to be re-baptised as a symbol of an adult decision to give her life to Jesus. They had a great time at that camp, and made some good friends amongst the young people that had come to the Discipleship School from all over the world. There was a large group connected with Reading University, which included Nick Small, Matthew Wright, and his sister Annie. Jenny Cardinal, Philip Smethurst, and Chris and Eric Eskelund were there from South Africa.

Barry (the bush-bungler!) Lowe, Tracey Theodorsen and Peter Ardle were there from Australia, as well as Leslie, of course. There were lots of Americans too, including Cindy Rogers, Mark Connell and John Muench. All of them were hungry for what God wanted to teach them, and prepared to go to the ends of the earth if He told them to. Many of them did. It was an amazing, life-changing summer. Andy Elmes was there, too, of course, and Nicky got to know him well. He was radically changed by his time there, and significantly for his future, spent one night on his face in the barn, asking God for all that He had for him, and vowing to do whatever he was told. Gerald really took Andy under his wing. He was given opportunities to speak and lead in various capacities, and he stayed on after the camp finished, joining Gerald's team. Amy came back home after 6 weeks, matured and strengthened in so many ways. Going out there on her own gave her a great sense of adventure, and she had become very self-assured in ways that most of her friends weren't. She survived near electrocution in the makeshift showers in the barn, and 6 weeks of junk food, amongst other dangers! I thought she would be eating some kind of frugal healthy diet on top of the mountain, but all the girls would regularly pile into someone's car and ride down the mountain for Pizza, candies and Pepsi. She also survived Mike and Jane Petzer's oversight of the camp! They were living in the main house and in charge of the day to day routines, as Gerald and Wanda had moved into rented accommodation in Windham. Jane was a wreck – she wasn't equipped or willing to be responsible for all these young people, and Mike was taking the flak, as well as operating out of his then rigid and frigid way of relating to people. They were newly married, and should never have had that kind of stress placed on their relationship, but they became a bit of a secret laughing stock, and Amy in particular was a great trial to Mike! However, God is so amazing, He takes us through things that we would never have chosen to happen, and when we "come out at the other side" we realise that He has built something lasting and precious into us. Amy's 4 hour wait at Newark airport, living in a hut on top of a mountain, and then her hair-raising return journey home, have made her realise she can do anything if God is in it. She was diverted to Germany on the way back, had to wait for hours on her own for a connection, and eventually got to Heathrow about 12 hours later, totally exhausted and without her luggage! All at just 16 years old! We had sent our girls off in faith, believing that the wonderful message of the real Gospel would change them and equip them for life, and it did. They both have such a confidence in God's love for them through Jesus, and a growing relationship with Him, which will keep them safe through thick and thin, and helped to lead their younger sisters, children, and friends into the same life-saving, joyful confidence. Amy started at Southdowns College that September after doing well in her GCSEs, and leaving Oaklands with mixed feelings of sadness and relief that she didn't have to cope with the religious mumbo jumbo any more. She had decided to do a B. Tech. National Diploma in Health Studies, with a view to going into nursing.

Nicky came home when her visa expired. She didn't really want to come back to England, but it seemed right for her to return, to start thinking about both her future and about Lauren's. She enrolled for a catering course at Southdowns College, and began going to the 17+ meetings at the Elim Church. They were a great bunch of young people and she made some good friends. We loved having her and Lauren back with us, and Zoe loved having someone to play with whilst Sarah was at school. The little ones were growing up. Sarah was doing well at school and was very happy, Zoe was turning into quite a character. I remember watching her in the snow that winter, wearing a blue snow-suit and a red woolly hat that matched her little red nose! I've got happy memories of pulling Zoe and Sarah along in the snow on a sled, dropping Sarah off at school, and then going off into the fields behind Wecock and spending the morning sledding with Zoe. She made us laugh a lot, but gave us some headaches, too. She had started talking quite early, and seemed to pick up all the wrong things, both from the TV and from us. Her favourite word was "bollocks", and she would wander round saying it over and over again with great relish. We tried to pretend we thought she was saying something else, and would quickly say things like "yes, darling, wallop, wallop, wallop" – especially if we had Christian friends staying with us! The other thing she used to shout out, if she saw a cat in the garden, was "Hey you bloody cats, get off my lawn!" quoting a line from Harry Enfield's "Dr. Doolittle Talks to the Animals" comedy sketch. It was so hard to stop laughing sometimes, and if we did have visitors and saw a cat in the garden everyone panicked and rushed Zoe out of the way, so that she couldn't see it! Around this time Mike and Jane Petzer came to stay with us for over a month. Jane was pregnant with their first child, and they were on their way back to America so that the baby would be born there. They had been in Israel, staying with people from Mount Zion Fellowship, where, as I have mentioned, Gerald, Wanda, and Bee had trained for the ministry. Mike and Jane had not been cared for! Jane said that they had almost starved, as nobody seemed to understand that they had no income, but had come to Israel hoping to learn from Ruth Heflin and her sidekicks (on Gerald's recommendation). Jane was particularly traumatised by all of this. In fact, they had been taught a lot by the experience – that a lot of people who made a lot of noise about the gifts of the Holy Spirit showed very little evidence of His loving and compassionate presence in their every day lives. Hellooo! It was interesting that Mount Zion fellowship seemed to be a common denominator in their learning process and in ours at Green Pastures. They were both really in need of some TLC but found it hard to admit it, and poor Mike tried to keep up his macho image. They ate like horses (they came to the right place), and we got through a bag of Satsumas every day for a month, as Jane's body was craving vitamin C. She started to do cross-stitch with me, but her contact lenses were so old and scratched that she couldn't see properly to sew. I think we were all learning that some of these super-spiritual people had given us a completely wrong idea of living by faith. God's Word says that He will provide everything we need, and I think that would include a new pair of contact lenses now and again, but Jane had not wanted to ask because it would have been considered self-indulgent. I hate religion, it gives people such a lousy impression of God!

23 – Out of Africa

In February 1993 Nicky and Amy went to a Valentine's Dinner & Dance at Elim, organised by the 17+ group. During the evening a girl we knew gave a heartfelt rendition of the song "I've Seen Jesus" (which was written from Mary Magdalene's point of view, when she met Jesus in the garden after the resurrection). She thought she had a good voice, and in truth it wasn't bad, but not nearly as good as she thought it was! When she came to the rising crescendo at the end of the song, culminating in a high, soprano exclamation that she had seen Jesus, she was shrieking, and Nicky and Amy were almost helpless with barely suppressed laughter. I love this about my girls! Everyone else was sitting primly, trying to look holy and appreciative, and my girls were wetting themselves laughing – which was what everyone else really wanted to do. After they recovered, Andy Elmes' friend, Wayne Keeping, came over and asked Nicky to dance, and they spent the rest of the evening together. After that they started to become friends. Wayne picked Nicky up a few times and they went out for a drive or a drink – just getting to know one another. Their relationship was so "different". Nicky told us that they really liked each other, but neither of them could see the point of dating and getting involved with one another if it was all going to end in them splitting up and moving on to the next relationship. They often took Lauren with them when they went out. Wayne was so lovely with her, and she loved him. Eventually Nicky told us that Wayne was going to formally ask Robb for "her hand in marriage". We were so pleased, but we waited and waited!

In the meantime Robb went to Africa on a mission trip, staying in Zimbabwe with Elijah Mukabi and others, and then with Dave Hart in Zambia. Dave was a friend of Angelo Parisi. He and Angelo had been Rastafarians before being born-again, set free from drugs, and going on several mission trips with Gerald. On one of these trips he met Janet – a Zambian lady who pastored a church in Livingstone. He married her and didn't go back to America! Robbie fell in love with Zimbabwe, and said he would love to take me there some day. He almost got arrested in Harare when he set up a shoe-shine stall just to get a captive audience to preach the Gospel to. He made a full page spread on the front page of the local newspaper, because it had never been seen before – a white guy cleaning the shoes of black people! He came up against the typical black African attitude towards the west whilst he was there, a feeling that the west was their source of supply. This was quite understandable, but wrong, as Zimbabwe had once been called "the bread basket of Africa". Robb really reprimanded them, because when he tried to hand over the stall to them they just tried to steal everything and run away. He reminded them of Jesus' teaching to serve one another in love, and to give rather than take. God must have had angels around him to protect him, because he could easily have been attacked at that point! He had already met with corruption in various forms, which is the real problem in Africa, not lack of supply. His stay with Elijah was difficult. Elijah, a black Shona African, lived like a king in a compound with high locked gates. He lived in a big house himself, but was waited on by servants who lived out in his courtyard and even cooked for him in the open air on a fire, whilst he enjoyed the comforts of home. I'd already had strong doubts about Elijah's integrity and discernment after his stay with us. Whilst in England he had seemed to be grabbing everything he could from whoever he could – not a problem on its own, as he was going back to Africa after all – but along with this was the way he treated the sweet young guy he brought with him. Gladstone was treated like a slave, scurrying around whilst Elijah barked out orders in Shona. Apparently Gladstone's father worked for Air Zimbabwe and had given Elijah the air tickets to come to England, thinking his son would get some training in ministry. He did, but not the kind he expected. Added to this, Elijah invited a local guy we knew to go to Zimbabwe and speak at his church. Bob (called "Fat Bob" by all who knew him) was one of the most phoney, ungodly, obese men I have ever met. Whilst staying with Elijah, Robb began to see that our colonial heritage in this country was to leave a model of autocratic behaviour which had been adopted by the very people who had once been subjugated by it. He travelled to various places in Zimbabwe, meeting many white nationals who were getting very worried about the way Mugabe's government was going. When Robb told me this I remembered meeting a guy in Bermuda who had left Zimbabwe when Ian Smith was ousted. He had smuggled out diamonds in a can of shaving foam, because no-one had been allowed to leave the country with any of their property, and were restricted to taking out £100, or some equally ridiculous amount. This was confirmed later by our friend Jane Franckeiss, whose parents had left Zimbabwe at that time with absolutely nothing, after spending years working hard there and building a lovely home for their family, which they simply had to abandon. After Zimbabwe Robb flew up to Zambia from Harare, and was regaled with the most amazing aerial view of Victoria Falls, before landing there and crossing the border into Zambia. There were very few people on the plane, and the pilot asked Robb up to the cockpit. He asked if he had seen the falls before, and when Robb told him he hadn't, he zoomed down over the falls themselves – an awesome sight. Crossing the border, and arriving in Livingstone, Zambia, was another adventure. Robbie got a lift from a couple in a Landrover, who couldn't believe he had no weapons to defend himself whilst carrying highly desirable medical supplies to give to the hospital in Livingstone. They had guns stashed in all kinds of hidden places in their truck! They were seasoned travellers in Africa and knew about the corruption and violence that was everywhere. Eventually Robbie arrived at Dave's home, and spent a week or so there, going into the local hospitals and prisons, praying for and talking to the inmates. Some of the things he saw were heartbreaking and horrifying, but he also saw God doing amazing things, and was kept safe through it all.

He called me a couple of times whilst he was away, first to tell me he was OK and to check that all of us at home were, too, but also to see if there had been any news from Wayne on the proposal front! Wayne was with us on one occasion when he phoned, and when I told Robb that he hadn't said anything else about marriage I was asked to hand the phone over to him. Robb simply said "Hi Wayne, did you have something to ask me?" and was rewarded with a request for Nicky's hand in marriage, to which he gladly said "Yes". Sometimes it's good to be pro-active! Needless to say we were delighted at the prospect of having Wayne as a son-in-law. He was a strong Christian man, who worked hard at the business he ran with his Dad, and, most importantly, he had shown us how much he loved Nicky and Lauren and was willing to commit himself to them and care for them as we would do. They got engaged, and the wedding was planned for the following August. We foolishly thought we had plenty of time to arrange it all, but life was a bit of a blur from then on! Robbie came home safely and went back to work at Netley, but from then on his heart was really in missions, and we realised that we both wanted to make ourselves available once again to go wherever God would send us. We had one of our caravan holidays down in Dorset with the two little ones, leaving Nicky, Amy and Lauren to hold the fort at home. We had become really fond of Dorset, especially Dorchester, Swanage, Wareham, and Lulworth Cove, but we also loved all the sleepy villages and beautiful coastline of Hardy country. One of my favourite movies when I was young had been "Far from the Madding Crowd" starring Julie Christie, Terence Stamp, and the then gorgeous Alan Bates as the shepherd, Gabriel Oake. It had been filmed in this area, so it was such a pleasure to visit all these places. We all have fond memories of silly raft races on the river at Wareham and Banana Boats at Swanage. We thought we had lost Sarah on one of these occasions, when everyone fell off the Banana Boat she was on. She was such a brave kid! She could swim fairly well and had on a lifejacket, but when everyone was picked up from the water we couldn't see from the beach whether she was back on board again because they were well out to sea. Eventually they got back to shore and she was with them, and OK, but she had been the last one to be picked up in spite of being the youngest, as she was so calm and everyone else was panicking! We came back home to the usual stories from Jan next door, about cars coming and going all night, dogs barking in the garden, and noisy parties. Whatever! The girls had learned to tidy up afterwards pretty well, and we knew that Jan was neurotic about it all anyway. The dog barking turned out to be a neighbour at the back of our house, and nothing to do with number 23, but I was a bit concerned when I found out that they'd had a "trifle fight" at one of their parties. Fortunately for them I didn't find any evidence. Amy and her friends got to know a bunch of Asian guys during all their clubbing activities, and we got to know one of them, Rufus, quite well. He was a lovely guy, one of several sons, born in England to a Bangladeshi family. He would often come to the house and bring gifts for us. He was a Moslem, but not particularly religious – much to his father's disapproval. A popular summer activity for us was going down to shows and concerts on the Southsea seafront with the little ones, and at one of these there was a big talent show put on by Rufus and his friends. Sarah wanted to enter the competition, doing her disco dancing, and in the end we let her, praying she wouldn't be laughed off the stage, but she actually won a prize! We couldn't believe it when we watched her – she was brilliant – Amy must have been giving her some training I think! Nicky and Wayne went out to New York for a couple of weeks so that Wayne could be best man at Andy Elmes' wedding to Gina Gardella, leaving Lauren at home with us. Andy had met Gina at a summer camp meeting and decided that she was "the one". She came from a big Italian family from Yonkers, was a Christian, was pure as the driven snow, and would sing beautiful solos at the meetings. All this made her a perfect candidate for an up and coming preacher's wife, as Andy by now was leading the little church in Queens, started by Gerald a couple of years before. They married at Higher Ground Farm, in the barn, which was decorated with wild flowers and looked amazing. Nicky and Wayne had a great time over there. Gerald was working more and more with a team of strong men, he was planting churches and they were growing. His reputation as a "loose cannon" was being replaced by the good reputation of the guys he was associated with, and they all seemed to be submitted to one another in love, the way it was supposed to be! We were longing to be over there and to be part of it.

We had another lovely Christmas. The little ones had such fun together. Sarah had her eighth birthday on 23rd December, Zoe was 4, Lauren was 2. Life was pretty hectic anyway, but then, as we went into 1994, Nicky and Wayne's wedding began to take over our lives. They wanted me to do the catering, and, after a bit of thought and prayer, I agreed to do a cold buffet, little knowing how much work would be involved! Wayne had always dreamed of having a cricket match at his wedding reception, and we realised that the place Robbie was working, the Netley Police Training School, would fit the bill perfectly for that, and also for what Nicky wanted. It was a lovely old building that had been adapted and modernised very tastefully. There was a big hall with a well stocked bar, and plenty of room to set out the tables for the 170+ guests that were to be invited, plus a well equipped kitchen off that. The hall was beautiful, with tall white columns around the central dance floor, above which was a raised vaulted ceiling surrounded by large gable windows. It was spacious and airy and full of light, plus it had French windows that opened out onto a lovely terrace with tables and seating. The terrace looked out over a lawn surrounded with tall trees and flowering shrubs, which was ideal for Wayne's cricket match. There was even room for a bouncy castle for the kids. We all loved it, and booked it for August 13th 1994. Because Robb was working there we got it for an amazingly low price – God was looking after us already! We started making decorations using a theme of pink bows, white hearts and green ivy. Nicky had brought a big, heart-shaped, papier-mache wreath back from Andy and Gina's wedding and we used it as a model for more hearts, to be hung on each of the white columns around the hall, after winding ivy around them and around the columns. It was a big and messy job, covering chicken wire hearts about 18 inches across with papier-mache, then painting them white, wrapping them in white tulle, and tying them with dusky pink paper ribbon bows. It was worth it, though, as they looked lovely. I was making the wedding cake too, so I started planning it on the same lines, patterned with bows, ivy, and hearts. Nicky started making the little bridesmaids dresses. There were to be four of them; our 3 little girls and Laura Keeping, Wayne's niece, who was the same age as Sarah. Again, we got a bargain! A load of lovely, pink flowered polished cotton which was perfect for the little ones' dresses, and some puffy white tulle for the necklines to match the wrapped heart decorations. Amy and Wayne's sister, Samantha, were to be the older bridesmaids, and we were hiring plain dark pink dresses for them. We shopped for Nicky's dress, and the first place we tried was a little Bridal Shop in Drayton, which was run by Christians from Drayton Methodist Church. Nicky had fairly set ideas of what she wanted, and tried on a few dresses that matched her planned style, but none of them looked particularly special. Then they brought out a dress that was nothing like what she wanted, and encouraged her to try it on. Just to be polite she did so, and when she came out of the changing room everyone in the shop burst into tears! She looked absolutely stunning, the most beautiful bride I had ever seen. When we asked how much it cost it took our breath away. It was twice the top amount we had budgeted. Nicky reluctantly took it off, and we left to start looking elsewhere. The trouble was that everyone knew that we had found the right dress! A few weeks later, not having found anything else suitable, we had a brainwave. Why not try phoning them to see if we could hire it. We called and they agreed, but it was still going to cost a lot of money – and we would have to return it after the wedding – plus pay for any damage. It wasn't the ideal set up, but we knew it was the ideal dress so we went ahead and reserved it. I started thinking about the food, and made my work plan. Looking back on it, I just don't know how I did it – but God was definitely involved. I was reading my Bible one morning and a line jumped out at me "and everyone will see that you are a people that the Lord has surely blessed". I knew that God was speaking to me about the wedding, and I felt so reassured that everything was going to be OK! I spoke to neighbours, and hijacked about 4 of their freezers, as well as buying an extra second hand fridge to put in the garage.

Robbie's time working at Netley was sadly coming to an end. He taught there for almost 4 years in total, and the maximum posting was supposed to be 2 years, so he was told that he needed to get back into regular police work. I had noticed over the years that both the Hampshire Constabulary and the Bermuda force seemed to specialise in stuffing square pegs into round holes (after digging out perfectly fitting round pegs!) This was another of these examples. Robbie, a gifted teacher, was sent to Cosham and made Custody Sergeant. It was everything he hated. He was stuck indoors, buried in paperwork, working with obnoxious prisoners, taking flak from them, and also from his boss, who hated him and seemed to delight in giving him major responsibilities whilst at the same time undermining his authority to make decisions. This "boss" was actually the nasty character who had lived at 23 Wheatsheaf before us – the one who drove his poor wife to suicide through his womanising. He was a high ranking freemason, and Robb had always made known his misgivings about freemasonry, not only in the context of the Police Force, but generally. The other thing this man hated was the fact that Robbie was a Christian who delighted in sharing his faith with anyone who wanted to hear about it. Poor Robb began to dread going to work, and in early summer he began to get terrible migraines as he got ready for his shift. The final straw came one evening when Robb was on duty and a teenage prisoner was brought in, having been caught red-handed, escaping from a house he was burgling, still carrying the stuff he had stolen. It seemed like a cut and dried case. The teenager came from a notorious Wecock Farm family of thieves, who began to teach their kids, when very small, to climb into other peoples houses through tiny open windows in order to open a door to let the adults in. The Police had been after this boy for a long time, suspecting him of many burglaries, but so far unable to prove anything. Robb tried to contact the boss to get authorisation to keep the boy in custody overnight, as he was so clearly guilty, however, the boss was nowhere to be found. Apparently, in spite of being on duty that evening, he had been in bed with his then girlfriend – a WPC who was also supposed to be on duty. Because the boss was unavailable, Robb made an executive decision, and kept the prisoner in the Police cells overnight. The next morning the poop hit the fan. The kid was marginally too young to be kept in the cells and should have been taken into specialised young offenders' custody. Of course, no blame was ever attached to the "boss", because his Freemason colleagues closed ranks, and, added to this, no-one ever spoke out against him as he was so unprincipled and vindictive that they were scared of him. Robbie got all the blame, and the little rat of a prisoner sued the Police force for unlawful imprisonment and won!!!

Robbie could hardly get to work by now, the migraines were so bad. One of his colleagues, who was involved with the Police Federation, advised him to go off sick with stress. He replied that he couldn't possibly do that, because, as a Christian, he felt it would be dishonest. Eventually, though, he decided to see our GP in order to get some sort of remedy. Our Doctor was still Tim Goulder, who had been present at both Sarah and Zoe's births. He was now a strong Christian, and he told Robbie that he was suffering from classic severe stress, and that he was going to give him a sick note for 3 weeks, after which he should go back to see him and possibly be given more time off! The timing of all this was so perfect, it meant that Robbie was around to help with all the arrangements and logistics of the wedding. We could see God in it once again, and, sure enough, as soon as the pressure of being persecuted at work was off, his migraines stopped and he felt fine! There's a scripture in the book of Romans that says "But we know that, in all things, God works for the good of all those that love Him and are called according to His purpose" and we knew it was true – even in being persecuted and stressed, then being put "off sick". Even Dr. Goulder's conversion was part of all this, because we trusted the judgment and integrity of a Christian doctor far more than we would have anyone else, so didn't feel the slightest bit guilty about taking sick leave after he prescribed it. Of course, as I'm writing this, in 2011, stress is recognised and is probably one of the chief reasons for people taking sick leave, but in 1994 it was generally regarded as a malingerer's excuse for skiving, on a par with "Yuppie Flu", which was what M.E. was then labelled. Robbie went back to see him after the initial 3 weeks and was given another 3 weeks off. Perfect!

August 13th was getting nearer. My freezers were filling up, the decorations and bridesmaids' dresses were almost finished, and it was time for Nicky to go back and try on her dress. When we got to the shop we got a wonderful surprise. The purchase price had been reduced by half! We could now buy it for only slightly more than it would cost to hire it, so that's what we did. Throughout the whole preparation for this wedding things happened that could only have been God organising and providing for us. Nanny agreed to arrange the flowers in the church, and her friend helped her. Some of the ladies from church offered to help with serving and clearing the food at the reception. The cake was finished and decorated and looked amazing. Everything was in place. The last couple of weeks were totally hectic, but the day eventually dawned and we were ready. Grandma, Auntie Eileen, Keith and Muriel, Mary and Jim, Liz and Dave, and Richard and Rachel had come down from Hull. Sue and John Headey were there from Huddersfield, but Lena couldn't come because she was filming in Italy. Di and Trevor came from Worthing. Gerald and Angelo were there from New York, and Dave Hart from Zambia. It was the most beautiful summer morning imaginable, it couldn't have been more perfect. Nicky's flowers were delivered, and she went to the hairdressers to have lovely dark pink roses and summer flowers wound into her loose auburn curls. When she finished getting dressed she took our breath away. I had never seen anything so beautiful. The bridesmaids looked absolutely lovely – Amy and Samantha in dark pink satin, Sarah and Laura in flowery pink polished cotton, and the two tiny ones, Zoe and Lauren, in pale pink satin, all with white tulle around their necklines, white baby's breath woven into their hair, and carrying pink rosebuds and white baby's breath. We arrived at the church, which looked lovely, and it was packed! As well as all the invited guests there were loads of members of the congregation, old neighbours, and acquaintances. We were overwhelmed. Wayne's face was such a picture of love and admiration as Nicky walked up the aisle to Mariah Carey singing "Music Box", a song that brought tears to just about every eye present. Zoe and Lauren went ahead of her, carrying little white baskets full of rose petals that they were supposed to scatter gently all the way down the aisle. Zoe was so nervous that she chucked great handfuls and ran out halfway, so Lauren copied her! Steve Potter conducted most of the service, Andy Elmes performed the actual marriage, with the vows and exchange of rings. Gerald stood up and prayed, pronouncing a blessing and prophesying that Wayne and Nicky's marriage would be strong and fruitful, both in the natural and spiritually. We sang "Great is Thy Faithfulness", and meant every word, with all our hearts. Steve Potter gave a short message, in which he said that both Nicky and Wayne had an extra dimension to their lives which gave them meaning, purpose, goals, security and significance, and that dimension was Jesus. It was one of the most clear and concise Gospel messages I have heard, and I was so blessed that my Hull family were there to hear it. I didn't know it at the time, of course, but three of them,

Richard, Auntie Eileen, and Uncle Keith, were to die within a couple of years of hearing that message. At the end of the ceremony Nicky and Wayne walked back down the aisle together to a song Wayne had been keeping secret, "My Girl" by the Temptations. Everyone loved it!

Over everything, and on through the reception, was the pervading, loving, presence of God. The sense of His love and beauty surrounding us was wonderful. At one point during the reception Wayne went into the men's toilets and found Amy's Moslem friend, Rufus, weeping. He actually cried on Wayne's shoulder, and said he had never experienced such a feeling of love surrounding him in his life. Nicky's gay friend from school, Mark, told her the same thing. In fact, about a year later, Mark was invited to a Christian rally at Portsmouth Guildhall by one of his hairdressing customers. Robbie and I were there, and as Mark came into the meeting he spotted us, ran over to us, and said excitedly "It feels like Nicky's wedding in here!" He gave his heart to Jesus that night. The reception went perfectly, and we could tell that everyone was enjoying it so much. There was such a buzz of conversation and so many expressions of delight and thanks for such a brilliant occasion. Auntie Eileen said she was lost in admiration for all we had done. It was the most positive comment I think I have ever had from a female Dawson – including my Mum! Sue and John sat with Rocky and Maureen and swapped Bermuda reminiscences. Trevor and Di sat with Mark and Viv and talked about Jesus! My family all sat together and talked to each other for the first time in ages. Richard fell in love with Samantha. The food was great, and there was plenty of it. Wayne got his cricket match, with all the guys joining in and the women watching from the terrace. The kids had a great time, dancing and playing together. The cake looked really lovely, and no-one seemed too upset when we cut it and found out it was a bit well-done! We were a bit disappointed that Nicky and Wayne refused to let Angelo play guitar and sing, but looking back on it, he could just as easily have ruined the whole occasion as wowed everyone with a beautiful song, by going off on one of his crazy "ad libs"! Actually – Gerald, Angelo and Andy were the only people at the wedding that didn't mix much with anyone else. Added to this they were first in the queue for food and piled their plates so high that I was worried there wouldn't be enough food left for the people at the last table to go up. Gerald also really upset my friend Lisa Moyes. Iris, Vaughan's Mum, had also been invited to the wedding, and was staying with her. Lisa was a girl who had a lot of problems going back to her childhood, and had been dramatically saved from a life on the streets after her boyfriend had died from a drug overdose in her presence. She had recently been given a flat of her own and was doing really well and getting her life sorted out, but the pressure of having a house guest, especially Gerald's Mum, proved to be too much for her, and she hadn't arranged things very well. Gerald was really harsh with her, and to be honest, seeing her so upset by him was a blot on my perfect day. We managed to sort things out, but all these little insights into Gerald's character were getting saved onto my hard drive. After a great Disco party in the evening, Nicky and Wayne went off in a white BMW full of balloons for a honeymoon in Tunisia. Lauren was snuggled up, asleep on my knee by this time, so soon afterwards we all went home, and gratefully to bed. The next day dawned, again sunny and warm and beautiful, and we all went over to Netley to clear up after the party. Even clearing up was a joyful experience, Wayne's family came over and helped, and we all sat out on the terrace in the sun afterwards with ice cold Gin and Tonics, and drank a toast to Nicky and Wayne. I've got a lovely photo of us all sitting there, with Zoe snuggled up to me. We all looked bombed – but really happy!

When they came home, two weeks later, they moved into Wayne's house on Lichfield Road with Lauren. It was just around the corner from the little shop where Nan and Pops used to take Nicky and Amy for ice-creams when we were home on holiday from Bermuda, near Baffin's Pond. They settled down to their new married life, Wayne worked so hard, and Nicky started fixing up her new home, which had been a typical bachelor pad. The two weeks of their honeymoon had been filled with frantic activity for us, and also for the Bakers. Far from relaxing after the hectic wedding preparations, we had organised a series of meetings at the Elim Church for Gerald and the guys, and Robbie and Keith were rushing around providing transport and meals and accommodation for them, and for people who came from all over the country to hear the exciting stuff they were preaching. The only people who weren't excited about the teaching were Steve Potter and Andre, and in fact, after the meetings had finished, Steve said he wouldn't allow Gerald to do any more teaching at Elim. He also warned us that he thought Gerald was a bad influence over us, and that he felt we were very vulnerable. It was actually a bit of a challenge – give up on Gerald or give up on Elim. Robbie and Keith Baker were also involved in the big Christian rally at the Guildhall where Nicky's friend Mark was saved, and they had been impressed with the number of volunteer helpers from the Bosham New Life Church. In particular we all got to know an older couple who were helping with prayer and counselling. They were Tom and Rachel Dale, and they lived in the old Rectory in Purbrook, one of my favourite houses in the world! We had a few meals with them and really liked them, and soon we started to go with them to a few of the New Life Sunday meetings. Keith and Diana and their kids came along too. Nicky and Wayne stayed on at Elim, as Wayne's family had been there since it started and they felt it was where God needed them to be. Amy wasn't going to church anywhere, as her Saturday night social life meant she spent half of Sunday recovering in bed! The church at Bosham was full of young people, a lot of them from South America – particularly Brazil – as there was also a Bible School on the large property owned by the church. Dan and April Holt and their 3 sons and daughter lived in the big house that housed the Bible School, and were part of a leadership team that included two other couples. We were really impressed with the loving relationships between all the leaders, and we felt welcomed by them, so decided to make it our temporary spiritual home. We weren't prepared to abandon our relationship with Gerald, and we felt really uncomfortable at Elim because of their attitude towards him. We enjoyed the meetings at Bosham, but there didn't seem to be an awful lot of Bible teaching, just very subjective preaching, and they also tended to jump on all the latest Christian bandwagons, in particular the Toronto Blessing. I had BIG misgivings about that. Why should anyone have to travel 3,000 miles to get a zap from the Holy Spirit when He was present everywhere? I also didn't like some of the "manifestations" people came back with, such as roaring like lions or falling down all over the place, but in other places we had also heard people barking like dogs and hissing like snakes, both of which seemed frankly demonic to me. The congregation also seemed to do things en masse, such as all starting to do identical dance moves at a particular point in a song, or all rushing out to the front to be prayed for by the speaker at the end of every meeting. But anyway – we felt fairly comfortable there for the time being, and Sarah and Zoe were happy. Amy fell in love with one of Dan and April's boys, all of whom were part of an excellent music group and were all gorgeous looking!

24 – The Reverend Porter

Robbie was still on sick leave, and because of the length of time he had been away from work he was referred to the Force Medical Officer for an assessment of his capability to return to work. By this time we were thinking that maybe it was time to get serious about making our move out to Higher Ground Farm. If the F.M.O. thought it appropriate, he could recommend that Robbie take early retirement and get his pension early on Medical Grounds, which would be the sign we needed to get us to America. We weren't getting any younger, and we were desperate to be part of what God was doing out there. The churches in Windham and Queens were growing, and working closely with Chris Scarinzi in Binghamton. The team around Gerald seemed to be getting stronger, and the Summer camps were having to turn people away because of lack of space. Towards the end of 1994 Gerald ran a Discipleship School at Crowcombe Manor in Somerset, which Robbie and I attended. There were loads of young people there, all wanting to get as much of Gerald's teaching as possible. He was preaching righteousness by grace alone, and it was so liberating. People were seeing that they had been striving all of their Christian lives to be what God had already made them, and so were set free to be themselves whilst walking hand in hand with Christ. The weather was freezing, and the manor was an old Youth Hostel with no central heating. Robbie and I had to sleep in the attic as all the other rooms were full, and I had never been so cold in my life. We put on every item of clothing we had brought with us and piled every blanket we could find on top of us, plus our coats, but we were still shivering. We snuggled up together and Robbie said "I must be mad thinking about going to New York – I hate being cold! I think I'll claim the islands for my inheritance" (by "islands" he meant the Caribbean or the South Pacific!). The next day he was ordained as a minister of "Life for the Nations" which was the name Gerald had given to the ministry that was growing up around him. Mike Petzer was there too, and he and Gerald prayed for Robbie and laid hands on him, then Gerald prophesied over him, finishing with the words "and my son you shall go to the islands" (bring it on!) I was now married to a Rev! During our time at Crowcombe Gerald officially invited us to go and live at his place, and to run the farming side of things, as well as asking Robbie to act in a Pastoral role to the people coming up there for teaching and ministry. Even though we had no idea how we could do it, financially or any other way, we gladly agreed, and decided that 1995 would be the year to aim for. We met a guy called Jimmy Rice whilst we were there, as well as a few Christians from the Somerset farming community. Jimmy was from Liverpool, and had been a prisoner in Dartmoor, but had become a Christian and was now part of a local church along with his wife, Jo, and their 3 daughters. He had written a book "Within these Streets", about his life and conversion, and the way God had led him to serve Him in the inner city before moving to rural Somerset. Each morning Robbie and I went running in the lovely country lanes, and normally we didn't see a soul, which was quite understandable, as Crowcombe was in the middle of nowhere, but on our last day we kept crossing the path of another runner. Eventually we were running with him, and we started chatting. He asked us what we were doing in the area, and we began telling him about the Discipleship School and our plans to go out to New York. He turned out to be George Verwer – the man who started the Christian organisation "Operation

Mobilisation", involved with taking young people all over the world to serve the Lord. So many "coincidences"! He said he would pray for us, and encouraged us that it would be a great adventure, but he also warned us to be prepared to have our hearts broken. Somehow I knew he was right.

Zoe had started school by this time, at Woodlands with Sarah. She seemed to be settling in well, but I started finding out about home-schooling, to prepare for when we went to New York and would be living on top of a mountain miles away from anywhere. I'd had a yen to try home-schooling anyway, because of all the heathen rubbish and political correctness that was creeping into school curricula more and more. Gerald's influence was strong on it too. He preached "Sheep keep their lambs with them, goats have crèches"! Wanda home-schooled all of her kids, and she was held up as some kind of desirable model for Christian mothers. I went to a couple of Accelerated Christian Education (ACE) conferences – which was the only curriculum option readily available in England that was also available in America. I found it a bit twee, and some of the people at the conference were kind of scary! One family in particular looked as if they had driven there in an Amish carriage, and their home-schooled teenage daughter had her hair in a sort of Florence Nightingale style net, topped with a Minnie Mouse bow. The fact that I didn't run a mile right there and then is a good indication of my state of willingness to be influenced by other religious Christians at that time. I look back on it and wonder where I left my common sense, but God honoured my openness and teachability, and saw that I was willing to be totally committed to whatever He wanted from us. I was helped a lot by Jo Rice, as she was home-schooling using ACE and was gloriously normal, as were her kids! She and Jimmy had been invited to work with Chris Scarinzi in Binghamton, NY, so we had a lot in common, and really got on well. Robbie went back to work, and thankfully was temporarily posted as Station Sergeant to Petersfield, a much less pressured position. Christmas came and went, and in January we heard that Robbie's final appointment with the FMO was to be on 2nd February. I remember driving up to Police HQ at Winchester that day surrounded by an overwhelming sense of God's presence. At one point I looked out of the car window onto rolling downlands and woods, and had a sort of revelation moment that it all belonged to me – that the world truly was my oyster, and that it contained the pearl of great price. That morning my Bible reading in Psalms was 37 – which begins "Do not fret because of evildoers, or be envious of the workers of iniquity, for they shall soon be cut down like grass, and wither as the green herb. Trust in the Lord and do good; dwell in the land and feed on His faithfulness. Delight yourself also in the Lord, and he shall give you the desires of your heart". It then goes on to say "For evildoers shall be destroyed, but those who wait on the Lord, they shall inherit the earth," and reassures the good man that he will never be forsaken, or see his descendants in need. Just to make sure I was in no doubt that God was at work in this whole situation, my reading in Proverbs included chapter 8, verses 20 & 21 – "I traverse the ways of righteousness, in the midst of the paths of justice, that I may cause those who love me to inherit wealth, that I may fill their treasuries". All of this was fulfilled when the FMO told Robb that he had recommended that he take early retirement and be given his pension early on medical grounds. He could see that if Robb continued working until his years of service were completed his health would be completely destroyed. We were overjoyed! The Government might not have credited his years of service to the Crown in Bermuda, but God had seen it, and counted it, and this was the proof! Of course, his pension would be smaller than if his full number of years had been completed, but it would be enough for us to live on until we got the farming going, and we had the option of taking half of it as a lump sum. We figured that this would be the best thing to do; we could tithe the lump sum and buy farm equipment, save the rest for a deposit on our new home, and still have a fairly adequate monthly income. At the same time Jimmy Rice told us about the U.S. "Christian Worker Visa", which was what he and Jo were applying for. We looked up the criteria for being granted these and they completely fitted our needs, so we sent for the forms and started the application process.

When I look back on all of these things, my faith in God is so reinforced. The timing of it all was absolutely incredible. Everything slotted into place. All of what might have been major problems were solved in the simplest ways. Nicky was settled in her new home and marriage, Lauren was happy and so loved by her "new" Daddy. I got the home-schooling for Sarah and Zoe sorted out, and found out that I could get all my supplies cheaper in the States from a couple of friends in Yonkers who ran a Christian School. Amy had finished college and had her Diploma in Health Studies, but didn't want to stay in England and start her nursing course just yet. She wanted to take a year out and come to America, but as well as not being eligible to be included on our visas because of her age, the last place she wanted to be was out in the sticks on top of a mountain with us! We heard about a scheme called "Au Pair America", and thought this would be a good way for her to get out there, so she applied, and was accepted immediately. The next step was that her CV was sent to families all over America whose requirements matched her abilities and qualifications. Very soon after that she got a call from a woman in Manhattan who needed a Nanny. She was President of a New York Bank, and her husband was an important member of the legal profession. She had seen Amy's CV and she told us that she wanted our daughter and was determined to get her. What's more, she said that if we wanted a reference she would ask her friend Eddie George to give us one. He was the Governor of the Bank of England! Amy accepted, and we were so blessed to think that, although she could have been sent anywhere in the States, including Alaska, she would be living less than 2 hours' drive away from where we would be living. Amy was overjoyed because she would be living in the land of her dreams – Manhattan, NY. By this time we had been up to the American Embassy in London to be interviewed for our visas. If they were granted, which was far from certain, it would be for 2 years, with a possible extension to 5 years. They were granted, and we were given the whole 5 years straight away! We didn't have to worry about selling our house, because it was a Police house, so all we had to do was move out when Robbie officially retired. We tried selling bits of furniture and having car boot sales and yard sales to get rid of the stuff we couldn't keep or send, but I found it soul destroying when people would haggle over paying 10p for something which, though perhaps intrinsically worthless, had lots of memories attached. I would get angry and slap it into their hands saying "Just take it – I don't want anything!" In the end we gave up trying to sell stuff and "sowed it or throwed it" – gave things away if they were worth giving, or chucked them away if they weren't. We packed up and shipped the stuff we were taking to America, and stored other precious things either in Nicky's loft or in Nan and Pops' roof storage space.

One thing that we did still makes me feel slightly embarrassed. We decided to have a big farewell party, and during that to auction off some silly stuff to raise funds for our venture. We thought of things like my autographs – from people like Chuck Berry, The Moody Blues, and Long John Baldry – even Russ Conway, a grinning pub-type pianist popular in the 60s, who most people at the party either had never heard of or forgotten. Pete Sharpe did the auctioning, and did a great job, but the money we raised in no way compensated for the embarrassment value of it all, and I feel we took advantage of our friends. Looking back on it, I can see that we had picked up a wrong attitude towards asking for financial support from Gerald and some of the people working with him. According to them, if you wanted to do anything for God which was going to cost money, it was OK to ask people for help. This was quite right in many instances, but they took it to extremes, and sometimes I felt that they intimidated people into giving. Right at the start of my Christian life I had read about George Muller, who ran an orphanage in Bristol, and never asked anyone for money – just prayed and told God what he needed, then had every single need met. I knew that this was a great example of faith. Later, during the course of homeschooling 5 year old Zoe, I realised just how wrong Gerald's attitude was. I was telling her the Bible story about Bartimaeus, the blind beggar, and was trying to explain to her what "begging" meant. I asked her "What is it called when you ask people for money?" and she replied "faith". We had been living at the farm for a while by then, and she too had picked up quite a few wrong ideas. What an eye-opener!

We sent out a Newsletter telling everyone what we were doing, and that we felt we would probably be going to the South Pacific eventually – maybe the Philippines or New Zealand, after training up for the mission field in New York for a while. We quoted Jim Elliott, a missionary who was killed by the Amazon tribe he was trying to reach for God; "He is no fool who gives up what he cannot keep to gain what he cannot lose". In lots of ways we did make fools of ourselves, but basically we knew that God had opened an exciting door for us and we were definitely going through it, even though it was to an uncertain future. Most of our friends thought we were mad anyway, doing something so radical at an age when most people were settling down! I still don't know how Nicky felt about her whole family disappearing over the Atlantic. At the time of writing this, Zoe is about the same age as Nicky was then, and I know I wouldn't dream of leaving her on her own with a new husband and a 3 year old daughter. We definitely expect and exact far more from our oldest children than our youngest! I hope Nicky has forgiven me. She was also left with total responsibility for Nan and Pops, although they were far more able-bodied then, and the Keeping family helped by taking them under their wing, and including them in things like Christmas celebrations.

The fellowship at Bosham had a goodbye service for us. They all gathered around and prayed for us, sending us out with a blessing, albeit reluctantly. Dan had counselled us to make sure we knew what we were doing after Robbie took Gerald to meet him when he was visiting us in England. Dan had not been able to get a word in because of Gerald's domineering monologue. Dan told us that he had never in his life met anyone so full of their own importance, and he was very concerned for us. I remembered Steve Potter's warnings. We reassured Dan that Gerald was surrounded by a strong team of men who kept him accountable, otherwise we wouldn't have considered joining him, having been "burned" before by someone who was unaccountable – Bee at Green Pastures. Sarah and Zoe finished at Woodlands, and the school held a farewell assembly for them, to which Robbie and I were invited. I had made a cross-stitch picture to present to the school at the assembly in thanks for their care of my girls and to remember them by. It showed a little boy painting a rainbow, and the scripture "The Heavens declare the Glory of God". Mrs. Morgan, the headmistress, aside from all her faults, was a great lover of classical music (and even Hitler appreciated Wagner), and had a different piece playing each week as the children walked into the hall for assemblies. As I walked into school with the girls that morning she was playing Gershwin's "Rhapsody in Blue" - New York epitomised! I thanked them for all they had done for the girls, and shared a little bit about where we were going and why, encouraging them that each one of them was loved and special to God, that He had a wonderful plan for their lives, and that what they could see in themselves now was something like a daffodil bulb – nothing like the beautiful thing God could make from their lives if they put their trust in Him. Woodlands had been such a happy place for the girls, and we were all really upset when we heard it had burned down in later years. Fortunately it was over the weekend, and no-one was hurt, but I wonder what happened to my cross-stitch!?

One of the last things we did before moving out of 23 Wheatsheaf Drive was to have a ceremonial burning of one of Robb's hats. Over the years he had picked up various pieces of weird headgear from places as upmarket as Triminghams of Bermuda and as downmarket as a skip he passed whilst on Police patrol in Havant! By far the worst, however, was his current favourite, a flat cap made of faux leopardskin, which looked as if it had started to develop mange. I couldn't allow this horrible object to go to America with us, so one afternoon when he was out, the girls and I put it in the garden, poured barbecue fuel over it, and set fire to it. We took photographs to show him that there was no hope of resurrecting it, but he came home just as it was collapsing into a pile of ash, and he still reminds me of the heartbreak it caused him! Leaving 23 was a really sad time for me. It had been such a happy home in spite of the traumatic beginning. We had moved in there after being forced to leave not only Hambledon, but a lot of our hopes and dreams (plus all of our money), but in spite of that our life at number 23 had been wonderful. Our lovely Zoe was born there, our first grandchild, Lauren, joined the family there, Nicky had been married from there, and we had so many memories of fun and celebrations and blessings with family and friends and guests. We were stepping into the unknown, and I was scared as well as excited. Looking back on my feelings at that time, I can see that they were very similar to when we moved out of 8 Craigwell Road. I was leaving a comfortable nest again. Once again, Nan and Pops were lovely. They must have been devastated by once more seeing their family disappearing across the Atlantic, but they did everything they could to help us. Nanny actually developed severe eczema almost overnight after we left, definitely caused by stress. We knew we were doing the right thing in going, though. The thought of sitting in our rocking chairs in our old age, having missed taking this amazing opportunity to fulfil our dreams, was more than enough to keep us focused. Added to this, though, we wanted to serve God with all our hearts and resources, and knew this was His opened door for us to achieve that. The day we actually flew to New York we saw God working for us in the most amazing way. Amy had gone to stay with Nicky and Wayne for the last 2 weeks before her departure, so we had few worries there, having finalised most of the arrangements for her. I can't remember saying goodbye to our lovely family, I think I must have blocked it out! We did our final packing at Wheatsheaf, with suitcases in every bedroom. Our furniture had long gone, and we were sleeping at "The Haven", but it was easier to spread out all our clothes and essentials in our empty house. Keith Baker was taking us to the airport in his people carrier, and he was to hand in the house keys to the Police afterwards. We got to the airport and started checking in our baggage, when we realised that we had left two suitcases in one of the bedrooms! They were the ones that contained all Sarah and Zoe's clothes, and I was frantic. There was no time to go back and get them, so we carried on and checked in with what we had, trying to devise a way to get the forgotten luggage to New York. We were only just within our weight limit without the 2 missing cases! Because Keith had our house key, he said he could pick up the cases and take them home with him, then would do his best to ship them out to us. As it turned out, he found out that someone we knew from Gerald's church in Queens, Angelo Paravalos, had been staying in Taunton with the Wrights and was flying back to New York the next day. He was a young guy coming back from a Mission trip, and had hardly any luggage, so he came to Portsmouth, picked up our luggage from Keith's house, and checked it in at Heathrow as his own. We got both cases back the next evening when his Mum dropped them off with us after picking him up from JFK, and it didn't cost us an extra penny!

Gerald had picked us up from JFK and taken us to Peter and Cathy Ardle's home in College Point, Queens, where we were to stay for the weekend. He was preaching at the little church in Queens on the Sunday, then we were to travel up to the farm on the Monday. The morning after we arrived we got up early and took the girls for a walk before breakfast. We spotted a "Dunkin' Donuts" and headed in there – knowing we would get a good cup of coffee. The Doughnuts were pretty good too, especially the Apple Fritters and French Crullers! I was so happy to be back in NY. There's such a special atmosphere in that city, I love it, and it always feels like home to me. As we walked back to Cathy and Peter's house we noticed that all the gardens were decorated for Easter, with pastel coloured eggs hanging in trees, plastic bunnies hopping around, and pretty banners covered with spring flowers everywhere. God bless America – only there do they go so O.T.T. with celebrating the season, which is another thing I love, they never do anything by halves! Signs of spring, new life, and new beginnings were everywhere, and we were part of it. Our new adventure was beginning!

George Dawson

William and Ruth Dawson

Annie Oaten

John Robert & John Richard (Jack) Osborne

Jack & Joan's Wedding

A Day at Hornsea

St. Mary's Girl (1958)

Jobson's Cove, Bermuda

Mr and Mrs Robert Porter

Nicky & Amy at the Police Beach

Nan & Pops

Sarah in front of Bethel

Joy in the Morning - Zoe's birth

Nicky & Wayne's Wedding